Contents

ACRYLIC FELT

This is a useful surface for machine embroidery as it can be cut easily without fraying for easy appliqué. It can be **free machined** without a **hoop** using a **darning foot**. It can be distressed with a **hot air tool**, or worked with a **soldering iron**, although, as it can become a little hard, it's best to use a bigger needle (100) or a **topstitch needle** to protect the thread from shredding. It can be **dyed, painted, applied** to or **glued**. It provides a firm surface for all these different treatments and can be **manipulated** with the machine-stitched lines if slightly tight tensions are used, which will pull shapes and mouldings into the surface of the felt. A number of different colours are available as it is frequently used for children's projects, but it can also be dyed to suit your own individual requirements.

 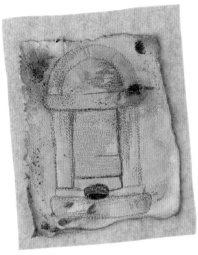

Left: Watercolour and oil pastel drawing for *Empty Shrine* series. Right: *Empty Shrine* embroidery on hot air tooled acrylic felt, with metal fabric paints and dyes. By the author.

ACRYLIC PAINT

This is a useful colouring medium, available in tubes, bottles or jars, which can be used to colour most surfaces. If used straight from the tube it will create a stiff surface that can be difficult to stitch into (depending on the fabric support used). If it is thinned with a little water, acrylic paint creates a less

Acrylic paint on paper with machine embroidery by Rebecca Franks, while a student at Manchester Metropolitan University.

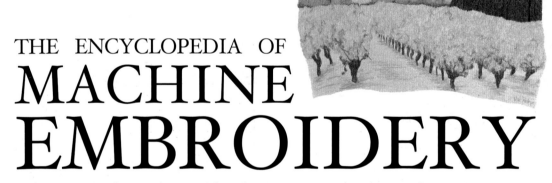

THE ENCYCLOPEDIA OF
MACHINE
EMBROIDERY

Techniques • Stitches • Fabrics & Threads • Sewing & Embroidery Machines • Accessories

VAL HOLMES

BATSFORD

First published in the United Kingdom in 2003
First published in paperback in 2008 by
Batsford
10 Southcombe Street
London
W14 0RA

An imprint of Anova Books Company Ltd

ISBN: 9781906388188

A CIP catalogue record for this book is available from the
British Library.

10 9 8 7 6 5 4 3 2 1

Printed and bound by Craft Print Ltd, Singapore.

This book can be ordered direct from the publisher at the
website: www.anovabooks.com, or try your local bookshop.

ACKNOWLEDGEMENTS

Firstly I must say thank you to Batsford for wanting this book!
Thanks also to Claude and my children for putting up with me
while I wrote it, Claude Vallin for over half of the technical
drawings, and Lucy and Joanne for joining in with the
experiments for Young Embroiderers. To Jill Boyes, Senior
Technician at the Manchester Metropolitan University School
of Embroidery, Manchester, for machine maintenance, Schiffli
and multihead machines, and general help everywhere; and Dr
Melanie Miller for additional help on contemporary industrial
machines. To Roma Edge for an encouraging reading of the
first draft as well as for the embroideries included. I would also
like to thank all the embroidery and textile artists who
contributed images of their work to this book. To all those who
described the techniques used and their ideas with generosity,
and particularly to Frankie Creith, Fanny Viollet, Lesley
George, Kelly Bales, Cas Holmes and Pascale Doire, for their
generosity in sharing their specific and personal techniques, and
whom I have quoted, to a greater or lesser extent.

Thanks also to Janome for a Memory Craft 10000, the
programs and their helpful training. Also to the Balarads for
the Embird and Sfumato plug-in programs. And to all other
machine manufacturers and dealers for their help and advice.

stiff surface and is more easily stitched without creating flakes, holes or dust. There are various qualities, and some are more supple than others. If you are planning to stitch into acrylic, use a good-quality paint such as Liquitex. It can 'glue' surfaces together – fabric to paper, muslin to calico or linen – if applied thickly enough, helping to create a homogeneous appearance (add **PVA** for greater security). It can be stitched through on paper or fabric – it is best to use large stitches and a 90 or **topstitch needle** to avoid excessive thread breakage. If used thickly, the holes made into the surface when stitching will be as important in the general appearance as the thread used for the stitching. By painting onto **Bondaweb** and bonding this to fabric, a smoother, easier to stitch surface is created. Layers of texture and colour can be built up in this way.

ACRYLIC THREADS

Strong synthetic fibre threads with a medium sheen and resistance to bleach, often used in thread manufacture, particularly for computerized sewing machines where a strong resistance is desirable. Acrylic threads are often blended with wool.

ADHESIVE WEBBING

See **Bondaweb, Soluweb.**

ALL-OVER DESIGN

A design worked all over the surface of a fabric to create a patterned fabric, rather than individual motifs. All-over designs can be made on domestic or industrial **embroidery machines**, or can be designed and created using ordinary set stitches or **free motion embroidery** techniques to create a unique and complete fabric which can be cut out afterwards to create

a garment or household item. If you are using this technique to create a garment, it can be useful to chalk in the garment piece shapes onto the fabric so that you only embroider the necessary areas and thus save time – whether this will work or not depends largely on the nature of the embroidery design.

ALPHABET

Alphabets, samplers, poems and letters all form part of an embroidery tradition that can find its place in machine embroidery as well as it does in hand stitching.

Girls destined for work in service would practise samplers of different alphabets, with a few chosen words or a moral lesson, for a future where they would be required to mark linen. Many richer samplers with pictures and whole poems were worked by girls of the wealthier classes, where embroidery

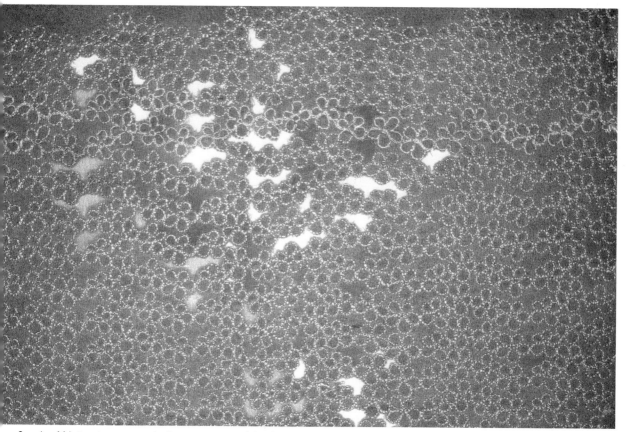

Sample of fabric using computerized patterns on a multihead machine by Vikki Lafford, while a student at Manchester Metropolitan University.

was also used to dictate the future place of women's work and efforts.

Lettering has always been required to mark linen and handkerchiefs, as well as being used in ecclesiastical and heraldic embroidery.

The use of lettering in machine embroidery will have to fit into this tradition, or at least be aware of it. The complexity of language and its use in contemporary conceptual art may also be an influence in the use of lettering and words in textile art nowadays.

Many modern machines now have letters available, often with a choice of font, in their **automatic patterns,** and it is possible to program words or phrases using the memory program of the machine.

Computerized machines have cards or software programs with many lettering styles available which can be used as they are for monogramming or writing, but they can also be adapted to make patterns. Using the possibilities of these programs you may be able to vary the placement of text within another programmed embroidery. Letters may also be flipped, rotated, or mirrored. They can remain as a unique **patch** or be built into **borders** or **all-over designs**. When the design is complete it can be transferred to the machine for embroidery.

You may also try importing your own lettering designs from other graphic sources and programs. Of course, writing and lettering can be achieved with free-machine techniques as well as programmable ones. See **writing freehand.**

ANGELINA
See **crystal strands.**

APPLIED PATCHWORK
Also known as **crazy patchwork**.

APPLIQUÉ
Appliqué is the act of applying a fabric to a background fabric by means of stitches. That's just the simple explanation! In hand

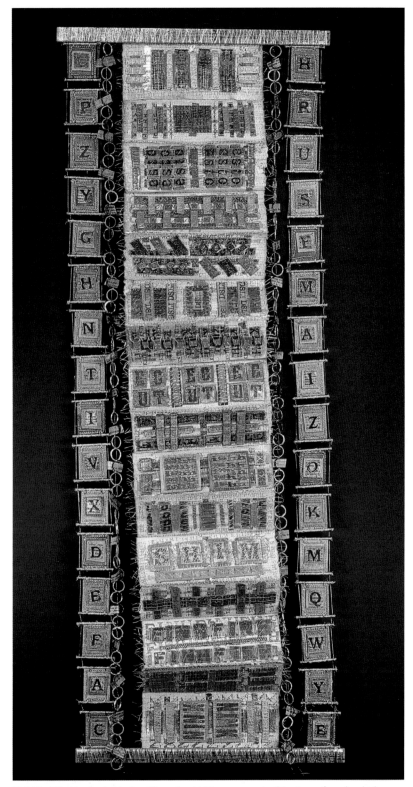

Unfolding Word by Angie Hughes. There is a hidden message in this piece of work, which says 'He that uses too many words like a cuttlefish hides himself in his own ink'. See picture on page 102 for detail and the techniques used.

stitching, one fabric is placed on top of another, the edges are turned in and the applied fabric is hemmed into place. The corresponding example in machine embroidery is the fabric that is placed onto the supporting fabric and **satin stitched** or **zigzagged** into place. This process can be easier if the fabric to be applied is first bonded into place using **Bondaweb** or a similar product, which sticks it to the supporting fabric. This stops the embroidery from slipping while it is being stitched, and prevents the bonded fabric from fraying and looking untidy.

In this state the bonded fabric is no longer going to fray, so it doesn't need to be stitched all around the outside – just some stitches to attach it to the base fabric and to integrate it into the rest of the design will be enough.

However, a fabric may not need to be completely bonded. It just needs holding down for the length of time it takes to get some stitches into it, and we may not care if it frays or not – small pieces of torn **Bondaweb** or **spray bonding glue** or **bonding powder** may be sufficient for this. Equally, fabrics can be held down with these techniques and then a transparent fabric or chiffon put over the top to give security to the appliquéd surface before stitching.

By using 505 or 606 spray glue, for example, pieces of fabric can also be bonded to **vanishing fabrics** which can help in the creation of a new fabric, integrating existing firm fabrics into a more lacy piece, or creating appliqué pictures more delicately with **piecing** on vanishing fabric.

Appliqué can also be worked on computerized **embroidery machines**. Many stitch patterns allow traditional appliqué or cutwork designs to be done using a pre-programmed card or disk, and digitizing programs include this technique for incorporation into your own designs.

Zigzag stitching along an edge for appliqué should lie on the applied fabric and just go into the background along the edge.

Satin stitch can be placed over the join as nothing of the join will be seen through the satin stitching.

Appliqué using Cornely machine by Sarah Birtwistle, while a student at Manchester Metropolitan University.

APPLIQUÉ FOOT

A presser foot made of clear plastic for better visibility for appliqué work. It has a raised heel to prevent the satin stitch from being flattened. It also works around corners and curves much more easily than a normal foot. See **embroidery foot**.

APPLYING

The act of applying one surface to another – see **appliqué**. We can also apply cords, **paper**, metal, mirrors, pieces of ceramic, pre-painted material, **plastic**, or paint. To create interesting surfaces or textiles with meaning we can apply almost anything to anything, using any kind of stitching or glue.

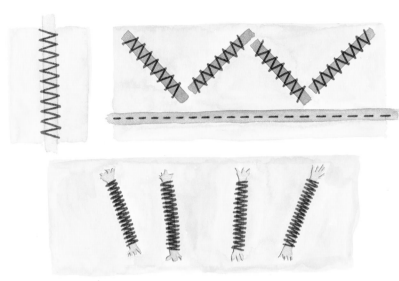

Applying ribbons with a zigzag or straight stitch. Bits of wool are attached with a closed zigzag.

APPLYING THREAD, CORD AND RIBBON

When a very fine cord is to be applied it can be threaded through the small hole in the **cording foot**. For a coarser cord or ribbon, place it over the bar of the foot and guide it under the needle. Stitch a straight line down the centre of the ribbon, or use an open **zigzag** or **blind hemming stitch** so that the ribbon or cord can still be seen. A closed zigzag stitch over a cord will give a padded satin stitch.

Cords can also be applied using the darning foot if they are too thick to pass under a normal presser foot. This gives a more flexible approach to the curves or shapes of the applied cord and also to the stitch: a satin stitch in some areas, an open zigzag in others.

Cords or ribbons could be left protruding from the stitching for more interest. See **embroidery foot**.

AQUAFILM

See **dissolvable film**.

ART EMBROIDERY

The name that has been given to picture embroidery created using the **free motion embroidery** technique. The earliest records of art embroidery have been dated to 1889 or just before, when a piece of machine embroidery was sent from America to an English lady interested in the technique. It is said that when she took it in to the Singer company in order to learn the technique they saw its value for prestige and advertising. The lady subsequently became the first manageress of the first **Singer workshops**. The Singer workshops continued and expanded in Britain from 1889 to 1962, while in the USA the workroom was closed around 1924.

Machine-made cords, ribbons and appliqué on a dyed surface, by Roma Edge.

ATA CP CARD

An ATA CP card is a method of transferring designs to an embroidery machine from the computer. It can contain the same amount of information as 22 floppy disks. For older computers you may need to buy a writer box in order to be able to create this format, and although all laptops accept the format, not all write it. The PC adapter holds a card – the most stable is the Compact Flash Card – which is the most common format of information storage for digital cameras. See also **disk**.

AUTOMATIC EMBROIDERY
See **computerized embroidery**.

AUTOMATIC PATTERNS AND STITCHES

All modern machines now come equipped with a straight stitch and a swing needle to enable a **zigzag** or **satin stitch**. Many machines include utilitarian or decorative stitches either through a card system or programs built into the machine. These automatic stitches dictate the needle position in terms of stitch width and length, and the direction of the **feed dog**, which will go backwards as well as forwards for certain automatic stitches.

Utilitarian stitches may include **overlock**-type stitches, **three-step zigzag** for stretch fabrics, double or triple running stitches for firm seams, smocking-style stitches to be used with shirring elastic in the bobbin, and so on.

The quantity of decorative patterns will vary according to the machine. The more computerized the machine is, the more automatic patterns and stitches can be included, and of course the price paid for the machine does make a difference, so you have to decide whether you have a use for a large quantity of decorative stitches.

On electronic or computerized machines you may be able to change the lengths and widths of these stitches, stretch them, mirror

them, or memorize them in a certain order mixed up with other decorative stitches.

It is also possible to experiment with different threads and thread tensions. **Whip stitch** and **cable stitch**, for example, can produce surprising results with many decorative stitches.

When using automatic patterns and stitches with **free motion embroidery**, do consider which ones will be suitable. The decorative stitches that require the machine feed to go backwards as well as forwards won't work well, as you will not be able to anticipate when to move the hoop backwards with the rhythm of the stitches, which often end up looking like a '**drunken wiggle**'. Stitches that rely on just one direction of feed, most notably stitches based on satin stitch, work very well in free motion embroidery. By programming a collection of **satin stitches** or elongating existing shapes (see **elongated forms**), elegant leaves or flowers can be created.

My Funny Valentine by the author. Automatic pattern of hearts worked on Mon Cheri wrapping papers, cut up and applied to a vanishing fabric grid (computerized embroidery machine). The background is dyed with metallic bronze powders, then stitched with programmed words. Worked on a Janome machine.

AUTOMATIC TENSIONS

Many modern machines now include automatic tensions that are chosen by the machine in relation to the fabric, thread and stitch length used. On certain machines the presser foot is automatically put into place and its pressure is also automatic; it is this that gives the signal for the stitch length and automatic tensions. Some machines can also be programmed with the type of fabric you are using.

These are great qualities when using the machine exactly as intended by the manufacturer for ordinary sewing or computerized designs. However, if you wish to be able to do free motion embroidery, or work with tension techniques, do make sure that your totally automatic machine can be overridden, or you may become frustrated when doing **free motion embroidery**. Most machines with automatic tensions do have the possibility to override this facility.

BACKGROUND

When a design or **motif** is worked onto a fabric the background is the part left unworked, although it may have an element of treatment already (see **background fabric**). The **negative shapes** left by the motif(s) on the background are an important element of the design and should be considered with the design.

BACKGROUND FABRIC

Surface used as support for the embroidery that may or may not show once the embroidery is complete. The choice of the background fabric for a piece of work is important. Consider the following:

■ Colour: Does the background fabric have its own colour, or does it takes dyes or paints in the manner required?

■ Texture: A fabric may have an interesting textural quality of its own – shot silk, hessian, raw silk, etc. –

or it may have special characteristics once it is stitched on that give an interesting texture – muslin, felt, scrim, etc. It may have an interesting texture if treated in some way, with heat or chemicals, for example. Thus a background will be created before stitching commences.

■ If the work is to include heavy stitching, bonding, or other materials, the fabric will need to be strong enough to support all these added elements.

■ Keeping its shape: For work that is going to be heavily stitched, the background fabric's ability to retain its shape or to be stretched back into shape may be important. If it already contains natural gum or starch, this will help in shape retention, or when stretching fabric

back into shape once the stitching is finished, or during the stitching process if this proves necessary. Linen, raw silk or good-quality cotton are all useful.

■ Going out of shape: choose a fabric that can be manipulated by directional stitching. Felt is an obvious choice, but many fabrics respond if worked with strong directional stitching. Choose a medium to heavyweight fabric.

■ Delicacy: It may be important for the design, but it doesn't necessarily mean that the fabric has to be fragile: habutai silks, organdie or organza, including those made with synthetic fibres, are all strong enough to stitch onto. Where stitching is to be delicate, almost any fabric can be used.

Matching scarf and bag by Anne Griffiths, worked on hand-dyed silk chiffon. The interior, in habutai silk, shows through the cutwork on the bag. For a detail see page 84.

■ Vanishing fabrics rely on creating a background of stitching to hold the work together.

■ Of course the background fabric doesn't have to be a fabric: it could be paper, plastic, metal, old vegetable nets – but then its selection and how to treat it becomes even more integrated into the design and subsequent work.

BACKING FABRIC
A backing used to give extra support to the surface to be embroidered on. See also **stabilizer**.

BAGS
Beautiful bags are a tradition in needlework, and are popular with modern embroiderers too. While experimenting with techniques and samples, it's not unusual to find yourself inundated with small, beautiful pieces of embroidered fabric that seem to have no apparent use unless it is to put them in the file with the other embroidered fragments. Turning such pieces into bags has become a popular solution if you have outgrown the need for sample files. Adding cords, buttons and beads can enrich the surfaces.

Constructions can be based on **pelmet Vilene** if you wish to give a firm structure to the bag. Drawstring bags are probably the easiest to make, and the most tactile in aspect, but envelope forms for clutch bags are attractive, and indeed almost any form can be made if you work it out on paper first. However, here we approach the notion of completely designing the bag in question from scratch – and why not, they deserve that sort of attention too.

BAKING PARCHMENT
A product used for baking that is completely 'non-stick' – not to be confused with greaseproof paper, which doesn't have the same non-stick qualities. Baking parchment is often used in cookery for products that have a high sugar content.

For the modern embroiderer it is an essential piece of equipment as it permits the use of an iron to heat surfaces that would otherwise stick to and damage the iron. The obvious examples are **Bondaweb, crystal strands, Fibrefilm** and **Fibretex, plastic** and **polythene, Soluweb, Tyvek, Xpandaprint** (puff paint), and any other fabric that is distressed using the heat from an iron.

BALLPOINT NEEDLE
A needle with a rounded end that divides the fabric it is going into between the threads, rather than splitting a thread as an ordinary pointed needle would. Invented specifically for synthetic and stretch fibres, these needles prevent snagging on any fibre that has a strong filament. They are therefore useful (and sometimes essential) for all synthetic fabrics and silks (although for raw silks they are not essential), synthetic quilt wadding and cold water **dissolvable film**. Like all needles they are available in a variety of sizes.

BARS
A bar is a reinforced length of thread across a space or hole. Bars can be worked across the space created by **eyelets**, between two fabrics in the manner of drawn hemstitch and **drawn fabric work**, or attached to complicated forms as in **cutwork** or **broderie anglaise**.

To create a bar, the fabrics to be joined should have two rows of machine running stitch along the edge, or should be turned in and hemmed. With the fabric(s) held taut in a ring, and without a foot or feed, work several rows of straight stitch backwards and forwards, going into the fabric (on the fabric side of the existing rows of stitching). At this stage the bar will hold, but you may also neaten it by satin stitching over it. In this case, don't work into the fabric with the satin stitch, especially if you intend to neaten up the fabric afterwards by satin stitching along the edge, as unsightly bumps will show. You may also add picots by stitching little circles onto the bars. If the areas to be held are too complicated to be held in a ring without support, you can stitch the bars across vanishing fabric in the same way. See **cutwork**.

BARTACK
Made with a wide **zigzag** setting and **free motion embroidery** by stitching on the spot to form a bar. See **bead stitch, satin stitch blocks, satin stitch daisies**.

BASTING
See **tacking**.

BATTING
See **quilt wadding**.

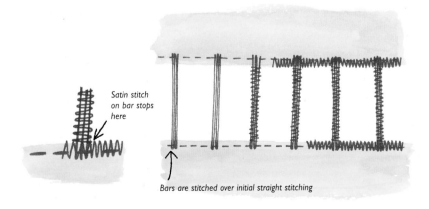

Satin stitch on bar stops here

Bars are stitched over initial straight stitching

Method for working bars across a hole or on vanishing fabric.

BEAD STITCH

Traditionally six or more zigzag stitches worked over each other to form a raised seeding stitch in **free motion embroidery**. The work must be kept absolutely still while the stitches are being made.

BEADS

Beads can be applied to a surface by machine. Thread the beads as required onto a firm thread, then place them on the surface of the fabric, wiggling in and out with your free motion stitch to hold down the joining thread onto the surface of the fabric. You can't really use a darning foot for this technique, so the fabric will have to be very stiff, in a hoop, or use a **spring needle**. To help in placing the beads, make sure you have an adequate length of thread holding the beads together so that you can move them around as you stitch. A

cocktail stick can also be useful to hold the beads into place as you stitch around them. The stitching should be at medium speed – if the beads are hard this will allow the needle to slide off them if it should hit one, rather than break.

Beads can also be incorporated into machined cords or **edges** by threading them onto a thread and incorporating them into the zigzag stitching. Sequins and other materials can be added to embroidery using the same method – see **mirror glass**.

A beading foot is available with some machines that allows the stitching into place of pre-strung beads up to 4mm ($^1/_8$ inch) in diameter, by zigzagging in between them. See picture on page 43.

BEAN STITCH

An automatic stitch frequently used in computerized embroidery. It

consists of three stitches worked between two points, and the needle then moves on to create the next three stitches. This can be used as a solid outline stitch for designs, for appliqué or cutwork.

BIAS

The bias of a woven fabric is at 45° to the edges, and even a tightly woven fabric will stretch and give a little in this direction, but organdie and lightweight fabrics are particularly good. For cutting bias strips, see **bound edges**. Slashing on the bias and then embroidering along the edges can produce interesting rolled raised edges; areas of heavy embroidery could be placed underneath such slashes. Cutting wide bias strips and pulling them as you machine straight stitch, zigzag or satin stitch along the edge causes them to curl and stretch. These could be added to other work

Beads threaded onto a thread (in red) with machine stitching holding the thread to the fabric in between the beads. Can be worked without a darning foot, and with a spring needle if necessary.

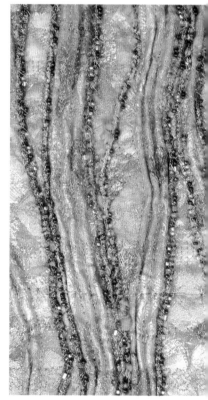

Beads stitched in with a cord added to pintucking over crazy patchwork. By Rosemarie Brewer.

to create sculptural interest. This technique will also work on stretch knits that can be pulled as you stitch.

A special bias binding foot is available to help put binding along an edge for neatening the edge or adding colour.

BIRD'S NEST

This is the accepted term for the mess that can occur on the underside of the work and which may jam the machine. It may be due to incorrect tension, fabric that has been badly put in the hoop on an embroidery machine, or, most commonly, when the presser foot lever has not been put down while working **free motion embroidery**. In all of the above cases, stop the machine, free the fabric and clean the bobbin area of threads. Try to ascertain the cause of the problem – and start again.

BLACKWORK

A traditional counted thread technique, worked in black thread and created with a double running stitch which forms a continuous line. Some automatic stitch patterns taken from traditional blackwork patterns are programmed into machines. It is also possible with a computerized embroidery machine to create motifs based on blackwork techniques. In fact almost any linear design could be used as a basis; the advantage of this method is that you don't have to program in colour changes!

Working with free motion embroidery in black or very dark blue thread to create linear drawings or motifs can also be an interesting way to anchor your work within an embroidery tradition.

Note that traditional 16th-century blackwork was frequently spotted with seed pearls or beads, or the odd stitch of red thread for richness. This fact is often ignored as the embroideries were frequently the victims of the late 18th-century craze for 'drizzling', where all items

Porcelain blackwork sampler by the author. Hand and machine embroidered pieces of fabric are dipped in porcelain slip, fired, then broken open to reveal the inside. The result is coloured and then refired.

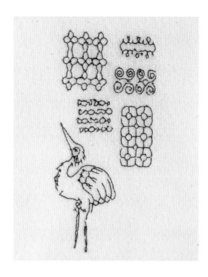

Blackwork sampler taken from Moyra McNeill and Elizabeth Geddes *Blackwork* book (permission granted). A tracing was scanned into the Janome Customizer program. It was cleaned up, and then the lines were traced in a chosen order to avoid too many jumps between the stitching. The second image was worked in gold thread on muslin over a calico ground with bronze powders. The 'blackwork' automatic stitches around the outside were also worked on the Janome. By the author.

of worth were unpicked from embroideries for pin money – a fashion invented by a dispossessed French aristocracy.

BLIND HEMMING STITCH
An automatic stitch is made up of two straight stitches to one side, then a zigzag that crosses to the other side. It is used to stitch a hem on garments by machine and can be almost invisible (see your machine handbook for details). It can also be useful for creative embroidery – see **applying thread, cord and ribbon** and **faggoting**.

BLOCK STITCH
See **satin stitch blocks**.

BOBBIN
A double-ended spool that holds the bobbin thread and fits underneath the machine bed, vertically or horizontally. The bobbin thread forms the part of the stitch on the underside of the fabric.

BOBBIN CASE
The bobbin case holds the bobbin on the underside of the sewing

machine and makes appropriate movements to create a loop around the top thread, thus forming a **lock stitch**. The bobbin case may be placed in the machine horizontally or vertically, depending on the type of machine.

A vertical bobbin case, which fits into the front of the machine, is withdrawn to put the bobbin in place. It has a screw that can be adjusted to change the tension of the bobbin thread for **tension techniques**, or for adjustments for the thickness of thread used. Some bobbin cases have a sort of horseshoe opening, in which case the tension spring can be easily bypassed to create a **feather stitch** or **cable stitch**. Because it is easily withdrawn from the machine it is easy to reset the tension. See **bobbin tension, correct tension.**

Horizontal bobbin cases are not withdrawn from the machine. The bobbin is merely placed in it for sewing. These also have a screw that can be adjusted, although resetting it is more difficult, and it is wise to take notes about its original position. Some horizontal bobbin

cases can be withdrawn fairly easily from the machine and reset as for vertical bobbin cases – see right. If you wish to change the screw regularly on a horizontal race machine, it's a good idea to keep a separate bobbin case to be used only for normal sewing.

BOBBIN TENSION
CORRECT TENSION
On a machine with a horizontal bobbin race there is often a screw mechanism with coloured marks, which show where the tension will be correctly set. Where there are numbers, the higher the number the tighter the tension, the lower the number the looser the tension. The tension screw can be adjusted on the bobbin case if necessary, but for normal sewing this should not be required. On some machines, the bobbin case can be removed easily from the machine and adjusted as described below.

Machines with vertical bobbin races are easier to gauge and can be more easily adjusted to suit yarns of different thickness and maintain a correct tension. Thread the bobbin case as usual and then suspend the bobbin case by holding the thread in one hand over the other hand – just in case the bobbin falls out, or if the tension is too loose the case will fall. For a correct tension the case should not drop when held in this way, and the thread should barely run through when the hand suspending the bobbin case makes the motion of a small sharp tap. To tighten the bobbin tension: turn the screw (a) in a clockwise direction; to loosen, turn it anti-clockwise.

ADJUSTING THE TENSION
For the best results, a good tension is essential. The bobbin tension often needs adjusting because of the fineness of the threads used. If it is not correctly adjusted, unwanted spots of bobbin thread can show on the surface of the work. For details of how to adjust for a correct tension, see above.

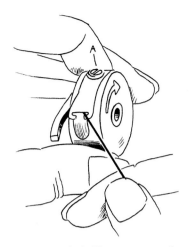

The screw on the bobbin case is turned clockwise to loosen the tension, anticlockwise to tighten the tension.

Bobbin tensions may also be adjusted in order to create textures in embroidery. By loosening the bobbin tension (turning screw (a) anti-clockwise) the bobbin thread will come through to the top surface of the fabric. This effect can be enhanced further by tightening the top tension. See **tension techniques** for details.

BYPASSING THE TENSION
In this technique, the bobbin thread comes directly off the bobbin and does not go through the tension spring on the bobbin case, but is left loose to be picked up by the top thread. The technique can be used for **feather stitch** or **cable stitch**. However, not all machines can accept having the bobbin tension bypassed. As a general rule it is worth a try on most horizontal race sewing machines (go slowly at first in case it doesn't accept it and gets in a tangle). On certain horizontal race machines the effect can be changed according to the speed of the machine. A fast machine speed and slow motion will produce a **whip stitch** or **heavy whip stitch**, while a slow speed will produce a **feather stitch**.

On vertical race machines it is impossible to bypass closed bobbin cases. If the case is open or has a horseshoe form around the tension spring, it should work. Some recent machines allow this, notably Pfaff. **Irish machines** also have this option.

Do try this on your machine, but start off slowly in case of difficulties. You should very easily get a loose **feather stitch** and may also produce good results for **cable stitch** if your machine accepts this method.

BONDAWEB

This is one of the more common names for a fusible weblike structure, sticky when heated with an iron, that can be used to bond two fabrics together. It is especially useful for **appliqué**. The webbing is backed with a non-stick parchment that allows it to be ironed to one surface without the risk of it sticking to and damaging the iron. Normally the product is ironed to one fabric, which is then cut out. The backing is then peeled away and the fabric piece can be ironed onto another fabric for decoration. Bondaweb has the advantage of fusing the fabric it is ironed to, so there is little danger of fraying. The

Empty Shrine by the author. Ink-stained Bondaweb makes the first layer of colour on cotton fabric. The second layer is acrylic painted on Bondaweb fused on top of the first layer. The inked surface can be seen through the imperfections. Further ink has been rubbed into this surface. Any flaking of the acrylic paint when stitching reveals the inked surface underneath. Stitched with a 'drunken wiggle'.

appliqué stitching that follows can take this into consideration – the appliqué does not need to be completely surrounded by stitching to prevent fraying or to hold it down to the background fabric. When used in this way the surface can become quite firm and flat, and can also be quite hard to stitch into. Fine threads will wear and break easily if precautions are not taken. The easiest way to stitch on a Bondawebbed surface is to use a **darning foot** or free embroidery foot to hold the fabric firmly at the point of stitching, with or without a hoop. Then there are no problems with quite heavy stitching. Using a larger-eyed embroidery needle can also help.

In practice Bondaweb has many and varied uses. The webbing can be torn into small pieces and used to hold down surfaces before stitching. This creates surfaces and designs that are much less rigid. If the bonding fabric is detached from its parchment backing in this way, do remember to use the special parchment or **baking parchment** to protect the iron and ironing board. Tearing the webbing instead of cutting it prevents noticeable solid edges.

Bondaweb can be used as a fabric surface in its own right with interesting results. Bits of fabric, threads, beads, or sequins can be trapped between two layers of Bondaweb (remember to use baking parchment to protect the iron and the ironing surface). Fine fabric or chiffon could be bonded on each side of this sandwich to stabilize the result before stitching, though this is not essential. Bondaweb can also be distressed with a **hot air tool** if this is required.

Bondaweb can be coloured with paint, ink and **fabric paint**. Different results are obtained depending on whether the paints are wet or dryish, whether the surface is left on its backing paper or not. The resulting coloured fabric can be bonded to a surface and stitched, or torn or cut into

shapes and then bonded. A see-through fabric such as fine chiffon can be added, or the bonded surface could be the subject of heavy stitching. The quality of painted surface obtained in this way can be quite textural and interesting, as well as being easier to stitch into than an ordinary painted surface.

BONDING
The act of fusing one surface to another, for decoration or to create mixtures of textures and colours. See **Bondaweb, bonding powder, Soluweb, spray bonding glue.**

BONDING POWDER
A **bonding** glue in a powder form, generally provided in a container similar to a salt shaker with different-sized openings. Bonding powder sticks two fabric surfaces together when it is placed between them and ironed. As it can be lightly dusted it is not perceivable in the same way as pieces of **Bondaweb**, and does not change the surface of the fabric by making it stiff, so subsequent machine stitching is much easier. It is a more suitable method for lightweight or transparent fabrics where Bondaweb can be visible. It can also a useful for applying **metallic transfer film**, as it gives a subtle surface, the metallic film only sticking to the points where the bonding powder has been shaken.

Fabrics using linen, cotton, wool or silk tops can be created using fibres drawn at opposing angles with bonding powder sprinkled in between. It is easy to make an extremely delicate structure in this way, which can then be machine stitched.

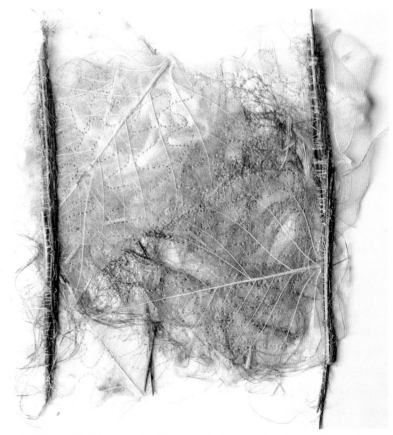

Linen, Leaf, Cotton, Thistle by the author. Worked with the stated ingredients in layers with bonding powder. Stitched with a vermicelli stitch.

BOOKS

Books can be a wonderful project for art pieces. After all, there's so much that you can say in a book! Bookbinding is a subject on its own, so this entry is more concerned about easily realizable book projects.

The simplest idea is an entirely fabric book, such as those made for children, with overlocked or bound edges. Not too many pages should be involved as the seam of the book will be stitched together – think about how many layers of fabric your machine can stitch through. A4 pieces of fabric, layered together and stitched through the middle across the width, will form an A5 book. Different fabrics or papers could be used. Or make it entirely of calico, but papers could be stitched onto certain pages. Instead of using a normal sketchbook all

Book, by Frances Pickering.

Inside of book by Frances Pickering.

the time how about trying this for a week or two? Include threads and a needle in your pencil case! A ringbound sketchbook of greater proportions could be made by making eyelets or buttonholes across one side for the rings. This could be a useful way of storing samples.

Loose covers can be made for any existing books. Firstly make a paper cover for the given book, so that you have a pattern shape that works. The paper will need to cover the book (closed as well as open) and then turn in for about a third to halfway on the inside of each cover. There will be a join top and bottom along this turned-in part, holding it to the outside part of the book cover. It is these pockets that slip over the book cover when the loose cover is made. Make sure you leave enough fabric for a seam allowance or for zigzagging or overlocking the edge. Any decoration on the cover should be worked before you sew the book cover together. The loose cover could be based on **pelmet Vilene** for extra strength if required.

The cover could be a removable one used for sketchbooks, or a special cover for a special book. Inspiration for cover decoration could be drawn from the contents of the book itself.

BORDERS

A decorative border may be placed around a design or picture to contain it or to add some meaning to its content. A **repeat motif** can be used, something that recalls an element in the existing embroidery. Words or a poem can be used to form a border, offering a further insight into the embroidery. The border could be rather plain, with perhaps just a few marks or lightweight stitching that recall the busier surface of the embroidery on the inside.

A border can finish off the edges of fabric in a decorative way. The border could be created on the fabric itself with **free motion**

Fountain, Vines and Olive Trees by the author. Worked on linen with a variety of free motion straight stitch fillings.

A border design to be worked as a vanishing fabric edge, based on a repeat motif that has been mirrored.

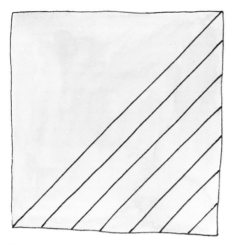 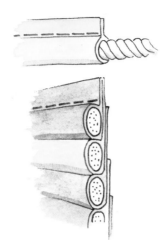

Strips are cut on the bias of the fabric and used to cover piping cord, which can then be placed together in layers.

embroidery, **appliqué** or **computerized embroidery;** applied with **braids;** be part of the stitching that forms the edge; or may go beyond the edge into a lace design using vanishing fabrics. Such borders are generally based on repeat motifs, although free forms can also work very well when following a theme, for example: wave shapes, leaves, flames. See also **insertions** and **lace edges.**

BOUND EDGES

Edges can be bound with straight or bias strips of fabric to add colour and stability to an edge. Strips of different colours can be folded over and stitched together in layers to form a multicoloured or textured edge. A piping cord could be placed within the fold to add bulk. When placing a piping cord inside a strip of fabric, or applying it to an edge, use a zipper foot and the needle to one side in order to stitch close to the piping cord.

A very useful bound edge, particularly on a garment, which avoids the necessity for linings, is to just turn in the edge using an iron, then satin stitch over this edge. From the inside of the edge of the garment, cut back to this stitching line. To firm up and neaten up the edge even more, you can then follow with a second row of satin

stitch, slightly wider than the first, if desired.

BOXES

Making boxes is a traditional technique that seems to be included in all embroidery courses. Using accurately cut card, ladder stitch and an unwieldy curved needle, most of us have had sore fingers to testify to our rite of passage! However, extraordinary boxes and containers can be made by machine using any variety of techniques. For more complicated box shapes, make a model first in stiff paper or card to try out the shapes and sizes required. If you are including a lid that will fit over the outside of the box, or over an inner sleeve, make sure it is large enough. Seams of some boxes may be on the outside of the work, and this can have a decorative effect.

Here are a few ideas to experiment with, though I'm sure that the list is far from exhaustive.

TRADITIONAL TECHNIQUES WITH FABRIC-COVERED CARD

You can sandwich a piece of card between layers of fabric and stitch around the edge. Use a zipper foot with the needle offset to one side, as if putting in a zip or working up to a cord. Four sandwiched layers can then be used to make a box in the

Box by Kelly Bales. 'The boxes are based on the theme of rust and deterioration, worked in machine embroidery on cold water soluble fabric. The pattern, based on mechanical and metal objects, is traced from the original painting. Materials such as velvet and tarnished metal plate are incorporated into the embroidery. The fabric is dissolved and allowed to dry as a solid sheet, rigid and fairly rough in texture. Acrylic paint is added in places to accentuate this and to contribute to the overall rusted effect. The boxes are made out of thick card and glue. Pieces are cut out of the embroidered fabric and applied to the containers with PVA medium. All edges and corners are neatly finished with a combination of hand and machine stitching. The fasteners are the main features of the boxes. The zips, bolts, locks and hooks are fixed to the boxes with glue and invisible thread.'

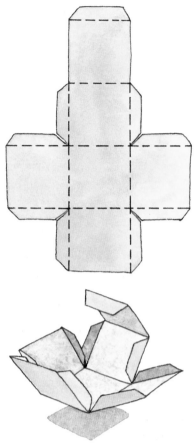

Cutting and folding for a box in one piece. The flaps can be turned out and stitched together by machine, leaving a seam, or turned in and stitched with ladder or slip stitch. This is easier if there is stitching along the dotted lines.

usual way with the seams turned towards the inside. A fifth sandwich can make the bottom of the box, but the seam will have to be worked by hand. A second collection of slightly smaller sandwiches (calculated according to the width of the card and fabric) can be made and placed with seams towards the outside or the inside of the existing box if you wish to hide the seams. You can experiment with this basic notion, leaving the seams apparent on the inside or the outside and decorating them in some way. Four sheets of card can be placed side by side within a long fabric sandwich, thus leaving only one edge and the base to be seamed.

Close-up of box by Kelly Bales.

Quilt wadding can be incorporated into the sandwich for a softer, more tactile result. The fabric could be embroidered before making up the sandwiched layers.

PELMET VILENE

Pelmet Vilene is an excellent material for making boxes. Before you start, decide on the form of your box, and make a stiff paper template to try out the shapes and sizes involved. If possible, try to make the box shape out of one piece of paper, just by folding. The same box can then be made with pelmet Vilene. It can be cut out, painted, covered with a fabric or embroidered and decorated. Where the fold lines are on the paper, stitch a machine line, so that the Vilene will fold at this point. Any two edges can be stitched together using a zigzag stitch. The needle should go into each of the sides, but allow a small space between them as you stitch so that the edge you have created can be folded. Another decorative way of joining the sides is to outline all the sides to be joined with a machine-wrapped **cord** zigzagged into place. These cords can then easily be stitched together by hand, or with another layer of zigzag machine stitching.

VANISHING FABRIC

Cold water **dissolvable film** or **Solusheet**, both of which leave a residue in the fibres, can be useful for creating boxes and vessels. Laces or fabrics created on these surfaces will be stiff enough to stand up, and therefore are useful for making small boxes, containers or bowls.

For boxes, additional stiffness can be added by incorporating wire in the lace for the edges of the box, stitching over the wire slowly and carefully with a satin stitch, and then painting with **PVA medium** for added stiffness. You can make separate box sides and stitch them together, either by hand or machine, a method which gives better corners and hinges. The embroidery should be exactly the shape required, with the wire incorporated along the edge; it is the wire that will be joined to the wire of the next side of the box, so there that will be no seams to hide.

Vessels and bowls can be sculpted in vanishing fabric lace. When the excess fabric has been vanished, place the lace in or on a mould to dry. Use several layers if necessary. Once this is dry and removed from the mould you can paint it with PVA medium for stiffness and to secure its shape. The best moulds are those made from plaster of Paris because they absorb the water and don't stick, but almost anything will do – including balloons, which can be popped once the work is dry.

FELT

Some varieties of felt can be particularly stiff, especially homemade ones and acrylic felts, even more so if they are treated with a **hot air tool**. More stiffness can be added with PVA medium if it is required. Felt doesn't fray, so it won't cause difficulties with seams. A box can be made out of felt on the machine with all the seams on the outside, neatly cut back with scissors or a soldering iron. The slightly soft, sculptural nature of this medium can add a greater textural quality to boxes made from it. Felt can also be wetted and heated and then sculpted into other forms – this method works most obviously for hats, but why not try it for bowls and other vessels? In Siberia they even use felt for making traditional snowboots!

SOFTSCULPT

The thinner version of Softsculpt can be moulded to take on different forms, and it is easily stitched

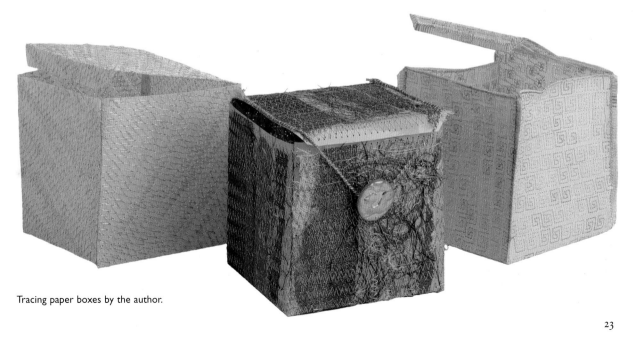

Tracing paper boxes by the author.

together or to other fabrics. Layered between fabrics as in card boxes, it may prove a softer, more textural way of producing boxes than using card. The fabrics themselves can be seamed to the next sandwich to produce good corners and hinges. Softsculpt can also be moulded when heated to take on any shape. For more details see the main entry on **Softsculpt**.

MACHINE-STITCHED WIRE MESH

Fine **wire mesh** can be stitched on and hinged to adjoining pieces using **zigzag**, **satin stitch** or **blind hemming stitch** to form the sides or lid of a box. The bottom will have to be stitched into place by hand. It can also be bent and sculpted into other forms and vessels. Or make a cross shape as for the paper boxes, so that only the sides have to be stitched together and not the bottom.

PAPER

You can use the above methods to create paper boxes, seaming pieces together in much the same way as felt. The perforation of the needle can cause the paper to become fragile at its most stressed points – the corners and edges – so make sure you use a good-quality paper: a thick tracing paper is ideal and these are available in a variety of colours. If the paper has an all-over stitch design before being turned into a box, this stitching can be used for slip stitching the sides together.

Paper and papier-mâché are superb materials for sculpting into different forms and vessels. Use plaster of Paris moulds to be sure that the bowl will come unstuck easily, or work over a balloon that you can pop afterwards. Pieces of lace, stitched fabric or other textiles and paint or dye could be incorporated as you build up a paper surface. The final vessel or bowl could also be embroidered afterwards. If you need to add more stiffness to the bowl once it is finished, use **PVA medium**.

BRAIDS

A braid is a flat decorated band that can be used to decorate a surface or edge. Braids made with heavy stitched patterns can be worked on ordinary fabrics or ribbons using existing **automatic patterns,** or you can create your own using the computer facilities on the machine. It is wise to use a strong **backing fabric** or **stabilizer** for the stitching process so that the braid holds its shape (width) and doesn't pull in as you are working.

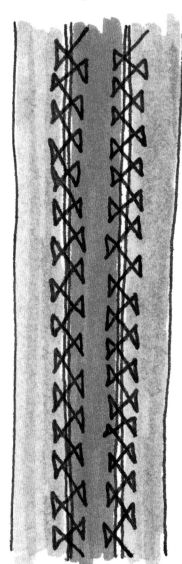

Ribbons or threads laid side by side under the machine and stitched with an automatic decorative stitch to form a wider braid.

Braids can also be made by placing ribbons or threads side by side and stitching them together with **zigzag** stitches. Alternatively, place them on a firm **vanishing fabric** (so that you don't need a hoop) and stitch over them, holding the braids together with any form of free stitching.

BRICKING

On embroideries that involve large areas of **straight stitch filling**, a hoop should be used. If an area to be filled cannot be placed in the hoop all at once, the stitching should be 'bricked' to join it neatly together without an apparent join, rather than stitched solidly up to the edge of the hoop. Stitch alternate rows, or every third row up to the edge, the next row a little in from the edge, the third row a little further in from the edge, and then start again. When you move the ring onwards you can fill up to this stitching and there won't be a harsh line. Note that in practice any staggered finish will work to avoid a line.

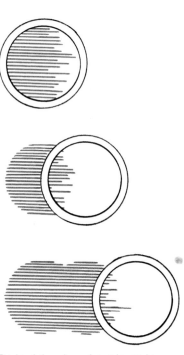

'Bricking' the edges of straight stitching as you move the hoop along prevents joins in the stitching being visible.

Filling in small areas at a time and deliberately creating lines within one colour area can become an element within a design. Alice Kettle exaggerates this quality in her work with her use of cable stitch.

BRODERIE ANGLAISE

A traditional white **openwork** technique involving the creating of holes and **eyelets** surrounded with satin stitch and sparsely decorated with lines and padded satin stitch to create an impression of lace, with borders in a wavy or scallop design. Broderie anglaise was and still is frequently worked on industrial machines to create metres of wide ribbon or fabric with holes and eyelets, with effective padded satin stitch. This is often known as Swiss work because it was originally produced in Switzerland. Many of

today's domestic machines can produce good eyelets, using an eyelet foot or computerized designs, although this technique is no longer fashionable, and the ribbons and lengths of fabric available in shops today are relatively cheap, so there is less need for home production. The techniques of eyelet and buttonhole embroidery on delicate surfaces can still be charming on special garments – and, after all, they don't have to be all in white!

BRONZING POWDERS
See **metallic powders**.

BUILDING UP SURFACES

One of the beauties of embroidery and textiles is the interest and intensity that can be developed on a surface. A sumptuous effect can be achieved just by stitching in different colours. Other techniques

include dyeing, **bonding** bits and pieces to the surface, and adding previously embroidered fabrics to be re-embroidered. **Glue, paint, gesso, metallic powders, crystal strands, plastics, scrim, muslin, paper, leather** and **metal wires** can all play a part. A built-up surface can look lovely and integrated, or may just be a collection of bits and bobs that include all the latest gimmicks. The important difference between the two will be the integrity of the design. Whatever the surface created and however scrunchy and gorgeous it is when you are close to it, it must still work as a whole when viewed from further away. Indeed the joy of embroidery is that it offers us this duality of vision.

To be sure that the surface is well integrated, a see-through fabric such as chiffon could be placed over the

Pink floral broderie Anglaise edge, by Vikki Lafford, while a student at Manchester Metropolitan University.

Growth and Decay by Frankie Creith. 'Gardens inspire this work. Actual plant fibres and leaves are used to explore plant life through the cycle of growth and decay. The notion of life and existence is indicated through a definite and planned pattern of leaves and twigs, while decay is illustrated by bland, distressed and limp "fabric", with a subtle gradation of colour between the two. Through this work the artist questions our human existence and its purpose. For like this artwork our lives go through periods of growth and learning, structure and deliberate planning, to eventual separation from this world toward a time when our earthly bodies too will decay.' The first image shows the area of growth. The work measures 400 x 30cm (157 x 12 inches).

whole surface and stitched to integrate the whole. Or just use masses of machine or even hand and machine stitching so that the whole piece becomes meshed together. See **worker stitches.**

Look at the work from a distance to ensure that it has not just become a mass of colour and texture, but that there is line and shape which work as a composition, and that some areas are less heavily worked to offer relief from the heavy textures or colours in other areas.

Good use of drawings or your sketchbook or notebook, with experimentation and design sheet work will be essential for the success of any large project.

THE MAKING OF *GROWTH AND DECAY*
'Growth and Decay' (left) by Frankie Creith was created using the following method:

1. Batches of paper pulp were made by tearing up soft kitchen paper and mixing it with a small amount of water in a kitchen blender until a fine pulp was achieved.

2. A sheet of polythene was placed on a flat surface (large enough to suit the overall size of the finished work). Small amounts of the pulp were placed in a dish of water (Note that larger proportions of water to pulp create a finer paper, so this can be regulated to suit the requirements of the work.) A paper-making screen was used to lift the paper pulp from the water (a picture frame covered in dress netting could also be used), and then it was transferred to the polythene. The process was repeated until the desired size was achieved. At this point there is usually a lot of water, which can be mopped up using kitchen cloths.

3. Other materials were placed onto this water-laden surface. The choice can vary according to the nature of the work. Leaves and petals were used in 'Growth and Decay', but

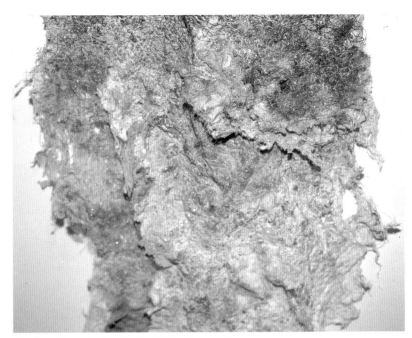

Growth and Decay by Frankie Creith. Detail shows *Decay*.

7. Free motion stitching, in both straight and zigzag, was used in an all-over random manner to enhance the existing surface and create further texture, as well as to change and grade the colour using a variety of coloured cotton threads. 'Fabric' created in this way can also be manipulated using techniques such as pleats and tucks, or it may be cut up and reassembled (in this case straight stitch was used and the stitch length set to 3–4). Beads and embellishments may also be added.

BULLION KNOTS

The effect of hand-stitched bullion knots can be imitated by stitching long thin **satin stitch blocks.** These can also be worked over a small cord or thick thread to give a raised finish. The cord or thread could even peep out at each end of the 'bullion knot' for added texture.

BURNING

Burning textiles, plastics and other surfaces can create a distressed effect which is interesting simply as a textural change within the embroidery, or may be useful as part of the statement that the

other suitable materials might include cellophane, foil, coloured papers, wool, pieces of fabric, etc. The choice of materials is endless, and the only limitation is that they should be pliable enough to allow a sewing needle to pass through them. On the top of this layering, a fine layer of sewing thread was added – this may be in long continuous strands (often several reels are used) or cut into shorter lengths. This layer acts as a sealer for the layers underneath.

4. Dress netting was placed on top of this 'fabric' of wet paper pulp, followed by a second layer of polythene, with some form of flat sheeting on top (this can be wood, Perspex, MDF or other suitable material), and then weight was applied. It should be left like this for at least one week, giving time for the water to evaporate and the layered materials to fuse together.

5. When the fabric was totally dry, the weight, sheeting and polythene was removed. A layer of Bondaweb was applied and ironed to fix. The fabric was then turned over and the Bondaweb process was repeated on the underside, making the created fabric now fully pliable and secure.

6. Most media may be used to colour the fabric: paints, inks and dyes are the most effective. Well diluted acrylic paints and coloured inks were used in this work.

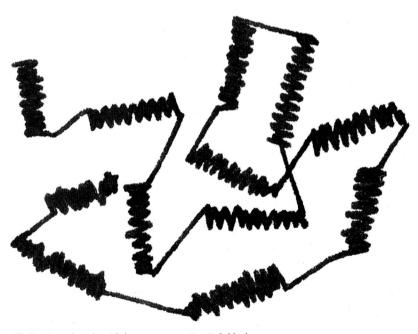

'Bullion knots' made with long narrow satin stitch blocks.

Dragonflies by Janice Lewis. Worked on layers of see-through fabrics with burnt cutwork.

embroidery wishes to make. Burning can be worked with matches, candles, joss sticks, using an **iron, soldering iron** or a **hot air tool.** Useful precautions are to work near a ceramic or stainless steel sink or over a metal tray, and to have a water spray or a bowl of water ready. A water spray will allow you to control which areas continue to burn, if it is used judiciously. A mask should be worn because some materials may give off toxic odours. Embroideries can be given a distressed look, have their edges sealed or textures changed. These

are all very useful, but as with all gimmicks, do make sure that the results are well integrated into your work, texturally or conceptually, so that they have a real role to play.

BURNT CUTWORK

A method of creating **cutwork** or **openwork** by burning a suitable fabric (synthetics, polyester organdie, nylon chiffon, etc.) to create open spaces in the fabric. The burnt holes will not fray because the burning finishes them off. The best tool for this is a **soldering iron.** Layers can be burnt and stitched

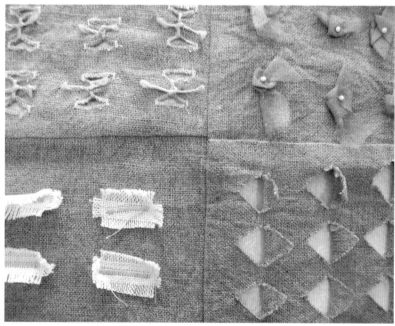

Sample of buttonhole stitching on linen by Simone Mosse.

together. Because the fabrics used are synthetic, it is best to use a fine ballpoint needle for any stitching. See also **burning.**

BUTTONHOLES

Most modern machines have at least one automatic or semi-automatic buttonhole. Details of how to work it on your machine will be in the instruction handbook, but they are usually very simple – often you just select the type of buttonhole you require, select the length, press the button and off you go! The length may also be selected by placing the button in a guide on the buttonhole foot. On older or simpler machines you may have to change between different buttons on the machine as you do the sides or ends of the buttonhole, and you decide the length as you go.

Buttonholes can be used for many decorative effects. They can create a depth in the surface by placing other colours behind them. The holes may be placed closely together and then tied open or laced through. Using a variety of lengths of opening can be interesting too. On many machines you are in control of the length, and even when the buttonhole is entirely automatic, a long length of buttonhole can be set.

You may even like to include buttons in your work and create flaps or openings to peep into that can be buttoned or unbuttoned.

CABLE STITCH

Cable stitch is worked when a thicker or more delicate thread than would normally go through the needle is wound onto the bobbin. The bobbin tension is changed to accommodate the thicker thread. The thick thread stays in place on the underside of the fabric, which now becomes the right side. This has the obvious disadvantage of not being able to see the right side of the embroidery as you work. For this reason it is always necessary to practise first on a spare piece of fabric to see what the result of stitch shapes and tension will be, before going ahead on the real piece. Marks can be made on the back of the fabric to guide you, or existing stitching on the work may also serve as a guide. Note that you need to turn the fabric over in the **hoop** so that you are still working into the well on the flat bed of the machine.

To create a cable stitch choose a hand stitch thread such as stranded cotton or rayon, soft embroidery or pearl cotton, knitting threads or ribbons – in fact anything that doesn't have lumps, bumps or loose filaments. This can be wound by hand onto the bobbin and placed in the bobbin case. If you do this after working a sample of **feather stitch** you will find that the bobbin tension spring which was loose on a fine embroidery thread is now tight. Put the top thread tension to normal or slightly tight (5 or 6).

Stitch a sample slowly so that you can stop immediately if the machine blocks or the fabric pulls through with difficulty. In this case the thread may be caught – perhaps there are loose filaments, or the bobbin tension spring may still be too tight – so loosen it further. The best thing to do is a series of wavy lines or U shapes and a little **vermicelli stitching**. This will give you an idea of the tension that you have on the

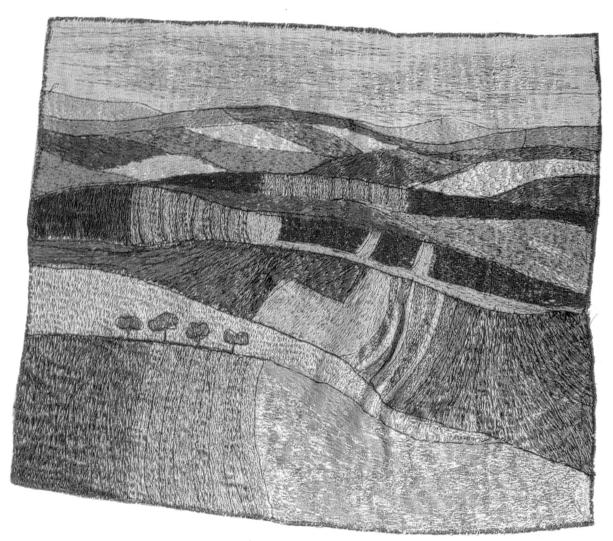

Beyond the Torridge by Carol Naylor, worked from the reverse of the embroidery with floss threads and cable stitch.

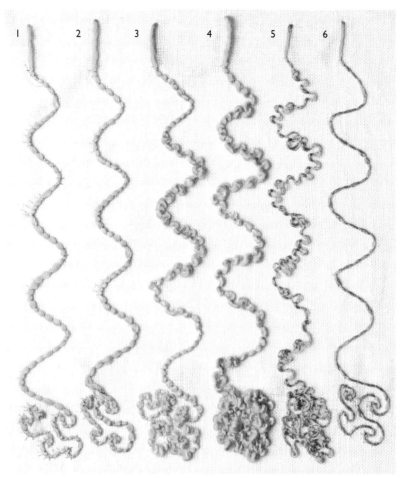

1 2 3 4 5 6

Cable stitch samples with curves and vermicelli stitch to show the results of tension settings. The first examples are worked with a soft silk. 1. Overtight bobbin tension with slightly loose top tension creates feather stitch. 2. Perfectly equalized tension, with top tension at 5 or 6 creates a couched line. 3. The bobbin tension is loosened some more to create bobbles. 4. The bobbin tension is bypassed (on a Pfaff machine) to create a very bobbly result. The final two examples are worked with stranded rayon. 5. Bypassed tension on a Pfaff machine. 6. A perfect couched tension.

bobbin. Keep the stitches fairly long, as this will allow the bobbin thread to show.

■ If the bobbin tension is perfect for **couching**, you will have a perfectly couched line, with the top thread neatly wrapping the bobbin thread and holding it securely in place.

■ If the bobbin thread is tight it will pull as you stitch and the top thread will be pulled through to the bottom to give you a (reverse) **feather stitch**. This result can be enhanced by loosening the top tension if desired.

■ If the bobbin thread is a little loose it will bobble on the surface of the fabric from time to time.

■ If the bobbin thread is very loose or if the **bobbin tension** is bypassed, bobbles will appear on the fabric's under-surface. If you use a **vermicelli stitch** this can even become a very quick textured filling.

Cable stitch, as couching or a highly textured filling, can be a very useful tool and is well worth the time taken to master. It can also be used as a **gimp thread** in **vanishing fabric** lace embroidery.

CAD
Computer-aided design can be used to design images for embroidery. Using computerized machines – **Schiffli, multihead** or computerized domestic **embroidery machines** – these designed images can be transferred, using special computer programs, into a format that can be embroidered directly by the machine.

CALICO
This simple and cheap cotton fabric, which can be bleached or unbleached, is particularly useful for embroidery or machine embroidery practice and for **fabric manipulation**. It takes dyes, paint dyes and **paints** relatively easily. It comes in different weights, from light through medium to heavyweight. It contains a starch in its unwashed state that can be useful when **stretching** the final work as it helps the embroidery to keep its shape afterwards.

CANDLING
See **burning.**

CANVAS WORK
Any type and gauge of canvas can be stitched on by hand and applied to other embroideries. A slip is a traditional motif completely worked on canvas which is then applied to another ground, most notably in **stumpwork**. One idea is to leave areas unworked, apply the whole to a firm fabric backing and then machine stitch into the unworked areas to integrate the whole into another surface.

Canvas work is a type of embroidery that many people start with when they begin embroidering. The structure of the canvas, and the simple basic stitches, are easy to become comfortable with. Little by little an embroiderer can become

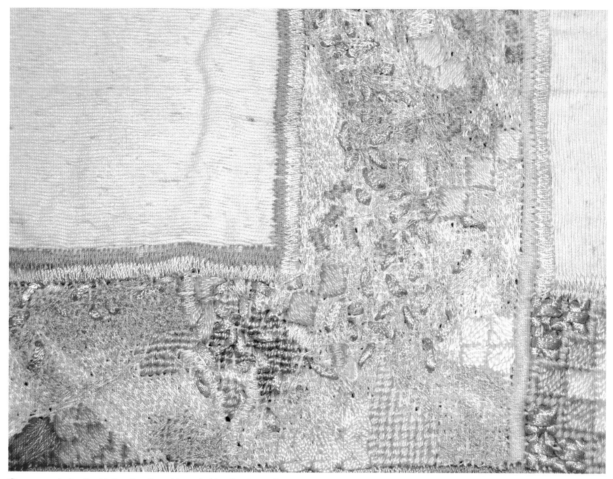

Canvas work detail with hand and machine stitching, by the author.

more creative with the canvas, using different canvaswork stitches, and employing different threads. Often when beginners are nervous about branching out too far into creative or machine embroidery I have found that using canvas as a starting point is very effective as an eye-opener and a path to creativity. Not only can traditional canvas stitches be used on canvas, but appliqué and other hand stitches can also be added, using any number of machine embroidery techniques.

For machine embroidery it is best to use a canvas that has a medium gauge (5–7 threads to 1cm, 14 or 18 to an inch being ideal). It is better if it is a lockweave (interlock) canvas as this will not create pulled work as it is being stitched on. Pulled work

may be interesting, but it will make further hand stitching difficult. Areas can be covered with **straight stitch, zigzag, satin stitch** and automatic stitches. The stitches created may resemble hand stitching, or be very clearly machine stitched. You can machine stitch into and on top of existing hand stitching, or hand stitch into spaces left in machine stitching. The informality of these methods can free up even the most traditional embroiderer!

Appliqué can be easily worked on canvas, but it is best to apply any fabrics before too much stitching is done, as the canvas will inevitably go out of shape, and it can be pulled back into shape once the work is finished (see **stretching**). However, if the appliqué is added near the end of the embroidery

process there is a risk that this will have been cut and applied out of shape, and it will not allow the canvas to find its original shape in the stretching process.

The needle should be of medium size, and it should also be sharp to penetrate the threads of the canvas. The work does not need to be in a hoop as the firmness of the canvas will make it possible to stitch without one. A darning foot is useful for keeping the canvas against the bed of the machine, in order to prevent catching the needle in between the threads and breaking it. See also **rug canvas**.

CHAIN STITCH
The very first sewing machines worked by producing a chain stitch, in the same way as handmade

tambour embroidery. Machine embroidery of this type is still produced today using **Cornely machines.**

CHIFFON

This very lightweight, see-through fabric is available in silk or nylon (it can often be purchased in the form of cheap nylon scarves). It is an extremely useful fabric which can be layered in colours in its own right, working a little like layers of watercolour. See also **organdie.**

It can also be used over the surface of other materials, to hold them down and keep them in place while stitching, without really adding colour, or only just enough to help the whole piece become more integrated.

When used on top of **Tyvek** it helps to soften the surface and gives a more textural look.

CHOOSING A SEWING MACHINE

The careful choice of a sewing machine is essential, particularly in view of the costs involved these days. The following points will help you to decide if your existing machine is suitable for machine embroidery, and can also help as a guide when purchasing a new machine.

■ The machine must be electrically operated. Although the first machine embroideries in the **Singer workshops** were created on treadle machines, hand- or foot-operated machines do make the job more difficult. These days most non-electrical machines are already in museums!

■ The machine motion should stop as soon as the foot pressure is taken off the pedal and should not run on. It is desirable to have a choice of speeds. Most machines have at least two speeds, and some modern machines have a variable speed control (as well as the pedal), though this is probably unnecessary except for computerized machine

embroidery, because one quickly learns to control the pedal.

■ Most modern electronic machines will give you a choice of finishing with the needle in or out of the work. You will be able to do just one stitch or, on some, half a stitch (from down to up or vice versa). This is very useful for accurate working and more exacting techniques.

■ All modern machines now do **zigzag** as well as **straight stitch** and this could be considered essential for machine embroidery, although of course a machine can embroider without it. Examples of **appliqué** with **satin stitch** exist from the Singer workshops done on machines that only had straight stitch: the fabric was moved from side to side to create the satin stitch known as **jump stitch.**

A smoothly graded control on the width of the stitch is preferable to one that is stepped, although if the 'steps' are small enough (1–2mm) they will hardly be detectable.

■ The top tension should be easily and reliably adjustable. If choosing a machine with **automatic tension** control, make sure that it is possible to override it – otherwise your attempts at tension techniques will be frustrating. The tension should pass through wheels on the top of the machine (usual on today's machines). If your old machine has a wheel on the front, so be it, but they do tend to wear.

■ It should be easy to adjust the bobbin tension by means of a screw on the casing, and this will be easier if the bobbin case is removable. Generally, therefore, a vertical bobbin race is preferable. A horizontal bobbin race should have a visible screw and a series of marks to help adjustment. This is important when buying a new machine, but if your old one is difficult to adjust, bear in mind that many interesting machine embroidery techniques can

be achieved without adjusting the tension. On horizontal race machines where the bobbin case screw is difficult to adjust and reset, you can always buy a second bobbin case for working the various tension techniques. See **horizontal bobbin race.**

■ Make sure that you know how to dismantle the bobbin casing, or if it does not dismantle, can rogue threads be removed by rocking the mechanism backwards and forwards? This is vital – everyone forgets to put the presser foot down on a machine from time to time!

■ Access to the workings of the machine is also important. Machine embroidery can create a lot of lint that needs cleaning out, and machines need regular oiling when they are used for long periods. Check the oiling requirements on your machine.

■ The machine must have a control to lower the **feed dog** (vertical bobbin race machines) or a plate to cover it (old horizontal race machines – most new ones now have the facility of lowering the feed dog). The cover plate leaves a small bump, so look for a machine where you can lower the feed dog.

■ The more robust the machine the better. It is going to work a lot harder as the tool of a machine embroiderer than it did for plain sewing. A sewing machine has a rest while the next seam is being prepared, but a machine used for machine embroidery may work all the hours that you do, with only your coffee breaks for relief!

Consider your normal way of working. A free arm can be useful for working into small areas; and for most free motion embroidery the larger the table or flat bed (included or bought separately) the better.

■ Automatic patterns can be fun, but are not essential, as most free machine embroidery is done with straight or satin stitch. So consider your investment carefully.

■ Finally, the difficult questions concerning embroidery machines. Do I need a new machine? Am I prepared to invest the cost involved? This is a matter of personal choice. Whether you consider that your own work could benefit from this additional technology is a matter for some consideration. Existing embroidered designs tend to be rather obvious and repetitive in nature. So to really benefit from the technology a computer is an essential tool for designing, either from scratch or from scanned images, as well as the investment in the programs that go with your choice of machine in order to get the best out of it. Many

computerized embroidery machines can be updated as the technology changes, so this could help in the choice of a new machine. Further information on the choices to be made can be found in the Appendix on Embroidery Machines on pages 188–190.

CIRCLES OR GRANITE STITCH

Worked with **free motion embroidery** (with the feed dog down or covered, and using a darning foot, or no foot at all), circles (or granite stitch) are best worked with the fabric in a **hoop**, which can be more easily manipulated to make the small movements necessary to produce the stitch. The machine speed should be fast and the hoop is moved in little circular movements which will gradually **colour in** the fabric. This is quite a difficult stitch to master, but

with the correct hand position on the hoop, the thumbs push towards the back, the middle fingers towards the front, the left index pulls to the left, and the right index pulls to the right. Between the six digits any movement is possible – including circles.

When they make their first attempts at circles, students produce very angular shapes, more often than not **triangles**, and although this effect can look attractive, it's not quite the same thing! The fault always lies with a machine speed that is not fast enough as the stitches must be very small if circles are to be produced. The movement of the hoop itself can be relatively slow.

Once the stitch has been mastered it can fill in slightly textural backgrounds and other colours can be added using

Detail of olive trees from *Vines, Olives and Cypress Trees* by the author, showing a crazy stitch meandering in granite stitch or circles, worked on vanishing fabric. See page 139 for the work in full.

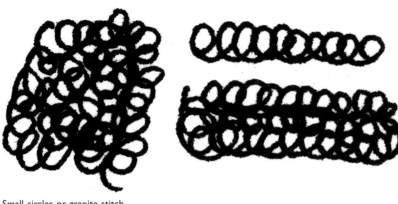

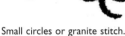

Small circles or granite stitch.

'drunken wiggle', **vermicelli** or **crazy stitch**. It holds together well on vanishing fabrics, so other work can be added on top with granite stitch as a base. Used with **whip stitch** or **whip stitch cord** it creates a more textural and very attractive stitch. It can be used to flatten areas in quilting, leaving the unstitched areas standing proud.

Stitching in diminishing circles or spirals that work back out on themselves can also create an interesting surface. If used densely, and particularly with a tight tension, the fabric will become distorted.

CLEAR DARNING FOOT
Some machines are provided with a clear plastic **darning** or free motion **embroidery foot** which helps enormously with the field of vision when it is necessary to use a darning foot. If your machine doesn't have this, or an open-toed darning foot, it will be worth investigating if you can buy one or the other for your machine. You will quickly become aware of the advantage over the closed embroidery or darning foot.

COLD WATER VANISHING FABRICS
See **dissolvable film, Solusheet, Soluweb.**

COLLAGE
The word *collage* comes from the French word *colle*, meaning *glue*, or *coller* – the verb *to glue*. It dates from the early 20th century, when artists in the Dada, Surrealist and Cubist movements started to glue mixed-media pieces such as wood, adverts or newspapers onto canvases, and even to create collage sculpture. The word has lost something of its original meaning and is now frequently used to describe the act of gluing anything together, often in the manner of a child, which can be a fun, relatively quick way of making pictures.

Collage is still the word frequently used to describe a picture made of mixed media glued to a surface, and there is no reason why the surface can't be textile, and the mixed-media object suitable for stitching as well as gluing. Machine stitching can obviously be added to such collages to delineate areas, add lines, marks, detail or texture, or to bring together disparate features.

COLOUR CIRCLE
The colour circle is a useful device to keep at hand until you have learnt it off by heart.

■ The inner triangle represents the three primary colours which cannot be reproduced by any mixing, and which are required for mixing other colours.

■ The secondary colours are represented in the next triangles, situated in between the two primary colours that are required to mix each of them.

■ The circle on the outside includes the tertiary colours, which are created by mixing a primary colour and a secondary colour.

The complementary colours are opposites in the colour circle. Each one can be used to give the notion of shadow to its complement, or to create movement within a piece of work. If you spend some time looking at one colour, when you look away at a white wall you will see its complement. The brain needs the two colours to feel comfortable, and we like images where two complementary colours are present, though they don't have to be obviously in equal proportions.

■ The brightest colour in the circle (the one that your eye picks up first) is yellow. Its opposite is violet. Green and red have equal values.

■ Harmonious colour schemes are those where the majority of colours used come from one area of the colour circle (think of Monet's water lilies). Clashes occur when many and varied complementary colours are used together.

■ The warmest colour in a colour circle is red/orange, the next warmest are next to red/orange on the colour circle, and so on. The coolest colour is turquoise/green, and the colours that are next to it are the next coolest, and so on. This can help to create movement or distance in a piece of work. In

On the other hand there are ways of making the investment stretch further. Instead of buying lots of different brands and thicknesses of thread, start off with just one type of thread in the one thickness that suits you best. At the most, choose one thickness of thread in silky and matt varieties. Then, when you have a project in mind, buy all the colours that you need for that project. When you plan your next project, buy the colours you need that you don't already have, and so on. Little by little you will need to buy fewer threads, and you can consider branching out into other thread types and sizes.

Fine threads (40s or 50s) mix well together on the work and are ideal for the type of work that requires the fine mixing of colours. If thicker threads are needed, or for covering large areas with the same (or similar) colours, two or three threads can be passed through the needle at once – though the result is obviously not the same as a heavily twisted thicker thread, which can be lovely for scrunchy **laces** or **quilting**. Over time you will gradually find the best solution for the type of work that you do.

To extend the appearance of your colour range, try putting different colours in the needle at the same time (a pale and a darker thread, or two colours next to each other on the **colour circle**, a plain and a shaded thread). **Colour spotting** is also a method of adding nuances to colours.

COLOURING IN

A term used for filling in an area with (usually) one colour – just as children colour in a colouring book. There are many **straight stitch** or **zigzag** stitch fillings that can be used to colour in an area with **free motion embroidery**.

For colouring in with computerized embroidery, the programs available offer different patterns of **straight stitch fillings**. These are used to fill in the

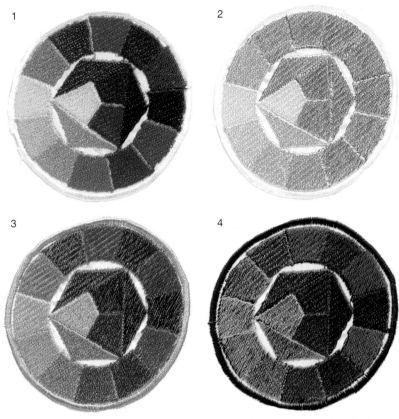

Colour circles programmed by scanning a drawing into a digitizing program. Once in the machine the design was enlarged while retaining the same *stitch count*. With a lower stitch density two layers of stitching could be worked in each area, allowing the first layer to be seen through the second. In order the circles are: 1 Two layers of colour. 2 The first layer of colour is covered with a layer of white to create an impression of tints. 3 A layer of grey is covered with colour to create an impression of shade. 4 A layer of black is covered with a layer of colour to create an impression of shade.

landscapes, cool objects are always imagined to be further away, as the layers of atmosphere between where we are and the horizon offer a cooling effect. Warm and cool colours can be used for something as simple as modelling a tree. The light will shine on the top of the tree and on the side facing the sun. If the greens are warmed up a bit, or specks of orange, yellow or even pink added, the effect will be of sunlight. Conversely, the greens can have more blue added, or blues and violets may even be used in specks or marks in the areas that are in shade and away from the sun.

■ Tints are created by adding white to colours.

■ Shades are created by adding black to colours.

Colours and colour schemes can be used to create many different moods and emotions. It's worth experimenting with various colour schemes, or looking at the work of other artists, to see what is successful, and trying to understand why. Note that the primaries described above are not the same as those colours used in printing or with light sources.

COLOUR: IMPROVING YOUR COLOUR RANGE

There aren't too many secrets to having a good colour range; it simply takes time and investment.

designated area using the 'paint pot' method of computer colouring, where the area to be filled has to be completely enclosed with an unbroken line.

COLOUR SPOTTING

Using a slightly tight top tension, small loops of bobbin thread can be pulled through to the surface of the embroidery over the top thread. If the bobbin thread is a different colour to the top threads, small spots of this colour will appear. Smaller stitches will create more spots in an area, larger stitches will mean fewer spots. If you use only the top tension wheel to change the tension (and not a looser bobbin tension) you will be able to make the effect of colour spotting come and go as you please just by adjusting the top tension back to normal or tightening it up again. When working filling stitches in straight lines, **circles** or **vermicelli stitch**, colour spotting can be a useful method of adding more colour. The apparent colour on the surface can be changed in appearance – a medium green will appear paler if spotted with a pale green, but not as pale as the pale green itself; this is useful if you have a limited colour range. It can also be used for shading by simply adjusting the amount of a darker colour on the bobbin, which will show in different areas on the top of the work, using the methods described. It is also a subtle way of adding a hint of metallic if the **metallic thread** is put on the bobbin and just appears on the surface in delicate spots.

The technique can also be interesting with a loose **bobbin tension** and a tight top tension set for **heavy whip stitch**. Working with long stitches backwards and forwards and at speed, spots of colour will appear in the middle of a line of stitching, and at each end of a line a large amount of the bobbin thread will be pulled through as the direction of the stitching changes.

Example of colour spotting by the author. Worked on dyed silk, with metallic thread on the bobbin. The area is worked with the Sfumato program on a Janome, with bypassed bobbin tension and tightened top tension. The other details are worked with free motion embroidery.

COMPUTERIZED EMBROIDERY

Also known as **automatic embroidery**. Stitched designs on a computerized **embroidery machine** can be done automatically by the machine itself from a **program** introduced into the machine by special card, disk or by a direct link to a computer.

COMPUTER PRINTOUT

A sheet of paper printed out from an embroidery program which can be used as a template for placing the embroidery on the fabric, or for storing a visual record of the embroidery design.

CONSERVATION

The conservation of textiles is an area full of different techniques according to the varying requirements of and for the object. An object can be preserved in the state in which it was found, whatever that might be, or a piece in a good state of repair can be carefully conserved to make sure it stays in that state for as long as possible. Textiles may also be restored to their original or nearly original glory. In textile, art and building conservation, arguments are always rife about the best approach to take, and the responses can be as many and varied as the objects to be treated.

Conservation is a question that needs to be addressed for your own work. The answers to these questions will be relative to the importance that you place on any finished piece of work, from a technical sample to a finished piece, or the importance that may be placed on it, from a small embroidery given as a gift to a large wall hanging commissioned for a public space. Techniques for marking the work, certain treatments, distressing or colouring techniques, certain materials used or the way the whole piece is held together, may not be conducive to long conservation. If this is the case, any purchaser has the right to know.

There is also, however, the conceptual issue of art forever, or art as a here and now statement. Is it always necessary or desirable to preserve a given piece of work? Art land works and installations often do not exist long after their first conception and realization except in photographic form, so you may feel that your textile creations also have a right to disintegrate as part of their artistic creative process. This could be fine, but it should be by design rather than by accident! So do think ahead about the techniques you wish to use for an object, and the longevity that you hope it will have.

CONTAINERS
See **boxes**.

CORDED PINTUCKS

For corded **pintucks** you will require a **grooved foot** to guide the **gimp thread** or cord. The cord is either threaded through the cover plate, or guided into place through a special plate that fits to the cover plate. Ensure that the cord chosen will run smoothly and use a 2mm ($^1/_{16}$ inch) **twin needle** – anything larger and the cord will be held too loosely to have much of an effect. As you stitch the pintuck, the cord will automatically fall into place

between the lines of stitches. Be careful when stitching curves and corners that the cord stays in place. See diagram.

CORDED WHIP STITCH
See **whip stitch cord**.

CORDING FOOT

This presser foot has a small hole in the front bar through which a fine cord can be passed for applying or for padded satin stitch. It is also useful for applying a cord to create a reinforced satin stitch edge. Larger sizes are available for some machines. See also **applying thread, cord and ribbon**.

CORDS – WRAPPING
See **wrapping threads and cords**.

CORNELY MACHINE

The long history of the Cornely machine starts perhaps with the hand technique of tambour work. For this the fabric is tightly held in a hoop (**tambour** in French) and a fine hook is passed through the fabric from underneath; a loop of thread from a continuous reel is passed around the hook and drawn back through the fabric to be passed through again, and the process continues. A small neat chain stitch can thus be produced

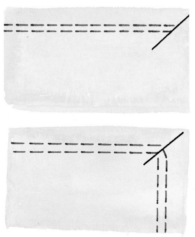

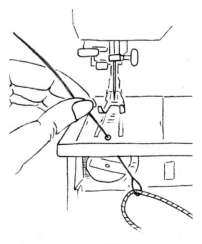

Threading a cord through the plate of the machine for corded pintucks. When it is threaded through to the back of the machine the cord will lie perfectly in place, although corners are a little delicate and have to be done in two movements.

on the top of the fabric. The embroidery created using this method, usually on fine muslin and net, was very popular from the end of the 18th century onwards.

It was inevitable that inventors would try to copy this technique by mechanical means so that it could be worked more quickly and economically. The first patent for

such a machine dates from 1790, although it was not actually built. More successful designs were produced from 1830 onwards. Early inventors struggled with the use of the chain stitch machine as a possible producer of seams, but the very nature of the chain stitch, and the ease with which it is undone, makes it unsuitable for such a purpose, so the **lock stitch sewing machine** inevitably won. The early versions of these machines produced a back stitch on the top of the work and a chain stitch underneath, using one (or sometimes two) continuous reels of thread.

In 1865 a French inventor called Bonnaz invented a reliable and practical embroidery machine which created a chain stitch on the top of the work, and this made decorative techniques easier. The machine had a universal feed driven by a padded foot whose direction was guided by a rotating hand-held lever under the machine. These early treadle-driven machines were manufactured by Ercole Cornely and immediately became popular in the embroidery industry, as they were compact enough to be used by outworkers in their own homes as well as in workshops. They could also produce **moss stitch** by a simple turn of the needle. There was a real fashion for all types of decorative embroidery work at the end of the 19th century and well into the 20th century, so several variations on the first machines were developed. These could add ribbons and sequins, sew complex cords, create rows of chenille (loop pile) or cut-pile embroidery, punch decorative holes for leather work and create a machine version of a decorative drawn thread hemstitch (this took no less than three different machines to achieve).

Other machine manufacturers have created Cornely-type machines, notably Singer. The success of Cornely machines has largely followed the ups and downs of embroidery in fashion, and in 1989

Dress with chain and moss stitch and appliqué, worked on a Cornely machine by Sarah Birtwistle while a student at Manchester Metropolitan University.

the Cornely company was taken over by the Japanese multihead industrial machine manufacturer Barudan, which now makes multihead computer-driven versions of the old Cornely-type machine.

Cornely machines were made until 1990, but old, working examples can still be found in use.

CORRECT TENSION SETTINGS

A correct thread tension will appear as in the diagram below, with no puckering of the fabric. The top tension should normally be set on 5, or where there is a strong line between the plus and minus. For **satin**, **zigzag** and **automatic stitches** a number 3 setting is usually preferable, and the top threads may appear on the underside of the fabric.

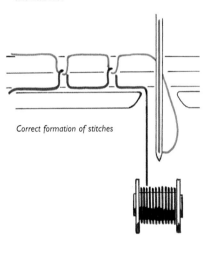

Correct formation of stitches

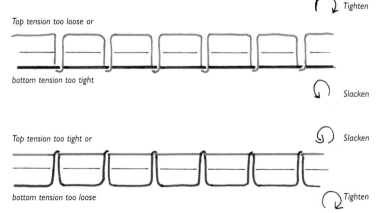

Top tension too loose or

bottom tension too tight

Tighten

Slacken

Slacken

Top tension too tight or

bottom tension too loose

Tighten

Correct tension setting for normal stitching. Tighten or slacken the top or bobbin tension a little at a time according to the diagram to obtain a perfect tension.

If the threads are being pulled through to one side of the fabric in straight stitching, check the bobbin tension as well as the top tension (see **bobbin tension**). Longer stitches, particularly on finer fabric, will require a very carefully set tension, with both top and bottom a little loose.

For **free motion embroidery** the top tension is best set as for **satin stitch** on 3 (there is often a buttonhole symbol in the right place). This ensures that the bobbin threads are not pulled through to the surface of the fabric (although the top threads may appear on the underside, this is of less importance).

Certain machines set the tension automatically, and within reasonable limits the threads will always have a correct tension.

For computerized embroidery programs the tensions are automatically set, although it is possible to override this if necessary.

COTTON

A natural fibre that is spun from cotton balls which grow on bushes in hot climates. It is sometimes mixed with other fibres, most notably polyester, for ease of care and ironing. It is available in many forms, thicknesses, densities, colours, bleached or unbleached,

and shows good resistance to most processes and can take heavy stitching. It also takes dyes and paints well. Containing a natural or re-introduced starch, it generally stretches well after embroidery and will keep its shape.

Cotton is also used to create a matt sewing thread as well as embroidery threads, which are available in 50 and 30 **thread thickness**. Cotton threads are very easy to use, being generally stronger than their rayon equivalents.

COTTON REEL

Until well into the latter half of the 20th century almost all sewing thread was cotton, and it was sold on reels – hence 'cotton reel', which is still a term that has stuck. As so little sewing thread now is actually cotton, and machine embroidery threads are made of a variety of fibres, this term is dated. **Spool** is the term usually applied now to differentiate from the **bobbin**, which holds the bottom thread underneath the machine.

COUCHING

The act of holding down a thicker thread by stitching over it with a finer one. The thicker thread is meant to be visible for decorative effect. There are various techniques that can be used on the sewing machine. See **applying thread, cord and ribbon, cable stitch, cording foot.**

COVER PLATE

The needle plate is under the needle of the sewing machine through which appears the **feed dog**, which moves the fabric under the foot. A cover is necessary on some sewing machines to cover the feed dog for **free motion embroidery**; on other machines the feed dog is simply lowered with a lever or button.

CRAZY PATCHWORK

Originally, pieces of fabrics – leftovers or surviving pieces from worn-out garments – were joined together using hand stitching and embroidered along the join with fly stitch, herringbone or similar. Thus fabric that was difficult to acquire and/or expensive could be reused. This was particularly important in America's pioneer days. The technique is also known as applied patchwork, as the process is easier if pieces of fabric are cut up and applied to a ground. Applied patchwork is the easiest method to use when working by machine. Crazy (usually triangular) shapes can be used as in the original crazy patchwork, and there are all kinds of **automatic patterns** that can be used to imitate the original hand stitching.

The method can also be developed along the lines of **Creating fabrics – patching and piecing.**

CRAZY STITCH

Crazy stitch is worked with **free motion embroidery,** and is not dissimilar to **vermicelli stitch,** although one may find a little less organization in its construction, and the threads may even cross over from time to time, which should not happen in vermicelli stitch.

CREATING FABRICS

Creating fabrics from scratch can be interesting and inspiring. They can be used afterwards as a surface for further embroidery, for creating garments or interior decor, or as wall hangings or pieces in their own right.

VANISHING FABRIC

To create fabrics on vanishing fabric, it is probably best to use hot water vanishing fabric as this accepts an enormous amount of stitching and can be completely dissolved, leaving no residue – essential if the created fabric is to retain qualities of drape once it has been vanished.

If you wish to add bits and pieces of fabric to hot water vanishing fabric this can be done with 505 or bonding glue, which will hold the pieces in place long

On the Process of Neglect. Patchwork by the author, worked in hand and machine embroidery out of recycled and found fabrics, with some burning, leather and canvas work. 'The patchwork represents someone's life of collected objects, like many quilts were intended to be. The life has been a sad one, full of regrets. The end of the poem that I wrote to accompany this piece reads: "As you come down from your bedroom to the breakfast neatly set; From behind your paper you complete the process of neglect" '.

Silent All These Years by the author. Created fabric worked on Soluweb. Small pieces of fabric are applied for the wisteria flowers and leaves, using a darning foot on the machine to hold the pieces in place. The bottom of the work, representing a wall and barrier, is worked in diagonal weave stitch on an Irish machine.

enough to work the stitching. Any fabrics or threads added to the hot water vanishing fabric must be able to withstand the boiling process at the end, when the fabric is vanished. Otherwise use a cold water soluble fabric.

To become familiar with the process you can chop up bits and pieces of fabric and thread in an imagined colour scheme, place them or glue them to the surface and stitch over with some form of stitching that will hold the whole piece together. This could be parallel straight lines, a **grid, circles, wave stitch,** or some **automatic patterns** might also be suitable. You can vary the type of stitching you use, and areas could be encrusted with densely worked **satin stitch** or **heavy whip stitch,** while other areas can be

left open and lacy, making full use of the qualities of vanishing fabric. If you are going to work a large piece you will need to do a sample first to make sure that the density of fabrics chosen and the stitches that you are planning to use will hold it all together. If there are lots of loose bits and pieces of fabric on the vanishing fabric you can hold them down with a cocktail stick as you sew. It is also easier if a darning foot is used while you do this.

If hot water vanishing fabric is unsuitable for the work because of the boiling process, you can use Solusheet and layers of Soluweb for the bonding. The resulting work will be a little more rigid, but this can sometimes be an advantage.

If you are making the fabric for a garment, you can draw out the lines

of the garment pieces that you require onto the fabric first (it works best if you use light marks made with a hard pencil). Be generous with the amount of fabric you embroider, as the fabric created is likely to shrink once it has been vanished. A certain amount of shrinkage can be recovered by pinning the work out to dry, but you will need generous seam allowances for this pinning.

PATCHING AND PIECING
New fabrics can be created by applying patches and pieces using an ordinary fabric as a base. The bits and pieces can be held on with bits of **Bondaweb** or **bonding powder** before the final stitching meshes the whole of the surface together. A darning foot may be

41

useful, or bits can be held in place with a cocktail stick to avoid getting your fingers too close to the needle. Suitable stitches are as for vanishing fabrics (see page 40), but this time a real fabric already exists, so there is less need to worry about the whole thing being held together by the stitching. Stitching can be more sparse, or **vermicelli stitch**, which does not hold together as a lacy stitch on vanishing fabrics, could be used. Any **automatic patterns** could also be used. The ground fabric could be an ordinary cotton or calico as it is probably not going to show if the work becomes heavy enough. On the

Midsummer Night's Dream bridal dress by Lesley George, with patched layered fabrics to form the bodice; threads are applied for more texture. Vanishing fabric lace, made separately, is attached to the edge. Around the neckline is more vanishing lace, finished with twisted, machine-wrapped threads. One of these has beads threaded on it and is stitched in by machine. The back is laced with machine-wrapped threads finished off with small tassels.

other hand, interesting surfaces can be built up on chiffon, scrim, muslin, organdie or other lightweight fabrics.

When the fabric is for an interior design fabric or for making a garment, the areas to be cut out afterwards can be marked with tailor's chalk or similar. That way the embroidery need not be heavily worked or indeed worked at all on the parts of the fabric that are going to be redundant (although these could be cut up and used again). However, be generous with seam allowances so that the work can be stretched flat and into shape before being made up.

CROSS STITCH

Cross stitch forms an X on the fabric when it is worked as a hand embroidery technique, traditionally on **evenweave fabric** for counted cross stitch. Cross stitch can also be a free stitch in hand embroidery, and many exciting hand embroidery experiments can be done with it. It's interesting to mix up both hand and machine stitched cross stitches. The X may be rather large and done with free motion running stitch, or try **bead stitch** to make the cross.

Cross stitches exist as preset stitches on many of the more sophisticated machines, and these can be mixed with hand stitches and free motion cross stitches too.

Using special computer programs, counted cross stitch-style designs can also be worked with the embroidery unit on computerized embroidery machines. These allow for colour changes, so sophisticated designs can be worked.

CRYSTAL STRANDS

Also known as 'Angelina', this relatively new product has a soft feel and an iridescent or metallic sparkle. It can be layered, trapped, bonded or included in paper or felt. With heat as a bonding agent, the iridescent fibres can be used to create a fabric in its own right. The metallic strands do not bond to themselves so need to be

Cross stitch sampler on Binca cloth. Some cross stitches are worked with a free satin stitch, others with an automatic set stitch. The beads are made from the coloured plastic surround of electrical wire, threaded onto a thread and stitched down with free motion stitching.

incorporated with the 'heat fix' ones in order to create a fabric.

It is best to place the fibres to be heat-set between two sheets of baking parchment, and use an iron on a silk setting. Too much heat or pressure can affect the colours, although this is not necessarily a disadvantage. Generally at low temperatures the fibres will only bond to themselves, but if nylon chiffon is included at this stage it will bond to that. A weblike

structure can be created by spreading the fibres thinly, or a more solid fabric can be produced by using a larger quantity of fibres, in which case it may be necessary to increase the iron temperature, or even iron from both sides.

Fabrics or other materials can be trapped between layers of fibre. The fibre is made from polyester, so it can be cut with a soldering iron. It can also be distorted with a **hot air tool**, and it will accept transfer

Guilt for Doris by the author. Worked on layers of crystal strands on a synthetic iridescent fabric with Japanese gold thread attached with a hemming stitch. Curled pieces of crystal strands are added to the surface. An idea for a bodice.

dyes. It can be moulded into firm shapes that will keep their shape when hot off the iron.

It stitches perfectly well but it is advisable to use a fine ballpoint needle for a good result.

CUPPING

The 'cupped' effect of distortion that can happen in computerized machine embroidery, usually caused by an insufficient **stabilizer**, or by a **stitch density** that is too great for the fabric, thread or design.

CURVES

Stitching curves requires special treatment if the work is to be successful. When stitching using a foot, and sewing with a **straight stitch, zigzag** or **satin stitch**, work the curves carefully over the fabric,

not pulling it too much, or you will pull across the grain and cause the fabric to stretch and pucker. Where there is a choice of presser foot pressure, choose a light pressure to help with movement.

When stitching curves or circles with a satin stitch, the fabric will distort if the work is pulled around too tight a curve. Where necessary, put the needle in the fabric on the outside of the curve, lift the foot, move the fabric a little to realign the centre of the foot with the curved line required, put the foot back down, and continue stitching. Repeat the process every time the satin stitch is in danger of not staying centred. The needle should not be placed on the inside of a curve or else there will be a gap in the stitching after the fabric has been moved.

Working a satin stitch around a tight circle for appliqué or for making a hole. It's not always possible to follow the curve just by turning the fabric, and if you try too hard it may pull the fabric out of shape. Where necessary, put the needle into the outside of the curve and turn the fabric a little more. Putting the needle into the inside of the curve and turning the fabric will leave gaps.

CUSTOMIZING DESIGNS

This is the changing of a purchased computerized design to your own requirements. It may include rotating, mirroring, enlarging or reducing, adding colours or lettering, or using selected parts of designs and putting them together in a different way. Stitch densities may have to be changed to accept the different results, and a change in stitch density can also become part of this customizing process. It's remarkable what can be achieved by changing a set design to make it more your own and more original.

Many customizing programs allow you to work from your own scanned or other imported bitmap images. So any drawing or designing that you have done on your computer or imported from other sources in bitmap can be worked with.

It may be possible to 'tidy up' the image if the program reads it badly. You can ask the machine to stitch the whole thing as it stands, or look at the image as a line drawing and work from that, filling it in with the colours and stitches of your choice. A customizer program will have a much reduced choice of stitch patterns compared with a digitizer program, and may be capable of registering only a limited width satin stitch in comparison to a digitizing program. When asked to create a colour or line image automatically the result can be a little messy, so tidying up the original image or recreating the order of work may be required if there are not to be too many jumps to be cut afterwards. Using a **graphic tablet** can be a successful way of introducing drawings directly into this program, and much easier than drawing with a computer mouse. If you are scanning an image, it will work best if there are not too many colours and if they have been applied simply. Try using felt pens rather than pastels or crayons. For a scanned line drawing, working with a pen on tracing paper creates the best results.

CUT AND SEW FOOT

Cut and sew foot attachments are available for certain models, to make edges. This is an elaborate foot with a small pair of scissors incorporated, which moves as the needle goes up and down. The machine then satin stitches neatly over the newly cut edge which is held in exactly the right position for stitching.

CUTTING OFF THREADS

Most machines have a thread cutter to the left or back of the needle bar or machine which you can very quickly become familiar with and use habitually for ordinary sewing, or where a length of thread is required for cutting off or threading through to the back. For **free motion embroidery,** or where a **holding stitch** has been used, the thread can be cut off right next to the fabric. Use a pair of small, sharp scissors, or a curved pair that avoids cutting other threads, or small clippers that are held in the hand rather than with a hole for finger and thumb. Everyone has his or her favourite tool – I prefer to use clippers.

It's important to cut off threads as you are going along, to avoid sewing over them, and connecting threads left too long will give a false impression about quantities of colour used, so they need to be cut off regularly. If the bobbin thread stays attached it will help prevent the work from unravelling, but if you are working on a light vanishing fabric lace you may need to cut bobbin threads off as well to avoid them being seen from the front, or getting caught into the work as you sew.

Many machines will cut off threads for you near the needle base, especially when working with computerized programs and when changing the colour.

CUTWORK

This traditional hand embroidery technique can be very time consuming and even tedious. It is much quicker to work the technique by machine, although it still requires patience and a great deal of care and attention to detail.

The following explanation and diagrams describe how to work a traditional cutwork design. The method can be adapted to a more contemporary approach that could include layering see-through fabrics, or creating an **appliqué** or dyed surface before starting cutwork. Many fabrics can be burnt into holes in a manageable way using a **soldering iron,** which would avoid the necessity to **satin stitch** all the edges afterwards; see **burnt cutwork.** Areas of machine-

For cutwork a straight stitch outline defines the areas to be kept. The unwanted areas (shown in blue) are cut away, leaving the vanishing fabric. The straight lines that join everything together can now be stitched and all the edges finally tidied up with a satin stitch.

Cutwork sample on silk, worked with vanishing fabric. By the author.

embroidered lace could be included to make a cutwork design that is even more open. The traditional white colour scheme could be replaced with pastel shades, or even rich reds, purples, black and gold.

Follow the instructions below for basic cutwork. Afterwards you can work design sheets and samples to help guide you to your own contemporary interpretation.

1. Trace the design onto the material using your favourite method. For this technique the design could be traced onto tissue paper or good-quality tracing paper.

2. This can be stitched onto the fabric, which is a layer of your chosen fabric, with vanishing fabric underneath. Using a darning foot and free motion embroidery, stitch all edges, but not the bars of the design. The tracing paper can easily be removed along the stitched lines.

Straight stitch all the design edges one more time to make sure that they are held firmly.

3. Cut away all unwanted areas of fabric in the design, back to the lines of stitching. Take care not to cut into the vanishing fabric as this holds everything together. If you do

accidentally snip into it, you can always repair it with another piece of vanishing fabric.

4. Straight stitch the bars between the fabric pieces, making sure that the needle goes into the fabric just on the inside of the holding stitches along the cut edges. Each bar should be stitched backwards and forwards about four times to hold the final satin stitch, then move on around the edge of the fabric to do the next bar. If you organize your order of work carefully you can avoid too much stopping and starting which leaves threads to tie off and hide.

5. Satin stitch over the straight stitch bars, but only on those areas that are to be vanished. If the satin stitch continues onto the fabric it will add bulk to the final satin stitching around the edges. Again, you can work around the edge of the design by changing to a straight stitch, and by carefully organizing your order of work, you can avoid too many stops and starts.

6. Finally, satin stitch around all fabric edges, into the fabric on the inside of existing straight stitches and back into the vanishing fabric – the technique at this stage resembles appliqué. Again, stitch over as many starts and finishes as possible to avoid too many thread ends – ends can be cut off once they have been stitched over.

7. Any remaining threads will have to be threaded through to the back of the work and correctly finished off to hide them.

8. The vanishing fabric can now be dissolved by the appropriate method for the fabric.

Don't give up until you get to this stage. Early on you may be a little disappointed in the quality of your satin stitching, especially if you are doing it as a free motion technique. In the end, though, this is a much easier and faster method for following difficult edges, and you can change to a straight stitch when necessary. This technique will really help you to perfect your satin stitch. Once the vanishing fabric has been dissolved, the satin stitch tightens up and the final appearance will be much better.

DARNING

Darning stitches are worked with a **darning foot**, generally with the small hoop that is provided by the machine manufacturer. The technique of moving the hoop backwards and forwards and from side to side without a **feed dog** is at

the basis of all **free motion embroidery** techniques. The technique still exists for patching holes (which after all can be done decoratively on that favourite old T-shirt that your daughter refuses to throw away!). The woven aspect of darning can be useful when meshing a lot of fabrics together to create a fabric, or **building up surface.** It is especially useful for working on **vanishing fabric.**

DARNING FOOT

A sprung foot in the form of a small hoop, less than 1cm (³/₈ inch) across, is now provided with all sewing machines. It will have some mechanism that allows it to 'bounce' yet firmly holds the fabric being sewn into as the needle enters the fabric. This mechanism is either an arm which fits against the needle screw that lifts the foot when the needle is lifted, or the foot itself is spring loaded and floating. This foot is used without the **feed dog,** so use the cover plate provided or the button that lowers the feed dog – see your handbook for details. An **open toe foot** can also be used which gives better visibility, while some darning feet are made of see-

through plastic which also helps with visibility. A larger **quilting foot** is available for some machines.

Many people prefer to use a darning foot as a matter of course, for comfort, less thread breakage, and a feeling of security for the protection of fingers which otherwise may get too close to the needle mechanism. However, much embroidery can be done without a darning foot, particularly when it is held in a hoop, and visibility is so much better when not using one that it is worth practising without. A **spring needle** can be used instead of a darning foot if the embroidery needs to be held firmly against the machine bed.

For some techniques a darning or embroidery foot is essential or at least very useful, and less frustrating because the threads break less often. For example:

■ Working on hard surfaces that can pull up with the needle and cause wear on the thread such as heavily bonded fabrics, papers, some heat treated surfaces such as felt, paper or fabric painted with acrylic paint or other medium, metals, grids, canvas or hard plastic.

Collection of darning feet for different machines.

■ Working on soft surfaces that are difficult to stretch fully flat (and without bounce) in a hoop, such as quilting, domette or silk wadding, and surfaces with small bits of fabric or thread held in place with just spots of glue or bonding or with nothing at all.

■ Finally, some surfaces are pulled up with the needle and may either tear or cause thread breakage, such as plastic and dissolvable film.

DECORATIVE FILL
Large areas of stitches that have a decorative pattern, on computerized machine embroidery. See also **straight stitch fillings.**

DELICATE FABRICS
Delicate fabrics need special treatment when they are being stitched. Synthetics and silk require the use of a ballpoint needle if they are not to snag. Other fabrics may pull out of shape with heavy stitching, or leave hoop burn marks. The kind of distressing and distortion possible on delicate fabrics may be why you chose to use them in the first place. However, if you wanted to do a beautiful piece of **free motion embroidery** or **computerized embroidery** without any distortion, the best thing to do is to use a backing that will support the fabric and can be got rid of afterwards. An obvious choice is fine **dissolvable film**, but check that there is not too much residue left in the fabric afterwards. **Soluweb** can be ironed on for a little more firmness, or use **Heataway**.

DESIGN
Good design is essential for good embroidery. Sampling different embroidery and background treatment effects can get you so far in technical knowledge and interesting surfaces, but a good design is the basis of any successful, mature piece of embroidery.

Improving design skills takes time, and students often think that an idea in their head will be easily translated onto fabric. It is rare that this will work successfully without passing through the middle process of drawing and design sheets or worksheets, and such failures can be very disappointing. If designing and sampling are developed thoroughly before a project is first embarked upon, the possibilities of failure or disappointment can be much reduced.

Possible design sources can be your own drawings, paintings or photographs, magazine cuttings, or work that you have scanned into the computer and worked on using the various programs available. Once you have found a satisfactory design source, you may wish to draw it a few times with different drawing or art media, in order to get to know it, its colours, the forms and the balance of the composition. The difference in textures in different parts of the design, and the balance of heavy textural or colour effects against plainer areas, are also important. Analysing these points through study will help you to understand your source material better and to know how to interpret it.

If you are starting only with an idea, and not a visual media source, drawings and research to formulate your idea and make it work will be particularly important, especially for installation and conceptual embroidery works.

On a practical level, keeping a sketchbook or notebook always handy is essential for any artist, and cutting out things that interest you for an ideas book can be useful – but be careful that this doesn't replace true and proper personal visual research.

DESIGN SHEET
The design sheet is a presentation sheet of design ideas from source material that can lead through to the proposition of the finished project. It can be decorative, and should be attractive. There should be a logic to the layout that allows the viewer or client to see the design process, to understand the project and have a good idea of how it will look (*in situ*, if it is for a hanging or installation in a given location). Design sheets may be required as part of an art syllabus or for a commissioned work. See also **worksheet.**

DIGITIZING DESIGNS
Digitizing is the process of designing a motif in a format that can be understood by the embroidery machine, including

Computer screen using Janone program. The drawing was put in using a graphic tablet.

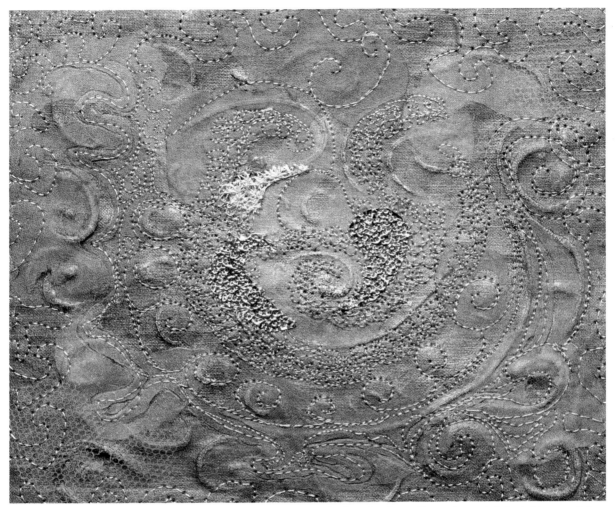

Pink Universe by the author. Dimensional fabric paint applied to a silk ground, coloured with metallic powders and stitched with crazy stitch. Polyester organdie cut with a soldering iron, and metal shim, have been added.

stitch type or fillings, density, any colour changes, or joining, and any **jump stitches** required for the needle to move from one area to another. Motifs already digitized for your embroidery machine will be provided with it. Extra motifs can be bought in a suitable format (see **disk**) or **downloaded** from websites on the **Internet**.

To digitize your own motifs you will require a special digitizing program for your sewing machine. Once installed on your computer the program will guide you through the process of digitizing your own designs for your machine, and these can often be formatted for other machines if desired.

DIMENSIONAL FABRIC PAINT

This works in the same way as **Xpandaprint**, but the result is less pronounced. It is often supplied in a tube applicator.

DISCHARGE DYEING

In this technique the colour is removed from the fabric, rather than being added to it. It is most successful on pure cotton fabrics, and one can even buy fabrics specially prepared for discharge dyeing. The randomness of the results, due to the unknown effects of the multitude of colours that may be used to make up one dyed colour, and the different techniques that can be used in discharge

dyeing, make for an interesting surface as a base for further embellishment and embroidery.

Bleach is applied to a fabric to take away the dye. The fabric can be crumpled, or protected with ties or stitching with a **long stitch** for gathering, as with tie-dyeing, to prevent bleach penetration in certain areas. The fabric can be dipped into bleach, or the bleach can be poured or carefully painted onto the fabric.

When the desired effect has been reached it is necessary to stop the discharge process immediately. Plunge the fabric into a bucket of cold water, rinse and squeeze out the excess water, then place it in a

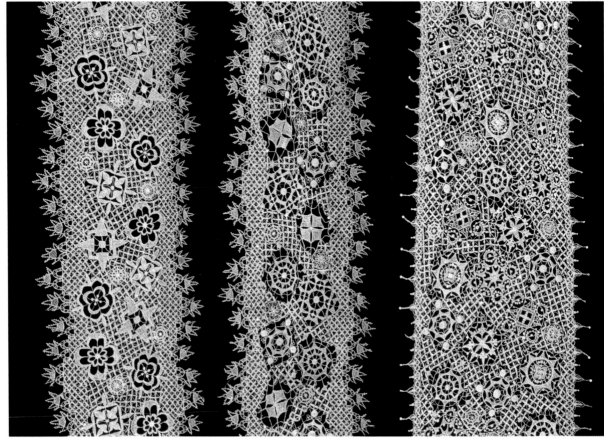

Importune Me No More. Part of a series by Carol Cann, worked on cold water soluble fabric. The titles come from a poem by Elizabeth I and the details are based on the patterns of her clothes. The left-hand piece is called *Go, go, go seek some other where*; the middle piece is called *When I was young and fair and favour graced me*; the right-hand one is *How many weeping eyes I made to pine with woe*. Photographs by Kevin Mead. For further details see page 91.

white vinegar solution (one part vinegar to three parts water) for 30–40 minutes. Rinse again, then wash on a short machine wash with detergent and leave to dry.

DISK

There are a number of ways of purchasing designs or transferring designs that you have downloaded from the Internet, digitized or customized yourself from the computer to an embroidery machine. The floppy disk is one such way and your embroidery machine may accept them. Reader/writer boxes and **ATA CP** cards are other ways of transferring information from your computer to your machine, or your machine may have a direct cable connection.

DISSOLVABLE FILM

Although the first cold water dissolvable film created in the 1980s was rather difficult to get on with, and certainly took some practice to get used to, it has since been replaced by a more forgiving generation of products. These products were developed as a **topping** for the machine embroidery industry, where embroidered motifs on towelling or velvet would disappear into the surface. A firm topping of cold water vanishing fabric keeps the embroidery on the surface of the fabric and disappears easily without changing the nature of the fabric.

The new dissolvable films are easier to use but the basic rules still apply. For sewing you should only

use a ballpoint needle, as piercing the film will lead to torn holes. Hoop up the plastic with a great deal of care, setting the screw on the hoop at the appropriate distance before attempting your final hooping up, and holding the film over the bottom hoop while pushing the top hoop into place. If you don't manage to get it perfect first time, undo it and start again; it is impossible to pull the film tightly into the hoop without distorting or tearing it.

The best way of dissolving this film is under a warm running tap. If the work is delicate you may first pin it to a polystyrene board so that it keeps its shape once the film has disappeared. The harshness left by the residue after the vanishing process can be improved by washing in fabric softener. These fabrics show little resistance to heavy stitching, especially in the finer weights. Bearing in mind the difficulties encountered when using **metallic threads** or polyester and synthetic fabrics on **hot water vanishing fabric**, cold water vanishing fabrics have a definite place in machine embroidery.

There are three grades of dissolvable film on the market. They are sold by weight or trade name:

Superweight or *Romeo* is a heavyweight film, which is easily stitched on without tearing and can be used without a hoop for some work. It needs more time to completely dissolve.

Mediumweight or *Guliette* is half the weight of the heavyweight. It is easy to use in a hoop with a ballpoint needle, and also easier to vanish, so is a good compromise.

Lightweight or *Verona* is half the weight of the mediumweight and much more delicate to use. It tears easily, but vanishes easily too, making it very useful as a topping. See also **Solusheet**.

DISTORTION

The change in shape that can be pulled into the fabric through stitching or fabric manipulation processes. Heavy directional stitching or working across the **bias** of the fabric can cause distortion that can become part of the piece. Other ways of adding distortion deliberately include **fabric manipulation**, **heat treatment**, **smocking**, **pintucking**, **elastic** and burning, pulling the fibres out of shape manually or with stitching, moulding using glues and heat for some fabrics, and so on.

Distortion may happen accidentally because of heavy stitching on **free motion embroidery** or in **computerized embroidery**. In order to avoid this use a strong backing or stabilizer. Once the work is finished it can be stretched to regain its former shape, though no amount of stretching will bring back really bad stitching.

DISTRESSING

The term given to the deliberate ageing, soiling or degrading of fabrics and surfaces to create an effect. Processes may include heat treatment with a **hot air tool**, a **soldering iron** or **burning** (in which case a mask should always be used to avoid dangerous fumes); oxidizing metallic surfaces using **heat treatment**; wetting and tearing or stitching into paper surfaces; partly destroying loosely woven fabrics by pulling threads out, or teasing threads apart. Edges of fabrics might be treated similarly to encourage fraying. Chemical treatments can be used to create crinkled surfaces, burn holes or bleach out dyes. Stitching or the punched holes made by the machine needle can also be used to distress certain surfaces such as thin metals, plastics or papers.

Distressing can harden up the surface of the fabric in some instances, in which case a large-eyed needle and a darning or embroidery foot are advisable for machining. In other instances the surface of the work can become very delicate, so use the finest needle possible.

Felt manipulated by tight circles of free motion embroidery with a tight tension top and bottom.

THE MAKING OF *RED SHOES,*
RED CARPET...

Red Shoes, Red Carpet... (below) by
Frankie Creith was created using
the following method:

1. A piece of lightweight cotton
fabric was cut to the approximate
size of the finished work. Onto this
base a variety of other fabrics such as
nylon, cotton, satin, organza,
hessian, etc. were cut into small

pieces of about 2cm (³/₄ inch) square
and placed closely side by side.

2. Further texture was added in the
form of coloured cellophane, foil
and wool. The choice is endless –
the only limitation is that it is
pliable enough to allow the use of
sewing needles through the surface.
On top of this texture layer, a fine
layer of sewing thread was added in
long continuous strands (several

reels were used). This layer of
threads acts as a sealer for the
layers underneath.

3. Dress netting was placed on top,
followed by a layer of Bondaweb,
and then ironed to fix. Free motion
stitching in a random fashion was
worked with a white cotton thread
(allowing easier colouring at a later
stage). The created fabric is now
fully pliable and secure.

Red Shoes, Red Carpet... by Frankie Creith. 'Red... the carpet of dignitaries, yet only in this world, for as time continues and we pass from our earthly home we will stand the same before our maker and our God.' In this very personal piece Creith considers the famous: their wealth, possessions, popularity and the influence they have among others – all of which, according to the scriptures, are meaningless, for we, regardless of our earthly fame, 'all share a common destiny' (Ecclesiastes 9:2). The resulting work – a 'carpet' whose length is symbolic of our lifespan, the shoes symbolic of our life in this world – begins to deteriorate as it reaches its close. The once grand now fades towards the unimportant. The notion of grandeur and wealth portrayed in this work through delicate layers and embellishment, both rich in colour and texture, are ironically constructed with materials of little value, echoing the belief the artist holds. The work measures 400 x 30 x 17cm (157 x 12 x 6³/₄ inches).

4. The created fabric was coloured with diluted acrylic paint. When dry this was overpainted with coloured inks. Finally, an oil bar was rubbed over the surface to enhance the textural qualities.

5. The surface was further embellished with machine stitching to enhance the texture. Thick layers of random zigzag were cut using a sharp blade to create a velvety texture, and areas of straight stitch worked to indicate direction and movement within the work. Both techniques were integrated using small repeated blocks of satin stitch, strengthened by a final overall layer of free motion straight stitch in various lengths. Beaded tassels were used to finish the edge of this piece.

DOMETTE

A wool-based quilt **wadding** for traditional **quilting**, available from specialist suppliers and providing a particularly warm quality to quilts that use it. It is held together by a knitted structure.

It can also be used as a fabric in its own right. It can be dyed, heated, felted and stitched. Because of its knitted structure it is easily put into an embroidery hoop, but it is rather bouncy so it's a good idea to use a **darning foot** or **free embroidery foot**. The fabric can be manipulated in much the same way as **felt**: areas can be flattened or allowed to be raised by the nature and forms of the embroidery.

DOWNLOADING DESIGNS

Many designs for computerized sewing machines are available on the Internet. Some designs are free, others have to be paid for and are available by credit card through secure websites. Downloading a design onto your own computer is relatively easy: you simply follow the instructions on the screen while you are connected to the website. Once downloaded you can open the program and transfer it in the relevant form to your embroidery

machine. If you encounter any problems with opening a paid-for program, the provider of the program should be able to give you advice. Note that programs of this nature were often made to be machine specific (Janome for Janome, Bernina for Bernina, Viking for Viking, etc.), but this is changing rapidly. Machine manufacturers now provide programs that can read and convert from other formats. Programs of this nature are relatively easy to find on the Internet – a search using key words such as 'machine embroidery' will bring many sites to the surface, or you can be machine-specific.

DRAWING

Being able to draw will improve your ability to design and the quality of your drawing on the sewing machine. Good drawing is not really a gift and there is, unfortunately, no secret formula to improving drawing technique, except work and practice. One useful tip is to do a drawing a day – every day. Start off with a sketchbook and a pencil (or several different pencils from HB through to 6B) and draw every day. Find a habit that suits you: just after lunch, before breakfast, or once or twice a week in the evening for a drawing that takes longer. Try to vary what you do, between drawings that take five or 10 minutes, and drawings that take an hour or two. Once you have mastered a pencil, change your habit to include colour pencils, then pastels, then paint, and so on. Organize yourself and your materials in such a way that there can be no excuse for not doing the drawing each day. The subjects don't always have to be ambitious; it might be something left on the table after dinner, for example, or draw different aspects of a room from fine details to large plans. Draw outside when you get the chance. Remember that the sketchbook is for you, so if the results aren't always good (and they

certainly won't be at the start) don't worry; practice is the most important thing, and you don't have to show the work to anyone. Over a year or two or three you will notice a huge difference in your abilities and confidence, and the constraints of the work will start to be worth it and a pleasure that you won't wish to give up.

DRAWN FABRIC WORK

Another name for pulled work, not to be confused with **drawn thread work**. This is a hand embroidery technique that can be adapted for machine use; see **pulled work**.

'DRUNKEN WIGGLE'

This rather attractive open **filling stitch** is created with **free motion embroidery**. It is simply a line that wiggles a little haphazardly from side to side as it goes forward and backwards. Small circular movements can be added here and there for more interest. This stitch is useful for progressing colour from one dyed area to another or to integrate areas of applied fabrics. Used openly it can be useful in

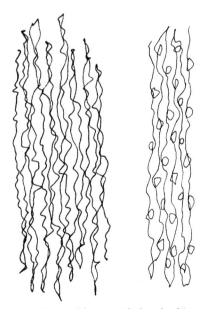

A 'drunken wiggle' is a straight line that has been drinking too much! In an even 'drunker' version the line even walks back on itself, creating little impromptu circles.

Courtyard at Tornac by the author. Appliqué with a variety of fabrics, including silk and worked scrim. 'Drunken wiggle' is worked around the flowerpots to add shading or move colours from one area to another. The plants are worked in granite stitch with crazy stitch shading.

The Matchmaker's Pocket by Diana Parkes. Hand-dyed silks, appliqué, printing, machine and hand stitching. Abstract rendering of garment portions.

quilting too. Variants can be tried using an open **zigzag** or **satin stitch** or working from side to side instead of up and down.

DUAL FEED FOOT
See **top feed** and **walking foot**.

DYES
Dyes actually go into the fibres of a fabric and change their colour, as opposed to a paint or fabric paint, which sits on the surface. While a paint – even fabric paint – can change, to a greater or lesser degree,

the feel of a fabric, a dye will not. It also has the advantage of being less changed by sunlight and in repeat washing. Real fabric dyes are more expensive and difficult to use, and not always appropriate to our needs – so a balance has to be found.

There are two main types of dye: one is applied by dipping or being brushed onto the fabric; the other is **transfer dye**. Dyes can be fibre specific, so do read the instructions to be sure that it will suit your fabric. Dyes are also available for dark and pale fabrics, but beware:

the product for dark fabrics is actually a fabric paint, not a dye!

Dyes can bleed more from the fabric than fabric paints, and will not be easily confined to specific areas. Blocking agents such as gutta (see **silk paints**) or wax can be used. But also test different fabrics, as some are more resistant to bleeding than others. Thickeners can be purchased to help prevent bleeding, but these can change the surface quality of the fabric in the same way as fabric paints.

All dyes need fixing at the end of the dyeing process. Even when they appear to be fast to water, they will not be light fast unless they are fixed according to the instructions.

Dyed surfaces can be very useful for all embroidery, including machine embroidery, as a dyed surface will lift any stitching in a different colour, but will also avoid the necessity for very dense stitching if you are trying to get an all-over colour effect. Dyes can give movement to a background which can then be reinforced with appropriate stitching. Dyes can even replace drawing, establishing much of the design before the stitching picks out details or adds textural interest.

EDGES

On most modern machines there are **automatic patterns** that will do **scalloped** or other **satin stitch edges**. The fabric can then be cut back to the edge. See also **blind hemming stitch**.

Cut and sew foot attachments are also available for certain models to make edges.

■ **Satin stitch** edges can be sewn along a piece of fabric and then cut back to the satin stitch using sharp stitches. The result may be slightly frayed, and can be improved by **burning** off the threads with a **soldering iron**. A better result can be achieved by straight stitching the desired edge first, then cutting the fabric back to this row of stitching, and satin stitching over the edge. A further wider satin stitch can be worked over the edge for greater firmness. This method can more easily be worked with paper or **Stitch and Tear** behind the edge for a firmer result. Work with the foot on and the **feed dog** up.

■ **Cords** may be attached to a previous satin-stitched edge as a decorative finish with blind hemming stitch or open **zigzag** where the cord is seen, or as a firm, nicely rounded off finish with a satin stitch where the cord is completely covered. Beads could be added in a string to the cords or along the edge and included with a **blind hemming stitch**.

■ **Stretch fabrics,** or those cut on the bias, can be pulled and stitched along the edge with a satin stitch, creating a wavy edge.

■ Turned **satin stitch** edges produce a firm edge. Just turn in the edge using an iron, then satin stitch over this edge. From the inside of the edge of the garment, cut back to this stitching line. To firm and neaten up the edge even more, you can then follow with a second row of satin stitch over this cut edge.

■ **Whip stitch** edges offer a freedom of movement for a freely shaped edge. Set up a **whip stitch cord** using a firm thread such as a buttonhole twist or number 12 pearl cotton on the top of the machine with a 100 or **topstitch** needle. The **whip stitch** should wrap the top thread evenly without big loops. Work the stitches very close together so that only the bobbin thread can be seen as it wraps the top thread, but keep the fabric on the move to avoid bobbles of thread. The work is done with a straight stitch in a **hoop**, so intricate shapes and loops can be worked. Once finished you can cut back to this delicate edge, which is nevertheless firmer than it looks. Use on fine fabrics and if necessary burn off any fraying threads with a **soldering iron.**

■ Edges on small pieces of fabric can be made with the help of vanishing fabrics. Place the desired cut shape onto a piece of **vanishing fabric** and bond or stitch it into place. The edges can be neatened with rows of **straight stitch, satin stitch** or small **circles** over the edge into the vanishing fabric. By using this technique you are effectively working **appliqué**, which is a little easier than trying to stitch along the edges of small bits of fabric. Once the backing fabric has been vanished the small pieces can be used as desired.

■ Non-fray edges can also be created on fine synthetics simply by passing a soldering iron along the edge to cut it and to seal the threads.

■ **Bonded fabrics** are a little firmer than a single piece of fabric, so it is possible to **satin stitch** along a bonded edge with the foot in place and the **feed dog** up.

■ **Quilt wadding** can be placed between two fabrics, and treated as for bonded fabrics, with a double satin stitch edge.

ELASTIC

Elastic is an interesting material for **fabric manipulation** as well as for ordinary garment making. It can be stitched into place from the underside of a fabric – the more you stretch it as you go, the greater will be its effect. Stitch in straight lines, circles and curves for different effects. Use a three-step zigzag to avoid thread breakage. It can also

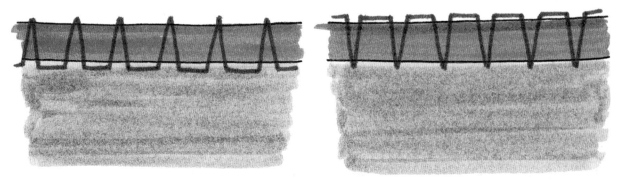

Two methods of applying a cord to an edge using a hemstitch. Note that beads could easily be included in the cord.

be used for manipulating fabric for **dyeing** or **discharge dyeing**, in which case use a long straight stitch that will be easy to break and undo after dyeing. Shirring elastic can be placed on the bobbin for **smocking** effects. A special bobbin case for elastic exists for some machines.

ELONGATING FORMS
Most electronic machines that include automatic patterns will include a means of elongating the pattern. This may simply double the length of the pattern that will be created, or may give you the choice of pattern length – in some cases up to 9cm (3½ inches), depending on the pattern and the machine. Some machines now give a choice of satin stitch shapes that can be programmed into a memory in different orders to provide longer stitch patterns and leaf shapes.

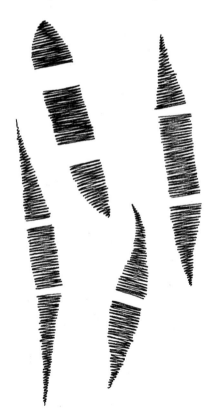

Satin stitch forms can be elongated and programmed into many machines in different sequences. These shapes can be used in free motion embroidery.

An interesting use for this technique is in the elongation of the satin stitch leaf shapes provided in automatic patterns. By elongating them and then using free motion embroidery, the leaf shapes can be drawn freely over a surface, obviating the need for manipulating the stitch width control as you stitch the different leaves over your embroidery. The shapes become much less rigid and more organic than when worked with a foot and the **feed dog** up.

On computerized machines many of the designs included with the machine can be elongated within the machine, without having recourse to a customizing program on a computer. This can be interesting as it will distort lettering and other designs, which in becoming unrecognizable may be more interesting as a base for further free motion embroidery.

EMBROIDERY
The dictionary definition of embroidery is: 'Decorate with needlework or fanciful embellishment' – meaning perhaps fanciful embellishment of stories, but it's a rather nice definition for textile work too. Embroidery is our embellished story, our embellished his(her)story.

EMBROIDERY FOOT
This foot has a wide space underneath it when the foot is lowered, to facilitate the application of cords, threads and braids, or to work over satin stitch or appliquéd edges.

A special embroidery foot is also available for computerized embroidery machines that is clear and not spring loaded, for use with programmed embroidery and the special hoops provided. See **darning foot** for **free motion embroidery**.

EMBROIDERY MACHINES
The origins of today's domestic embroidery machines can be found in the multihead single needle

machines of the 1970s and 1980s. These machines had the same appearance as ordinary domestic sewing machines working in a hoop. But the machines were lined up in rows of six or more, and the hoop was fixed to an arm driven by a pantograph or computer. As the technology improved, each head acquired more needles, so that re-threading became a thing of the past as the machine could pass from one colour to the next without intervention.

The technology involved separate guidance from what was, at that time, a powerful computer, and was limited to relatively simple embroidery designs such as badges and designs on baby clothes or sweatshirts, with few colours.

Multihead multineedle machines now exist in an enormous array of formats, including **lock stitch** and **chain stitch** machines as well as **Schiffli machines**. The technology has gradually been passed on to domestic machines, at first through manufacturers who produced machines both for industry and for the domestic market.

The first computerized machines of this type required a small pantograph device that allowed automatic repeat motif patterns to be created in one colour up to the width of the throat in the **needle plate**. Gradually more **feed dog** control was built into these machines so that the feed could work from left to right as well as backwards and forwards, and we now have arms to hold the embroidery hoop so that this can move too. With all the possible movements and colour changes now possible, a pantograph is no longer suitable as an instruction device, and indeed it is the improvement of computer technology and capacity, particularly in the home PC market, that makes this new type of machine possible. The domestic computerized sewing machine can now produce embroidery that was impossible even in industry only 20

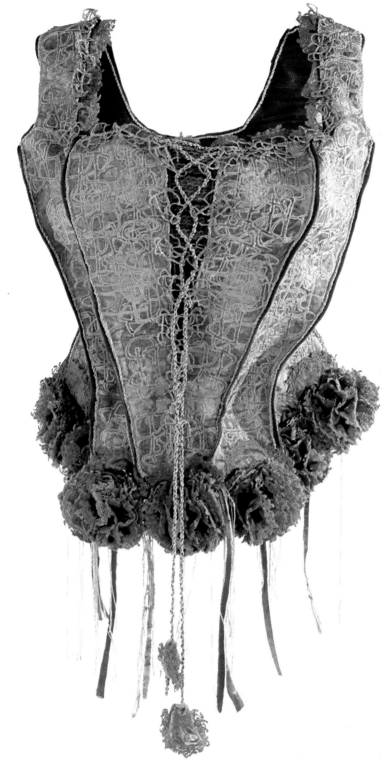

Mrs Pepys' Corset by Elli Woodsford. Worked on a Brother Super Galaxie 2100 computer machine. The square motif, designed from combining S and P for Samuel Pepys, was digitized and then stitched as both a solid form and an outline. These were then superimposed. Free motion embroidery was added to different parts of the corset panels. The Chinese lantern edging is a digitized shape with free motion embroidery inside the shape.

years ago. Any number of motifs and designs are available from a variety of sources, and you can of course design your own. But these machines do pose some questions:

How should we use them – not in the technical sense, but in the creative sense? The technical prowess of the machines can be so overwhelming that the artist is submerged. We need to step outside the technology and use its power to serve us. It is often interesting to use this computerized embroidery with other techniques that offer a more 'human' touch. This could include stitching onto previously worked, appliquéd, dyed or distressed backgrounds, or adding free motion embroidery or hand stitching to the computerized embroidery.

Is it art, or craft? The technology involved in computerized work takes away so much of the creative and design process that the result can look very 'industrial'. How can we reclaim this work and make it our own in a contemporary sense, or will it just remain a craft area? For something to work as a piece of art it must adhere to a concept formed by the artist. Accidents can be interesting or even beautiful, but there should be a conceptual purpose behind the work if we are to label it as art – and the term 'textile art' really shouldn't mean anything less than that. Even good craft work, whose only purpose is to decorate or serve as a useful object, needs good design.

What is the best way to master these techniques? This very powerful technology can very often simply control the operator, who designs to fit in with what he or she knows about the machine's capacities. This may be subliminal, but work can often be based on programs that are already in use, rather than designing and making the machine work towards the design. Good, solid designing is therefore essential if you are not going to fall into this trap.

HOW TO USE THEM

Embroidery machines have built-in **programs** that can be used as a guide to practising the techniques involved. The machine will have an arm, attached permanently to the machine or to be attached for embroidery, that a hoop in turn can be attached to. This arm moves the hoop in accordance with the programmed designs. The **hoop** is attached to this arm. There is usually a choice of sizes of hoop, and it is best to use the smallest possible for the design chosen, to avoid **flagging** of the fabric in the hoop. The fabric needs to be taut within the hoop. A **stabilizer** is recommended to keep the fabric firm and to avoid poor stitch quality and fabric flagging. The design you choose to do will have several colours, worked in a specific order, and the machine screen will guide you as to when to change them and what they should be.

Once you have understood how the machine moves and a little about the quality of the stitch that it can create, you will be able to start customizing programs, understanding colour changes, and the order of work that can be given to the machine to make the embroidery easier. Digitizing images can give even more choice of stitch filling and styles, as well as the possibility of working stitch by stitch if required. This may be worth pursuing if you are making a program for many repeats, but it can be time-consuming if you are just creating one-off or limited edition embroideries.

As you use programs you will learn which stitches and movements cause the most thread breakage and the best way of scanning images, as well as how to prepare images for the best scanning results.

The full capacity of these machines has yet to be exploited by skilled embroiderers, but they are fascinating and can certainly add a new dimension to creative embroidery. It is important to remember also that this is just one technique in our repertoire. Very few people use machine embroidery alone as a method, and it is more often mixed with dyeing techniques, created fabric or textural backgrounds, or hand stitching. Similarly, embroideries worked on computerized machines can be used by the creative embroiderer as part of a piece of work with **free motion embroidery** or **hand embroidery** added. **Dyeing** or **vanishing fabric**

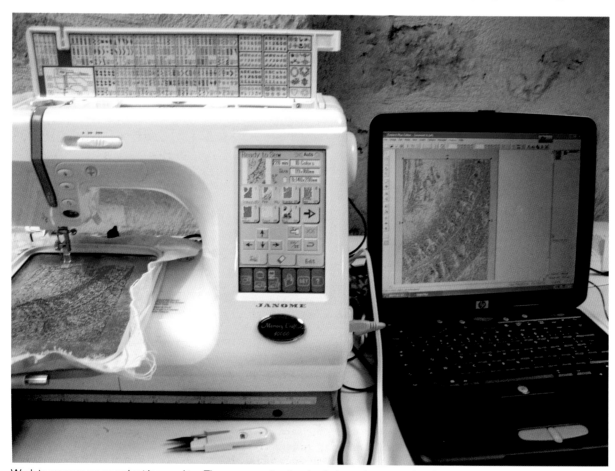

Work in progress on an embroidery machine. The computer showing the design no longer needs to be connected.

techniques can also be involved. The most important thing is not to be influenced by the existing programs, which tend to be kitsch and flat. Creative embroidery on these machines needs to be invented and reinvented, and will inevitably be related to the quality of the programs available. For more information see the Appendix on page 188.

EMBROIDERY NEEDLE
An embroidery needle has a bigger eye than usual for its size and a grooved shank that helps prevent thread wear on more delicate threads. Not being overlarge, it doesn't make unsightly holes in the fabric. It also causes less wear on metallic threads, and there is less overheating with this sort of needle. It is also useful when threading up with more than one thread in the needle, for all delicate threads, and on heavily stitched or difficult surfaces to avoid thread wear. The N or **topstitch** needles have particularly large eyes and are recommended for metallic threads, the E needles have a slightly smaller eye, but allow the passage of thicker threads.

EMBROIDERY PLATE
See **cover plate.**

EMBROIDERY RING
See **hoop.**

ENCAUSTIC COLOURING
'Encaustic' simply means coloured with hot wax. Coloured wax crayons, including metallic ones, can be used. Melt bits of crayon in an old frying pan or a foil-lined aluminium pan. As the crayons start to melt you can choose where you will add other crayons. You can design the surface by dragging a fork, or stirring with a spoon. When you have something interesting you can add the fabric. Cotton is probably best. Press the fabric down into the hot wax – you can leave areas proud if you want negative undyed shapes. If you are

Metallic oil pastels fused with heat onto a muslin ground with free motion embroidery.

not satisfied with the result you can add more crayons and try again. When you are satisfied, take the fabric out and iron it between layers of newspaper or kitchen towel until as much of the wax as possible is removed, as you don't want this gumming up the mechanism of your machine.

The resulting fabric should create an inspiring background for many free motion embroidery techniques.

For an easier version of this technique draw on fabric with oil or wax crayons and fix the colour by ironing – this is particularly good with metallic oil pastels which can also be fixed on paper with heat.

ENCROACHING CIRCLES
Small **circles or granite stitch** can be very effective when used as a texture or filling, and can also be useful to hold vanishing fabric lace or pictures together. Larger

Encroaching reworked circles will hold together on vanishing fabric.

encroaching circles can achieve the same purpose, but the circular shape is more exaggerated. It takes a little practice to decide how to move on from one circle to the next. Practise drawing the patterns you are trying to achieve on the machine with a pen on paper first.

Olive trees worked on an Irish machine by the author. The yellow ground is worked with encroaching satin stitch in matt and shiny threads.

Remember to use the correct hand position on the **hoop** – essential for drawing circles.

ENCROACHING SATIN STITCH
Wide rows of satin stitch can be worked overlapping into previous rows. This can quickly cover a ground and produces a smooth surface; use the widest possible satin stitch. For even more texture and colour variations try using a **whipped satin stitch.**

ENLARGING THE DESIGN
Many designs can be enlarged directly on the computerized machine, without recourse to **customizing** on a computer program. Usually the machine itself will be able to enlarge the design by about 20%; above this level of enlargement the change in **stitch density** will be such that the design will no longer work. If you wish to enlarge above this, for most machines you will have to use a **customizing** program, although this is an area that is changing, and some machines can now readjust the design to keep the stitch density the same, whatever the enlargement. See Appendix on page 188.

For enlarging your own designs for ordinary embroidery use, the time has passed when we used to

have to draw a small grid over the work and gradually transfer the design bit by bit onto a larger grid. Even if the original drawing or painting is in colour, you can simply trace a black ink drawing off it and enlarge or reduce it on a photocopier to see what the result would be, or to acquire the size you desire. As colour photocopying is still relatively expensive, it's best to play around with black and white until you have the result you want. For large pieces you may need a number of photocopies which you will need to mark in such a way that you can put them back together again. Once they are taped together I usually trace off from this again, and use the tracing paper to transfer my design to the embroidery fabric. See **elongating forms** and **transferring designs.**

EVENWEAVE FABRIC
Usually available in cotton or linen, evenweave fabric has a given number of threads to the centimetre or inch and is generally used for hand embroidery techniques such as counted **cross stitch, pulled work,** hardanger, and so on. Because the threads and the thread count need to be very even, it is generally a fairly expensive fabric. It can be used for machine embroidery, particularly for pulled work

techniques where you may achieve wonderful edges for tablecloths and so on in a style familiar to your grandmother (or great-grandmother). Cheaper, more stable versions are available in the form of Aida and Binca fabrics. Aida comes in finer thread counts than Binca. These evenweave fabrics can also be used for machine embroidery. A childish piece reminiscent of the samplers worked by schoolchildren years ago is illustrated on page 43.

EYELETS
Eyelets can be worked as for **free eyelets,** and this method does mean that you are in control of the size of eyelet and the hole. However, an eyelet attachment is available for most machines. It usually comprises a cover plate for the feed with a point for the location of the eyelet hole, or a larger hole into which other attachments with varying sizes of locating spikes can be fitted to give larger or smaller eyelets. An awl (a pointed tool) may also be supplied to make or cut the eyelet, and a special foot to fit the cover plate. With these attachments eyelets are easy, if a little predictable.

Put the work in a small **hoop,** make a suitable size of hole in the fabric and place it over the locating spike. Then check the needle

Machine stitched eyelets on muslin incorporated into acrylic painting and embroidery with fabrics. By Sarah Birtwistle while a student at Manchester Metropolitan University.

cotton and calico can be treated with heavy directional stitching.

Fabric can also be manipulated by **gathering (puffing)**, working on the **bias, pintucking** and tucking, **quilting, Italian quilting, burning,** slashing or including wire in the seams, stitching to form the fabric, or using such materials as **Tyvek,** other plastics and **Softsculpt.**

FABRIC PAINTS

Fabric paints are specially created paints for use on fabric, although they also work on paper or **Tyvek.** They are usually fixed using heat (from an iron) which has the benefit not only of fixing the paint against water damage, but also of preventing damage by exposure to light. Paints, unlike **dyes,** stay more easily where they are put and do not bleed into the fabric unless they are used in a diluted form. If pale tints are required, water can be added, but transparent extenders are available so that the quality of the paint remains the same. Another difference between fabric paint and fabric dye is that paints have a tendency to sit on the surface of the fabric and so change it to a certain extent. The more water that is added, the less this occurs. Spirit-based fabric paints are also available, but these are less pleasant to use than water-based ones.

FABRICS

Woven or non-woven fabrics are usually the base for our embroideries, although we can also use **plastics, paper,** some metals and **leather,** for example. The quality of the fabric should be chosen with a certain amount of care.

If it will be visible, and the embroidery only represents a small decorative part of the surface, the fabric will obviously play a major role and should be suitable for the task – perhaps it needs to be a delicate silk, or a rich satin or velvet. If the embroidery is to cover, or almost entirely cover, the surface of the fabric, the quality of the

position and stitch width to be sure they correspond to the holes in the cover plate. Sew a closed **zigzag** continuously and evenly while turning the hoop. Larger eyelets can be made, if a little untidily, by pulling the fabric against the locating spike as the stitching is worked. Fixing instructions are provided with these attachments when they are purchased.

Computerized machines are capable of doing eyelets of various sizes using machine programs.

Follow the instructions provided with your machine, or **download** designs from the **Internet.**

FABRIC MANIPULATION

Machine embroidery will stiffen fabric by virtue of heavy stitching alone. This stitching can be directional and the fabric can be manipulated to distort it and to take on new shapes. Tight tensions can be used to further enhance the effects. **Felt** works particularly well for this kind of work as it 'gives', but even

fabric is especially important. If the work is to be stretched to a flat, perfect surface afterwards it is important to use a strong, good-quality fabric – silk noil is ideal, or a good calico. Some fabrics (such as cheap polyester cotton) are just too weak to support a great deal of stitching, and will pucker and almost certainly not stretch flat and back into shape afterwards. Perhaps the fabric will be deliberately manipulated or the stitching is meant to take over and the fabric give way – in which case you could choose **felt, scrim** or **muslin**. The most important thing in the choice of fabric for your work is that it is a conscious choice, and that what you have chosen will work for what you have in mind. If you are not sure, do a sample first before embarking on a large project.

FABRIC TENSION

Good tension of the fabric in the **hoop** is essential for **free motion embroidery** in order for the stitches to be formed. **Missed stitches** are often the result of slack fabric tension in the hoop.

Good tension is also vital for **computerized embroidery** on an embroidery machine. Loose tension will lead to missed stitches, poor stitching, fabric puckering and poor design justification (lines failing to meet). See **stabilizer**.

FAGGOTING

Faggoting is a traditional decorative method of joining two fabrics together across a space, where the space was created by tacking (basting) the turned edges to paper, before creating a loose filling.

To achieve this technique with the sewing machine, two pieces of fabric with the edges turned under (ironed) are placed under a foot (a grooved **pintucking** foot is ideal) with a gap in between them. The stitch selected should enter each of the fabrics at its extremes, and stitch over the gap in the centre. There are usually several automatic

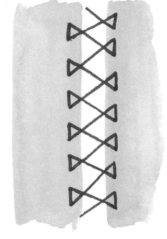

Putting two separate pieces of fabric under the machine and using an automatic stitch for a faggoted seam (a grooved foot can be useful).

stitches to choose from that will achieve this, or you can use an open **zigzag** or **blind hemming stitch**.

Faggoting can also be achieved using the **tailor's tacking foot** and a zigzag stitch. Do a few stitches on the spot to start or finish, then zigzag over the foot and into each fabric as above. When the fabrics are pulled apart they will be joined by the insertion stitches.

Note also that there are many different faggoting stitches, or potential faggoting stitches, included on modern electronic and computerized machines.

FEATHER STITCH

Feather stitch is created by tightening the top tension and

Bobbin thread comes through to the top edge

Stitch patterns worked in free motion embroidery suitable for feather stitch.

loosening the bobbin tension. Thus the bobbin thread is pulled through to the top of the fabric in large loops. (**Whip stitch** is created in the same way, but to a lesser extent, producing only small loops.)

By turning the top tension to about six or seven, and loosening the **bobbin tension** screw so that the thread flows easily when the

bobbin case is suspended, you will create a feather stitch. To achieve even greater loops, the top tension can be tightened further, or the bobbin tension can be loosened further. When loosening the bobbin tension screw, do so over a surface (the fabric stretched in the **hoop** will be ideal) so that if the tension screw does come

completely undone, it will fall into the hoop when it springs out. Always close the bobbin race cover (on vertical bobbin race machines there may be a tendency to leave it open); if the bobbin case should spring apart during sewing, you will hear the noise and the bits will be under the machine, and not on the floor.

On some machines the bobbin tension can be bypassed and this will also give a feather stitch. See **bobbin tension – bypassing the tension**.

A variety of different stitches and marks can be created with feather stitch. Working with **curves** and **circles** is perhaps the most rewarding, but rows of straight lines can also be interesting. Various set stitches work well, including **satin stitch**.

Removing the top thread after working will produce a **moss stitch**.

If you are working feather stitch onto **vanishing fabrics**, make sure that there is enough support already in place (pieces of fabric or existing heavy stitching) to be able to create and hold the feather stitch. It needs a 'fabric' surface in order to hold together and not just become a mess of unruly loops.

FEED DOG

The feed dog is the toothed feed system under the bed of the machine, visible under the needle plate, that moves the fabric backwards and forwards (and sometimes even from side to side) under the presser foot. It will consist of between two and seven individual sets of teeth which have a rotating movement to ensure that the fabric is held and moved evenly, or in accordance with the design of the stitch.

There is usually a button or knob somewhere on the machine that will allow you to lower the feed dog so that it does not interfere when the machine is being used for free motion embroidery. On older horizontal bobbin race machines

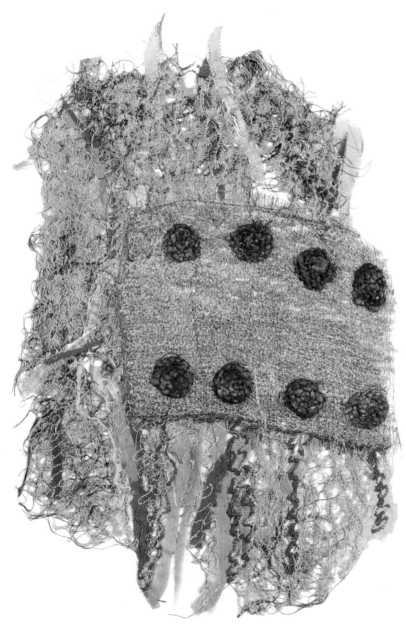

Door by the author. Worked with scrim and fabric strips applied to Solusheet in a Soluweb sandwich. Feather stitch is worked in U shapes or fleece stitch worked over the fabric strips.

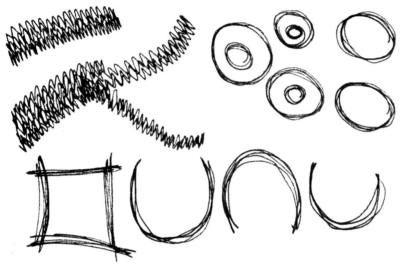

Stitch patterns worked in free motion embroidery suitable for manipulating felt.

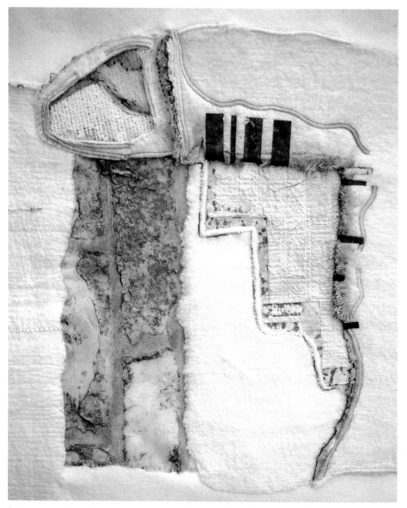

Felt and mixed media with twin needle stitching. By Lynda Mennell, while a student at Manchester Metropolitan University.

there is more frequently a cover plate to cover the feed dog for free motion embroidery. Your own handbook will give details.

FELT

Felt is a non-woven fabric, usually made of wool, but it can be made of silk or acrylic and often mixed fibres in acrylic/polyester or wool/viscose matted together using heat, moisture and pressure or a rubbing process. Many people enjoy making their own felt, in which case you can mould it, add colours, threads or bits of anything interesting within the surface of the fabric.

Because felt is firm it is easy to embroider without a hoop and with a **darning foot** or **embroidery foot**. An embroidery hoop can actually mark the felt and spoil its appearance. Using a slightly tight top and bottom tensions, large stitches, and stitching very strong lines, **curves** or **circles**, felt can be manipulated into shapes, bumps and bubbles – it's fun to experiment!

FIBREFILM AND FIBRETEX

These products are similar to **Tyvek**.

FILLINGS

See **straight stitch fillings – computerized embroidery** and **straight stitch fillings – free motion embroidery**.

FLAGGING

The loosening of the fabric in the hoop during stitching, resulting in poor stitching in free motion embroidery and poor alignment in computerized embroidery. Use a good stabilizer to prevent this on computerized machines. For free motion work, reset the hoop.

FLEECE STITCH

In **free motion embroidery**, fleece stitch is working in U shapes, or undulating U shapes, one over the other. This is a useful stitch for vanishing fabric lace structures, and particularly effective when worked in **whip stitch** or **heavy whip stitch**.

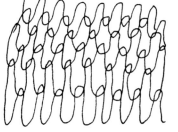 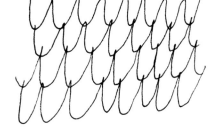

Fleece stitch and variant.

FLOSS THREADS

Floss is a non-twisted shiny thread in rayon or silk. Some floss threads may work through a topstitch needle with a loosened top tension – it's worth a try. If they break too frequently, put them on the bobbin and use them in the same way as for **cable stitch**. See pictures on pages 29 and 174.

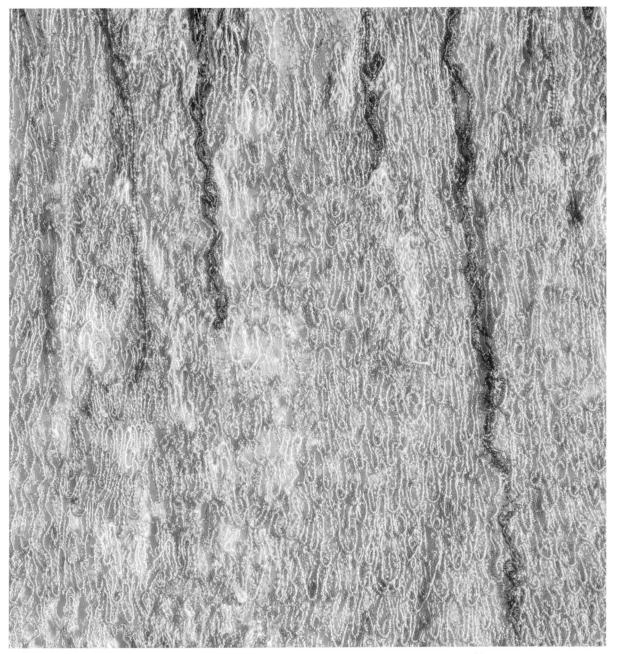

Detail of *Roussillon with Olive Trees* by the author. Fleece stitch worked with whip stitch on Solusheet vanishing fabric.

FOUR-DIRECTION SEWING

Some of the latest machines now offer the possibility of sewing sideways as well as forwards and backwards. This can be useful for working difficult seams and corners (see below), and even for putting boxes together.

FRAMING UP

See **hoop.**

FRAYING

Fraying is a natural process that can occur on woven fabrics along any cut edges, where either the warp or weft of the weave pulls away, leaving a sort of fringing of the remaining threads. The fraying process can be avoided by fusing **Bondaweb** onto the fabric to be cut out before you start cutting, or by applying thinned **PVA medium** along the edge after cutting. Fraying can also become part of the design. It can be allowed to happen naturally: bits and pieces of fabric are stitched together and whether they fray or not is left to chance. Or it can be exaggerated by pulling away the threads in one direction; this can be particularly interesting on shot fabrics (fabrics that have a different colours in the warp and weft). The fraying can be stopped at the desired point using glue, a bonding spray or web. Rows of **straight stitch** or a wide **satin stitch** can add a decorative edge to prevent fraying. On synthetic fabrics, fraying can be stopped by carefully cutting or melting the edge with a **soldering iron.**

FREE EYELETS

Free eyelets have a charm for me that surpasses machine-made **eyelets,** which tend to be very regular and industrial in appearance.

TO MAKE A FREE EYELET
1. Place the fabric tightly in a hoop, and carefully stitch two or three times around the desired size of circle.

2. Cut out the centre of the circle, close to the stitching.

3. Satin stitch around the edge of the circle. Holding the hoop correctly in the right hand and swivelling with two fingers of the left hand on each side of the needle, you should manage to stitch around the curve.

4. Filling holes can be done before the final satin stitching if desired.

Small coloured squares, heat treated to prevent fraying, by Liz Maidment.

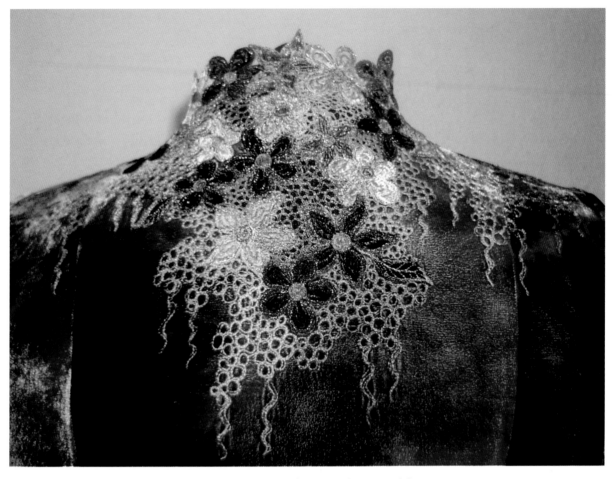

Detail of *Flower Coat* by Lesley George. An eyelet technique was used to create the openwork leaves.

Method for working a free eyelet and bars across the hole.

Eyelets of any size and almost any geometrical shape can be made using this method – round, oval, pearl shapes, squares, hexagons, and so on.

FREEHAND MACHINE EMBROIDERY

Freehand machine embroidery is another term for **free motion embroidery**, which distinguishes this process from **computerized embroidery**.

FREE MACHINE EMBROIDERY

Free machine embroidery is another term for **free motion embroidery**, again as distinguished from computerized embroidery.

FREE MOTION EMBROIDERY

Free motion embroidery is the term

that is used to explain the technique in which the **feed dog** is lowered on the sewing machine (older machines with a horizontal bobbin race may have a cover plate) and the presser foot is removed from the machine. There is now no feed at all to pull the fabric through the machine for you, so you are free to guide the fabric and stitch as you like.

When it is used for free motion embroidery, the machine often has difficulty in creating stitches if the fabric is not held taut enough, which is why most free motion embroidery is done using an embroidery **hoop**.

A **darning foot** or free motion embroidery foot may be used in the place of the presser foot. The foot holds the fabric on the bed of the machine while the stitch is being made, and can be quite useful if the fabric is layered or stiff enough to work without a hoop. See **darning foot** for more details.

The presser foot lever is lowered even when there is no presser foot, as this engages the top tension, and without this there will be a **bird's nest** on the reverse of the work and the machine may even jam. If you have accidentally not lowered the presser foot you will notice that the stitches on the surface appear slack, as one would expect with a loose top tension. This will be the first sign of your error.

As machines wear and age, the symptoms described above may appear even though you have put the presser foot lever down. In this case just lift the presser foot lever and put it down again sharply. Many patterns, shapes, fillings and stitch techniques can be done with free motion embroidery – see **straight stitch fillings** and **zigzag**

filling stitches as a starting point. See picture on page 154.

FREE MOTION SATIN STITCH

Working with a **zigzag** stitch to create a free motion satin stitch does require some practice if you are to obtain an even stitch length and smooth appearance. See how to hold the **hoop** correctly, which will help enormously, and practise in straight lines before attempting circles and curves. Bear in mind that your hands are the stitch length control for your machine when you are working **free motion embroidery**, so you must move them and the hoop very slowly to achieve a good satin stitch. Work with a slow machine speed while you get used to the technique – you can speed up later. The satin stitch will look better if you achieve it in one passage, and are not obliged to go over it a second time to fill in the gaps.

Once you have achieved this technique you can use it for many

textural effects – see **satin stitch** and **zigzag**. It is also useful for **appliqué**, **edges** and **cutwork**.

Working freehand gives a lot more flexibility than when using a foot and **feed dog**, and is much more interesting and faster than having constantly to change direction with the foot on. The fact that the work can be held in a hoop will also prevent puckering when working wider satin stitches. See also **jump stitch**.

FRENCH KNOTS

Effects similar to individual French knots can be achieved with small **satin stitch blocks** (see picture on page 133). See also **bead stitch**. Use a very narrow satin stitch and stitch the blocks on the spot.

For the effect of lots of heavy French knots together, try using a **cable stitch** with a very loose or bypassed tension to create bobbles.

Janome offer a lookalike French knot as a linear stitch on the

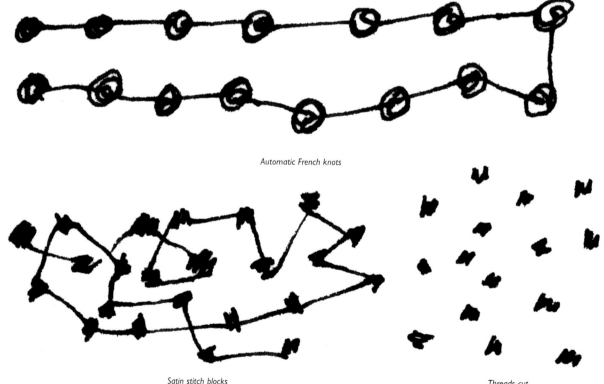

Automatic French knots

Satin stitch blocks

French knots worked by machine.

Threads cut

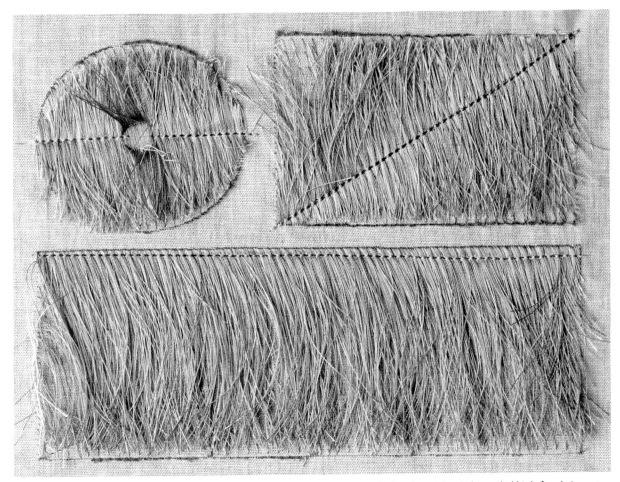

Fringing worked on a digitized program with a large satin stitch. The satin stitch is stitched with straight stitches to hold it before being cut into a fringe. Worked on a Janome machine.

computerized machines. It can be stitched individually, and the work can be moved under the foot to place them. The stitch cannot be worked with free motion embroidery as it relies on the machine working in a forwards and backwards motion.

FRINGING
Fringing involves producing a very large **satin stitch**, held at one end or in the middle by a series of small **running stitches**, then cutting the threads to leave a fringe. It is technique included on some ready-bought computerized embroidery programs, but it's relatively easy to program with a digitizer program that allows you to make an enormous satin stitch.

On **free motion embroidery**, if your machine has the **tacking** (basting) facility, you will be able to produce large stitches that can form a satin stitch, and be subsequently held down with a small running stitch, before being cut, just like the computerized version.

FUSIBLE WEB
See **Bondaweb** and **Soluweb**.

GARMENTS
For embroidering pieces for making into garments, see **all-over design** and **creating fabrics**. If you wish to embroider only part of a fabric piece for an existing garment, the garment piece itself should be marked out on the fabric so that the positioning of the embroidery is

perfect. If the embroidery is to be done by a computer program, it may be necessary to try out the embroidery first to ensure that the fabric, and the **stitch density,** will work. It will also help you to decide on the positioning of the hoop for the final garment and you can make sure that your chosen **stabilizer** is suitable. You should use the same type of fabric for the sample piece. This effort is never a waste of time and it can prevent ruining a larger fabric piece. These samples can also be used as a base for further embroidery, or **slips** or **patches.** Some fabrics shrink in the wash, so it may be a good idea to wash your fabric first before you begin. The fabric shop should be able to advise you on whether this is necessary.

Some embroidery machines have a mechanism for holding fabrics that are susceptible to hoop burn. If yours does not have such a device, use a stabilizer **backing fabric** and **topping** if the fabric is likely to suffer.

If you are working with **free motion embroidery** you will obviously already have planned your motif and technique beforehand, hopefully by stitching onto the same fabric. You will know if you need a stabilizer behind your work to prevent puckering. Make sure that the garment piece has large enough seam allowances if there is a risk that you may have to stretch the work after your embroidery. Carefully place the **hoop** onto the fabric, or if you have a fabric that is susceptible to hoop burn use a heavier stabilizer in place of a hoop. Binding the hoop with tape can prevent hoop burn on most fabrics.

If you wish to embroider on a readymade garment there are several rules to follow. First pre-wash the garment to avoid any excessive shrinking or colour bleeding once the embroidery has been worked. If the embroidery is to be worked by a computer program, do a test as above, on as similar a fabric as possible. Be particularly careful about the positioning of the fabric and consider hoop burn (as above). Use a suitable stabilizer for the fabric and the density of the stitches. When working on an existing garment with free motion embroidery the same rules apply as above. Also bear in mind that you will not be able to stretch the embroidery once it is finished, so pay particular attention to good thread tensions and use a suitable stabilizer for the area that is going to be embroidered.

GATHERING (PUFFING)

If you wish to gather material for dressmaking, for fabric manipulation or for effects before dyeing or discharge dyeing, there are a number of methods you can use. A gathering stitch is available on some machines (see your handbook), or set a long stitch with a loose bobbin tension for the same effect. A gathering foot or ruffler which gathers the fabric to a greater or lesser degree as you stitch is available for some machines, or a tucking foot which puts regular tucks into the fabric. See also **elastic**, **smocking** and **pintucking**.

GESSO

This acrylic and plaster medium is used for preparing surfaces before painting, leaving a white finish that paint can adhere to. It can be used as a light sculpting medium as it is supple and resists flaking and cracking. It can be coloured with powders or paint (metallic colours are best added to the surface before it is dry) or used under gold leaf as a sculpted support. Other sculpting, modelling and textured supports and gels are available for acrylic painting. These can be experimented with if you wish to add paint and painterly qualities to your embroideries.

GIMP THREAD

The term given to a thicker yarn used in lacemaking to define a design area and/or add strength to the design. This technique can also be used in lacy effects on **vanishing fabric** for the same reasons. Ways of adding the effect of a gimp are:

Empty Shrine by the author. Part of a series. Worked on felt with gesso and acrylic paint. The sculpted gesso was coloured with metallic powders before being dried. The whole piece was treated with PVA to hold the powders more firmly. Free motion stitching.

■ Rows of straight stitching one on top of another.

■ Several rows of straight stitching as before, bound together with a satin stitch.

■ **Whip stitch cord** (corded whip stitch).

■ Couched **cable stitch**.

■ Applying thread, cord or ribbon.

Note that gimp threads are best added after the rest of the lace has been created, to hold the work together. If you lay the gimps down before you make the rest of the lace, you will have to stitch over them to hold the various areas together and the result will be untidy.

Close-up of Romanesque church sculpture worksheet with details to show the use of a gimp on vanishing fabric lace. Examples include cable stitch and satin stitch over straight stitching. By the author.

GLAZED, COATED OR WAXED THREADS
These threads are pre-treated for hand quilting to give a stronger thread and firmer finish. However, they should not be used for machine quilting because they may damage the machine's mechanism.

GLUE
See **PVA medium**.

GOLD THREADS
See **metallic threads**.

GRAIN
The straight grain of the fabric is rarely taken into account by embroiderers, and yet it can be an important consideration, particularly in larger pieces, wall hangings or where good drape is required. The straight grain is in line with the woven edges of the fabric, or at right angles to this line. Ideally, anything cut to hang that is not deliberately cut on the bias for effect should be cut on the straight grain. Applied pieces should be cut on the same grain as the fabric underneath.

Of course this is not always possible – the design effects required from moving applied fabrics in different directions to catch the light may be more important than any technical requirements. However, the straight grain should be taken into consideration, and the finished work may have to be supported differently (for example on a frame rather than a hung support) if the grain is ignored.

GRANITE STITCH OR CIRCLES
See **circles**.

GRAPHIC TABLET
This is a useful add-on for your computer. They are available in sizes from A6 to A2, although A5 or A4 is quite a reasonable size for the needs of most embroiderers. They allow you to draw, either freehand or from a tracing, directly with a special 'pen' onto the pad, into a paint or embroidery program. They can also work as a mouse for the computer. The most costly versions allow for a 'pencil' feel and different qualities of mark according to how you use them. For embroidery programs you only need simple line quality, so this is probably not necessary. Do buy a good brand, though, that will pick up your drawn lines easily and without fault. See page 185 for a child's use of this tool.

GRIDS
Grids form an agreeable structure to work within and with which to experiment with colour, stitch or texture. We can find grid designs around us in buildings and industrial landscapes. Photos or

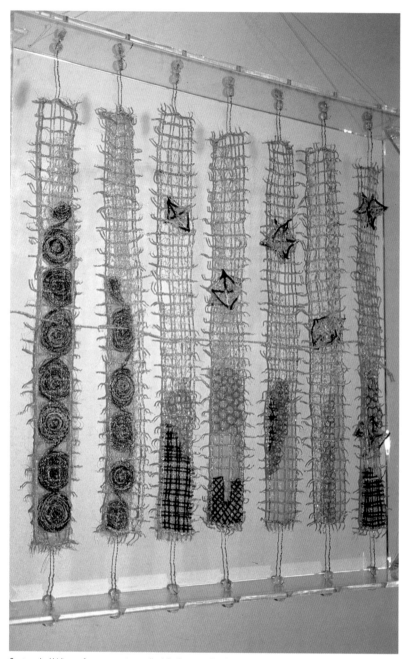

Suspended Winter from a series called *Reflection*. Grids worked on cold water dissolvable fabric by Lorna Rand while studying with Opus School of Textiles.

top. Machine-wrapped cords, wire or wooden kebab or cocktail sticks can be used to make independent grids. Grid structures can be used as sculpture or mobiles to appreciate the intersection of different lines, shapes and patterns within these structures.

Grids can be made on the sewing machine by any of these methods and can then be used as a base for hand embroidery.

GROOVED FOOT

Grooved feet come with a number of different grooves (in odd numbers from 3 to 9) and are useful for creating better effects than an ordinary foot when **pintucking** or making **corded pintucks** with a twin needle.

They can also help to keep things in place when **applying cords** or working **faggoting** over two edges of a seam.

GUIDE STITCH

This is a series of stitches used to align subsequent embroidery or to mark where appliqué motifs are to be placed on the fabric.

GUIPURE LACE

In about 1879 the first attempts at 'chemical lace' were made on a **hand machine** and then on a continuous thread or **Schiffli machine**. Paper was used as a background for the embroidery, and designs were made that would hold together when the paper was washed away. This process presented two problems: small pieces of paper would remain in the work even when the embroidery was thoroughly rubbed; and the paper did not form a solid enough ground for the embroidery, breaking into pieces and causing irregularities in the stitching.

The technique was of interest, however, because of the popularity of lace fabrics at the time, and the expense of producing them by hand or on slow, costly lace machines. The technique came to the attention

sketchbook material can be collected to form a base for textile work. Broken grids or organic grid forms such as tree bark or pool mosaics reflected through lightly troubled water create interesting spaces to examine ideas on harmony or routine, or look at colour and light relationships.

To make grids on normal fabrics the **presser foot** or **quilting guide** can help you to make equidistant lines in straight or satin stitch. Satin stitch over the threads of large-holed rug canvas to create a grid. Grid structures can be used as a base on **vanishing fabric** where other stitching can be worked on of Charles Wetter, who was determined that something better could be achieved. His first attempts were made with muslin that could be dissolved away after stitching, but only through a long and dangerous chemical process. Then by accident he became aware that silk dissolved in a chlorine solution. If the embroidery were worked in cotton, this, being vegetable-based, would not dissolve. It took some time to perfect the techniques necessary to stop the delicate lace structure from falling apart when the silk backing had been dissolved, and the chlorine solution proved injurious to health. The first problem was solved by using laceworkers to teach embroiderers some of their interlocking stitching techniques; the second by substituting caustic soda for the chlorine solution, and so the process was patented. From 1885 'chemical lace' was widely produced, most especially on Schiffli or continuous thread machines which were more suited to this technique, though some work continued on the hand machines.

At first copies of popular laces were produced, but eventually individual styles emerged that did not resemble anything handmade and these became known as 'guipure lace'.

Between 1885 and 1895 a 'chemical lace' was developed working in silk on a nitrated cotton base which could be dissolved with a blast of hot air in a special furnace (the forerunner of vanishing muslin); but the first chemical method remained the most popular.

HAND EMBROIDERY

The fine tracery of machine stitching contrasts well with the bolder textural mark that can be made with hand stitches. Generally the machine can quickly and easily produce unbroken lines of movement, although stitches such as **satin stitch blocks** are an exception.

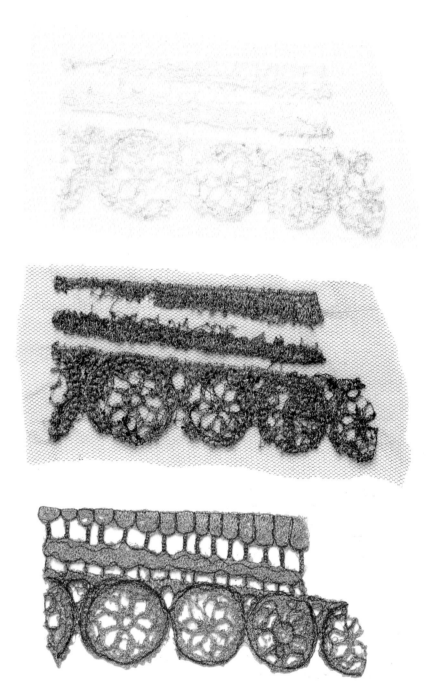

Guipure Lace. Three examples worked on a computerized embroidery machine (Janome 10000) from the Embird Sfumato program. A photo from the inside of a Romanesque church taken with a flash was manipulated in a paint program to give extreme light/dark contrast, and as much light (colour) as possible under these extremes. The program was then told that the fabric colour would be black, so all the black stitching was removed from the embroidery, but the white areas were now heavily embroidered, which made the lace design. Two examples are worked on net over dissolvable film, one in pale colours, one in gold and red on black to show the effect of different colourways. The final example was worked on vanishing fabric and stitched afterwards with free motion embroidery to firm it up.

Court d'Aron (detail) by the author. Hand embroidery in threads and fabric strips with machine embroidery in straight stitch and satin stitch blocks over the hand stitching.

One of the benefits of hand stitching is that it is possible to stitch broken lines and individual stitches. The choice of threads and thread textures is greater, too, than that available for machine work.

Most people work the bulk of the embroidery by sewing machine first – tracing in colour, form and movement. Hand stitching, when added to machine embroidery, is generally done at the end of the work, highlighting colours or contrasts, defining textural areas, and bringing significance to one area over another so that this will serve as the focal point of the work.

Considered the other way round, hand stitching can be worked first, perhaps in highly textured yarns or stitches, and machining into this will flatten certain areas and allow others to become significant. This technique can be particularly effective on **canvas work**.

Many machine embroidery techniques can imitate the bulk of some of the techniques used in hand embroidery – consider **applying cord or ribbon, cable stitch, padded satin stitch, satin stitch blocks**. These machine techniques can be useful techniques to mix in with hand stitches.

Whenever you are mixing hand and machine stitch techniques in this way, be sure that they are well integrated and that the hand stitches are not just a way of finishing off areas that you are incapable of doing by machine. In the past, there has been a tendency to believe that one is obliged to add hand stitches at some point to a piece of work, and that machine embroidery cannot stand alone, which is false. Be careful of following fashions just for the sake of it; there should always be a design sense to any of the choices that you make.

HAND EMBROIDERY TECHNIQUES

Many hand embroidery techniques, and even stitches, can lend themselves to reinvention on the sewing machine, and an interesting project to set yourself is to experiment with the hand techniques you know, to see how they can be adapted. You can, for instance, look at crewel embroidery, **blackwork, whitework,** bead embroidery, **openwork** and **broderie anglaise, pulled work, canvas work, stumpwork** ... the list is as long as your imagination.

HAND EMBROIDERY THREADS

There are now a huge number of hand embroidery threads available for your hand stitchery. Traditional stranded, pearl or soft embroidery cotton, different thicknesses of wool, stranded or pearl silk or rayon, and many knitting yarns, can also be used for embroidery. More hand-dyed and spun threads appear on the market all the time – and you can of course also prepare your own threads at home!

These threads can have a use in your embroidery by mixing **hand embroidery** with your machine embroidery or hand whipping embroidery stitches. You can also **apply threads** to embroidery, or many can be wound onto the bobbin and used with **cable stitch.**

HAND MACHINE

The hand embroidery machine was the first ever industrial multineedle embroidery machine and was developed during the Industrial Revolution. The first machine was used in 1828 and by 1830 they were widespread. They were known as hand stitch embroidery machines because the action of stitching mimics that of hand embroidery.

Rows of double-pointed needles, which had an eye in the middle for the thread, were passed right through the fabric and back again to form stitches. There was no bobbin or shuttle and the fabric was

held in position on a large frame moved by the use of a pantograph.

A flat knot held the thread in the needle in such a way that it could be passed through the fabric. The carriages holding the pincers were moved by hand and were required to move quite a way from the fabric for the first stitches, but less and less so as the stitching continued. Threads used were about 1 metre (3 feet) long, which meant that the machines needed constant re-threading. Eventually carriages were invented that worked by power, and the quality of movement and thus the delicacy of stitching improved. By 1865 between 600 and 650 hand embroidery machines were in use in St Gallen in Switzerland, with possibly as many as 19,000 units at the climax in the 1880s.

The technique, being based on hand embroidery, could imitate hand stitching. Techniques could include running stitch, back stitch, satin stitch, cross stitch worked in white threads on white at first, and then increasingly colourful work on different and darker fabrics and even delicate **reverse appliqué** with net or muslin.

Devices were invented that made a kind of drawn thread work possible and **guipure** lace was also produced for a time.

Much work produced on these machines can easily be mistaken for hand embroidery because of the use of a single thread and the nature of the stitches. Only experience with hand and hand machine work will help you to tell them apart. Note that chain and related stitches were not possible on these machines.

HAND-WHIPPED MACHINE STITCHES

Large straight stitches used as a base can be hand whipped with hand or machine embroidery threads. The machine stitching can be in adjacent parallel rows (use the foot or the **quilting guide** as a guide), or worked freely over the surface of the fabric and hand

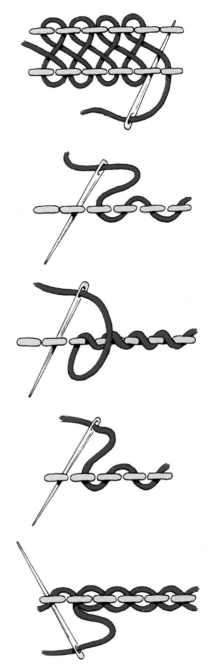

Different whipping techniques for hand whipped machine stitches. Note that the change in the direction of the needle will change the direction in the lie of the threads.

whipped freely too. There are many examples of whipped running or backstitch in hand embroidery handbooks that could be used as a starting point for a technical sampler. The interest of this technique can be in the way of adding hand stitch threads quickly and effectively. Because the needle with the hand stitch thread does not go through the fabric except at the start and finish of the thread, there is an economy of movement and thread. Use a fine tapestry needle, as this makes picking up the machine thread without piercing the fabric much easier to do.

HAND WINDING THE BOBBIN
It may be necessary to hand wind the bobbin when using hand embroidery threads on the bottom of the machine for **cable stitch** or when using shirring elastic. When

Hand-whipped free motion stitching on a transfer crayon-dyed background. By whipping beads onto a machine stitch the beads follow a line and can easily be applied, as the whipping stitching does not go through the fabric. The background is coloured with transfer crayons on a synthetic organdie over a cotton ground dyed with the same print. By the author.

the thread is in a skein and not on a reel or spool, this is probably the easiest option if tangles are to be prevented. Avoid leaving a long, loose length that might catch in the bobbin case, and try to wind the bobbin as evenly as possible.

HARDWARE

The pieces of equipment used for computerized machine embroidery are known as hardware. The obvious requirements are the machine and a computer, but you may also require a **scanner**, printer and a card reader/writer box to work between your computer and your machine if the machine does not take floppy

disks or **ATA CP cards,** CD-ROMs or have a direct link.

HEATAWAY
See **vanishing muslin.**

HEAT-TREATED FABRICS
Fabrics and other surfaces can be heat treated with an **iron,** a **soldering iron** or a **hot air tool.** They can also be subjected to **burning** for a distressed effect.

This technique can be used to change the quality of the surface to be embroidered, to create more texture, to create embossed effects on some fabrics, to finish off edges to prevent fraying, or to make holes

for changes in depth. Heat-treated fabrics can be machine embroidered into, but because the surface is now harder, a hoop may not be needed, but a darning foot will almost certainly prevent excessive thread shredding and breakage. An embroidery needle has a larger eye for its size and this can also help to protect the thread. See pictures on page 6 (top right) and page 28 (top).

HEAVY WHIP STITCH
A heavy whip stitch pulls more bobbin thread through to the surface of the fabric than an ordinary **whip stitch,** because the bobbin tension has been loosened a

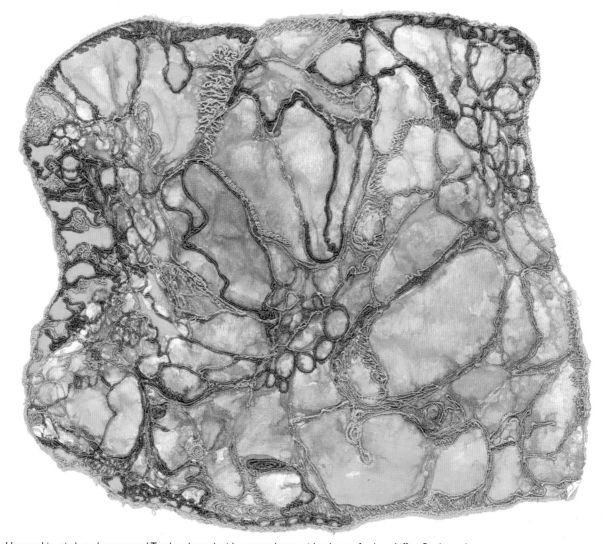

Heavy whip stitch on heat-treated Tyvek coloured with watercolours, with a layer of nylon chiffon. By the author.

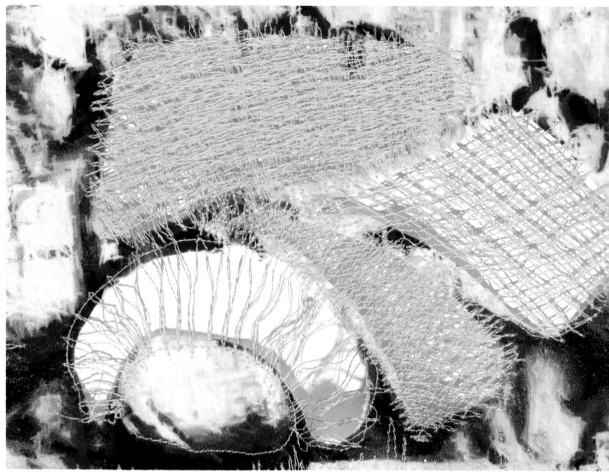

Stitching across holes.

little more, with a tight or very tight top tension, yet it is not as loose as a **feather stitch**.

HEMMING

See **blind hemming stitch** and **hemming foot**.

HEMMING FOOT

This foot has a sort of flattened corkscrew that turns a narrow, neat hem on a lightweight fabric. There are several different types, making different sorts of turnings and different-sized hems.

HEMSTITCH NEEDLE

These single or double-winged needles make the classic holes of hemming stitch when they are used with a **zigzag** stitch (single wing) or **straight stitch** (double wing).

HOLDING STITCH

See **thread tie-off**.

HOLES

Before the advent of vanishing fabrics that were safe and easy to use in the home, the only satisfactory method of creating lace structures was by using **openwork** techniques. One of these techniques involved creating a hole in a piece of fabric firmly held in a hoop. Three rows of straight stitch are worked around the hole to stabilize the edge. Stitching slowly with **free motion embroidery** techniques and small stitches, threads are laid across the hole, joining one side to the other. Further rows can be added to form a spider's web or woven structure. Additional stitched lines are then added to join these

threads in a decorative structure that will hold together once the lace had been cut away from the fabric support. This lace can then be used in its own right or added to another fabric for texture. **Starch** can be added if necessary. See also **broderie anglaise, buttonholes, cutwork, fabric manipulation, lacy effects, openwork, pulled work, soldering iron, vanishing fabric**.

HOOP

Traditionally, a hoop is a hand embroidery device which keeps the fabric tightly stretched; two rings are used, one inside the other, to frame up the fabric to be worked. Fabric needs to be carefully hooped up (see diagram opposite), and if it is not taut enough most fabrics can be pulled in towards the centre from opposite edges of the ring, to tighten them further. Note that for machine embroidery the hoop is used upside down in relation to its use in hand embroidery. The fabric lies against the bed of the machine, and the stitching is done into the well.

For free motion embroidery the fabric needs to be held taut if it is not going to pucker or distort. The fabric also needs to be held against the bed of the machine so that the bobbin thread can be picked up and the stitch made. Where there are missed stitches in free motion embroidery, the most common reason is that the fabric is not taut enough. If the fabric or surface to be stitched on is stiff, it may be used on its own with just a darning foot and no hoop. However, on most surfaces it is easier to use a hoop or an embroidery ring, and this gives you something firm to hold as you move the work around.

Most hoops have a screw device on the side to tighten the outer hoop against the inner hoop, and this can be adjusted to allow for a greater or lesser thickness of fabric. The screw should be set correctly before starting the hooping process. If it is tightened too much afterwards it can cause 'hoop burn' on some fibres. That is, it leaves a permanent trace on the fabric, particularly on delicate fabrics or those with a pile. Generally speaking, it is best not to leave a piece of fabric in a hoop for too long. When free machining, flick the hoop off the fabric if you are going to leave it for any length of time.

There are many styles, sizes and shapes of hoop. Round wooden ones offer the best grip for free motion work. If you are worried about hoop burn it is wise to bind the inner ring with tape before starting – this may also prevent a silky fabric from slipping. Plastic rings are available in round-cornered squares and rectangles, particularly for use with the embroidery unit of computerized

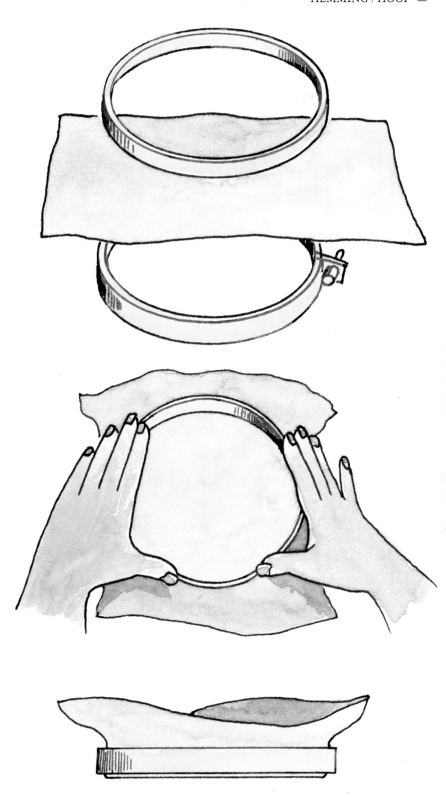

Placing the fabric firmly in a hoop for machine embroidery, working on a firm surface. When in the hoop, the inside circle should be just proud of the outside circle, so that the fabric will lie on the bed of the machine and the stitching can be done into the well.

machines, as good hooping is essential for the proper functioning of computer-generated embroidery. These can also be used for free motion embroidery. Round plastic rings with metal spring clip interiors tend to hold the fabric less well.

Do use a hoop that is appropriate to the size of the embroidery, or the space available between the needle position on the bed of the machine and the body of the machine on the right. It's not worth using a ring that has a diameter greater than this space, as you will be concentrating on your sewing at the moment when the ring hits the body of the machine and causes a jagged mark on your embroidery. For this reason 17.5cm (7 inches) is generally a good size of hoop to use on domestic machines, and a hoop of this size can be easily moved around the work if you are embroidering a large piece.

Note that the larger the hoop, the more difficult it is to hoop up and keep the fabric taut. For this reason, always use the smallest hoop possible for the design when hooping up for computerized machine embroidery.

The depth of the hoop is also important. Larger rings for hand stitching are often deeper in order to hold the fabric more tightly, but a greater depth of ring will not fit under the machine needle and shank. These deeper rings are also more likely to cause hoop burn.

Note that when working from the wrong side for certain embroidery techniques such as **cable stitch**, you will have to turn the embroidery over in the hoop so that you can work into the well of the fabric.

HOLDING THE HOOP
The correct position of the hands on the hoop for **free motion embroidery** is essential if you are going to succeed – and preferably without causing backache. Position your forearms on the table and adjust your seating position so that you are comfortable. With the hoop under the machine, hold it with both hands between your thumb and your middle finger; pushing with either digit will now give you control in a forwards or backwards movement. Now place your two index fingers against the inside of the hoop (see diagram below); pushing or pulling with either will give you a sideways movement in each direction. Between the six digits you now have total control of the hoop, and the edge of your palm should be resting on the bed of the machine. Making

small circles should become relatively easy. Remember that the hoop is not turned around, but always maintains the same position top and bottom and left and right, except when you are using **satin stitch** or **zigzag**, when you might need to change the direction of the stitching.

If the work is delicate you can bring an index finger in closer to the work.

For satin stitch, pushing with the thumbs against the resistance from the middle finger will give you good control. When working a satin stitch on a **curve** or circle, practise having enough 'stitch length' control in just your right hand to be able to place two fingers of your left hand on each side of the curve near the needle to turn the work. The same degree of control for the stitch length in your left hand will leave your right hand free to change the width of the stitches on the dial or push button of your machine while you are working.

Never be tempted to place the whole of your hands on the ring to move them. A lot of people do this at first and it is a very bad habit to get into. Control is difficult and tiring as your whole arm needs to move, and you will end up with aching shoulders.

HORIZONTAL BOBBIN RACE
Machines are constructed with either a vertical or horizontal bobbin race, in which the bobbin case and bobbin are placed, under the needle of the machine. On older machines, and even some newer ones, there are several disadvantages to this system.

■ Many such models require a **cover plate** for the **feed dog** because lowering the feed dog is not possible. This is a disadvantage, as the bump of the cover plate can be annoying when free motion embroidering. Many new computerized machines have a horizontal bobbin race and a lever

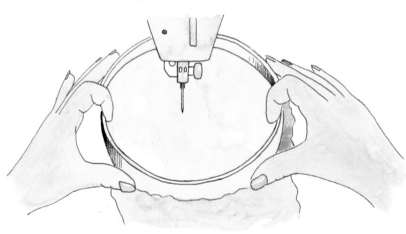

Using the correct hand position to guide the hoop for free motion embroidery gives you total control, working from the wrists and not the shoulders. This is much easier and much less tiring than working from the shoulders. Your forearms should rest on the table.

to lower the feed, so check when buying a new machine.

■ The bobbin tension is more difficult to set in these machines as the case is often difficult to remove and reset correctly. This can be a disadvantage when working with **tension techniques**. On some older models, numbers on the adjusting screw are there to help, and with many newer machines the bobbin case can be removed almost as easily as on a vertical-race machine and reset (see **correct tension settings**) in the same way. Ask your dealer's advice.

■ The work needs to be removed from the machine in order to replace an empty bobbin.

■ Horizontal-race machines are generally very unforgiving if you forget to put the foot down, and can be difficult to clean out, so do

take care. Again this is more true of older machines.

■ One advantage of horizontal-race machines is that they usually allow the bobbin tension to be bypassed, and then will usually produce different results according to the stitching speed. A **whip stitch** will result from a fast speed and a feather stitch from a slow speed. See **bobbin tension – bypassing**.

HOT AIR TOOL
A hot air tool is like a powerful hairdryer or paint remover tool with a nozzle (or sometimes a choice of nozzles) to direct hot air at a surface. It can be used to distress or change the surface of many fibres, including acrylic felt, plastic, Tyvek, plastic and synthetic fibres, or it can be used to raise textural paint (**puff paint**), or to vanish vanishing muslin.

Always put the work on a surface that won't be affected by the heat. Work in a well-ventilated area with a mask to avoid inhaling any toxic fumes, and have a water supply handy just in case of surprises! See **heat-treated fabrics** for embroidering.

HOT WATER VANISHING FABRIC
This fabric not only looks like a bluish organza, but also works like it. It can be placed in a hoop and stretched tight like any other fabric, and the hoop can be moved around easily and as often as necessary for larger pieces. You can use any needle, and any fabric and threads, bearing in mind the limiting factor of the vanishing process.

This fabric and all residues can be completely dissolved in boiling (not simmering) water. If the result is not perfect the first time, it is because the water is exhausted (too

Port Vendres by the author. Worked on hot water vanishing fabric with free motion straight stitch.

much product dissolved in it), so boil the work again in clean water. The end result is soft, and even usable in garment making, whereas some of the cold water dissolvable fabrics might prove too harsh to be comfortable. A little residue can be left in the fabric for stiffening purposes, if required, by not boiling at the high temperature required, or not for the full length of time, or in a small amount of water.

Some fabrics and threads will not withstand the boiling process, but do test fabrics before dismissing them – the results can be surprising. Most importantly, metallic threads and many metallic fabrics will not withstand this process, becoming hard and crumpled on boiling. Although this distortion may be interesting, if you wish to avoid it use small quantities of metallic threads (e.g. use a normal thread on the bobbin), and work lightweight stitching with them, rather than heavy solid areas. A microwave oven, or simmering water can be used for the vanishing process on delicate (non-metallic) threads or fabrics, but the dissolving is not as thorough. For delicate fabrics or metallic threads it is best to choose a cold water dissolving fabric.

The vanishing process can cause embroidery in cotton or rayon to shrink a little, too, especially if the embroidery is heavily worked, so take this into consideration if you are planning a large piece where size will be important (for example, parts of a garment). Smaller pieces can be pinned out on a polystyrene tile before being boiled so that they retain their shape while being boiled. I simply arrange and dry out the embroidery between layers of kitchen towel under a weight such as a book, so that it dries flat.

Many embroiderers find that the ease of stitching on this fabric, and the soft quality and handle of the resulting fabric, outweigh the constrictions imposed by the vanishing process.

INDUSTRIAL MACHINE EMBROIDERY
See **Cornely machine, guipure lace, hand machine, Irish machine, multihead machine, Schiffli machine, Singer workshops.**

INK
India ink is readily available and provides a strong and permanent colour when used on fabric, particularly in black. Other colours are also available, although they tend not to mix well. They are water soluble on fabric until they are dry. You can draw with a pen, a brush or a toothbrush, or spray onto wet or dry fabrics. Salt can be added to wet ink on fabric for an interesting effect. Different inks work differently on different fabrics, so experiment to see what results can be achieved. They can also be used on plastic. As ink dyes the fibres of the fabric rather than sitting on the surface like a paint, it does not require any special treatment in order to embroider onto it, so use ink dyes appropriately for the fabric you use. See also **Bondaweb.**

INLAY
An inlay is created when the fabric forming the pattern or design is placed on top of the background fabric and both are cut through simultaneously with a sharp blade. Thus the pattern pieces can be inlaid in the ground and oversewn together to form a smooth continuous fabric, unlike appliqué or reverse appliqué where there is a difference in levels. To hold the work together for easier machine stitching, the whole could be placed on a vanishing fabric, or a Bondaweb or Soluweb ground, to hold it together. Satin stitching is inappropriate as the appreciation of the continuity of the surface will be lost. Some open overlocking stitch

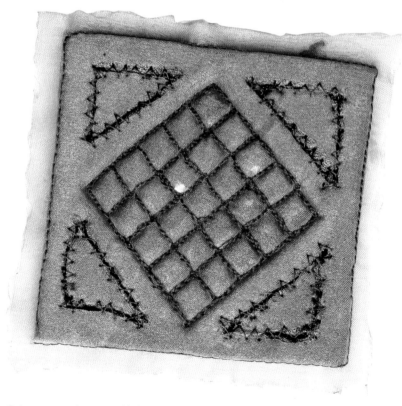

Polyester organdie-covered Softsculpt with an impressed grid. Cut triangles have been stitched back into place as an inlay.

The 'waste' produces the reverse of the design

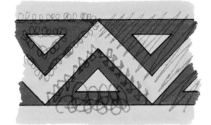

Possible stitch ideas

Design for inlay, showing the reverse design that can be made from the waste cuttings. Ideas for machine stitching (in green) will allow the join to show through the stitching so that there is an awareness that the fabrics are inlaid (on the same plane) and not appliquéd or cut to reverse appliqué.

could be used with the feed and foot. For **free motion embroidery,** try straight stitch machine lines or vermicelli that are not too heavy over the whole surface. Note that the waste from the two fabrics will form the same pattern as the first piece but in reverse colours.

INSERTIONS

A piece of lace, see-through fabric or machine-made vanishing fabric lace can be inserted into a fabric using the same method as the one used to create **reverse appliqué.**

Insertions can also be created with **vanishing fabrics** – hot water will keep the good drape qualities of the fabric ground if this is important and if it will resist the boiling water process.

To create a vanishing fabric insertion, tack (baste) two pieces of fabric on each side of a strip of vanishing fabric. Formal or informal designs can be used. The edges of the fabric can be turned in or not, according to the needs of the design. The fabric need not have straight edges if this is not appropriate. Indeed, you may stitch the vanishing fabric and fabric together using a free motion embroidery stitch, then

cut the fabric back to your stitching line, which could have any form that you wish. If you are using machine lines instead of hand tacking (which can be removed later), make sure that these lines will be covered by later stitching, or can form part of the stitching design.

For a simple formal piece, straight stitch along the edges of the fabric, applying it to the vanishing fabric. The insertion stitches can then be worked from the fabric, on the fabric side of the securing stitches, then across the vanishing fabric which will leave a space once the fabric is dissolved. Work backwards and forwards creating any type of lace appropriate to your

design. Any satin stitches should be worked across a number of rows of straight stitch so that they do not fall apart once the fabric is dissolved. The satin stitches, but not their straight stitch support, should stop at the edge of the fabric so as not to create an unsightly lump in the satin stitching that will finish off the edge of the fabric. The satin stitching to finish off the fabric edges goes into the fabric on the inside of the stabilizing stitching, and then into the vanishing fabric. Thus all stitching and edges are tidied up.

A freer design can be worked with the edges turned in and tacked (basted). The stitching can now be

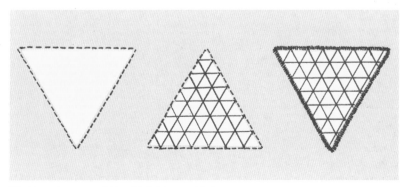

Working a lace on vanishing fabric into a cut hole.

worked haphazardly over these edges across the vanishing fabric and into the main body of the fabric to integrate the lace with the fabric, even leaving some edges showing.

Designs with securely stitched edges (not necessarily satin stitch – small **circles** work well, or several lines of straight stitch) can be made with fabric stitched to the vanishing fabric in a combination of shapes to allow an insertion across a vanishing fabric.

A soldering iron could be used to secure the edges on synthetic fabrics, in which case stitching is unnecessary for this purpose, allowing you to concentrate on creating the insertion stitches. The fabrics can be held together with **spray glue** (when using hot water vanishing fabric) for long enough to work the stitching.

As the space for the insertion gets bigger and more elaborate you could leave in bits of the original fabric, held with the insertion stitches across the space.

A piece of vanishing fabric can also be placed behind a normal fabric, stitched around, and the hole cut out of the fabric, leaving the vanishing fabric to be stitched for a lace filling.

To join two different fabrics across a seam, see **faggoting** and **simple insertions**.

INTEGRATING

Integrating a variety of techniques, surfaces and media within an embroidery is often a challenge. Beautiful stitching and surfaces can often be ruined by a lack of order to the work, exposing perhaps a weakness in the original concept or design. There may be too many competing focal points so that the

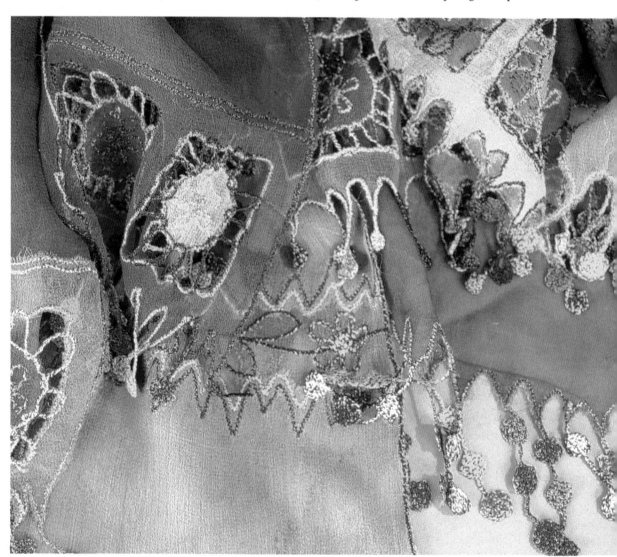

Detail of scarves by Anne Griffiths. Using chiffon, the holes are worked with dissolvable film, allowing for another piece of chiffon to be included in the centre. The fringe edges are also worked on dissolvable film.

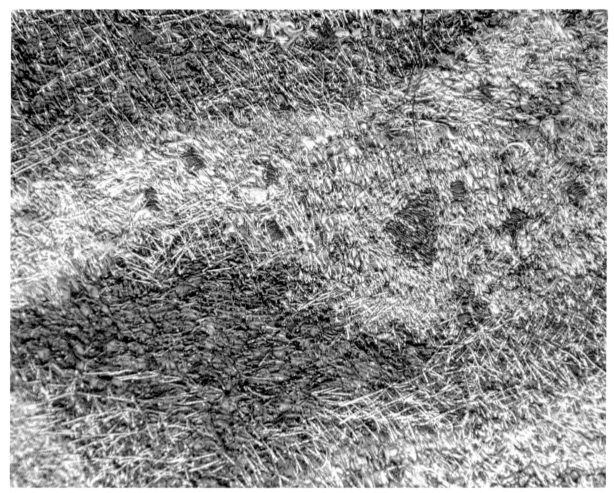

Worked on different-coloured linen scrims. Layers of zigzag and satin stitch create a textured surface which is then cut up and applied to a ground before being stitched over again with straight stitch in different lengths and with satin stitch, to apply additional texture to the fabric and integrate the whole surface.

composition seems too fragmented and 'busy'. If the work is well planned and well integrated, the eye will move comfortably from one area to another and be drawn to a focal point or the main area of interest. Colour schemes can be important in unifying a piece of work, but that doesn't mean you are restricted to the use of a few colours – it just means there needs to be a sense to the colours used. A working knowledge of colour and the **colour circle** can help.

Worker stitches are useful in integrating elements within an embroidery. They do not necessarily feature prominently, but by linking the background together and helping the eye to move from one area to another, they play an essential role. They can mesh bits and pieces of fabric into a ground, carry colour relationships across a piece of work, and integrate pieces of fabric or areas of colour that might otherwise be too prominent.

When working with crayons or paints on a paper surface, an artist usually makes a colour 'walk' across the surface of the paper; that is, a colour used in one place will be used again in another place, and then used again just a little bit further on, uniting the surface of the work. A colour may be used in only one place on a work, and if it is a prominent colour, complementary

to the other colours used, or deliberately out of harmony, it can provide an effect of shock or 'sparkle'. These uses and effects can also be applied in embroidery.

If the main area of interest seems too prominent in the embroidery, the best thing to do is to bring elements from that area to the rest of the embroidery, but in lesser degrees (in order to keep the main focal point). This could be in the form of fabrics or textures, or colours. For an area outside the focal point that is too dominant, try to integrate it further by using worker stitches over the surface.

The successful integration of all the elements of a piece of work is

Working on the Irish machine, a larger hoop fits easily on the machine bed. The embroidery being worked is *Best Dress, Baby Blues*.

paramount where mixed media are used – otherwise the embroidery risks being just a representation of the latest gimmick. In embroideries where just one technique is used, the problem is less extreme, but a good understanding of stitch and good colour work is essential.

INTERLACED MACHINE STITCHES
See **hand whipped machine stitches**.

INTERNET
The World Wide Web, available via a modem connection from your computer through a telephone socket, is fast becoming an essential tool for many of us. There are even domestic embroidery machines now capable of direct Internet access.

As well as providing quick and easy access to up-to-date information, suppliers, online magazines and other embroiderers, you can also access support systems for your machine, **download designs** from embroidery digitizing companies, or even download updates to your machine directly from the manufacturer.

Getting to know the Internet is quite simple. It is best to choose a good search engine (Google, Yahoo, etc.), where you type in what you're looking for and then just 'surf'. If you need more help, most local authorities offer courses or instruction days. Many libraries and other venues have Internet facilities available if you do not have your own computer.

IRISH MACHINE
This type of machine, also known as the 107 class trade machine (subsequent letters or numbers may be added). Dating from the beginning of the 20th century, Singer adapted an earlier model in 1908 to produce a machine capable of producing a zigzag stitch. Improvements continued to produce a quieter, efficient machine that worked a beautiful, even satin stitch. This machine has no feed or foot and produces only free embroidery, but very quickly. It has a stitch width of up to 1.25cm (¹/₂ inch) with a knee bar for smooth, easy adjustments as both hands are employed directing the work. This is much easier than adjusting the stitch width with a hand-controlled knob.

Patterns from the ancient world can provide excellent ideas for Italian quilting.

Much of the original work done on these machines was done in London, but it resembled the hand stitch worked on Irish linen, which may be the reason for the name 'Irish machine'.

These machines were quickly taken up by the industry, which was looking for a better method of producing satin stitch than **jump stitch**, which was difficult to master and very time-consuming. Irish machines were also used in technical and art colleges that were teaching embroidery techniques to industrial workers and designers.

Although it has not been in production since the 1970s (in industry it has been replaced by **multihead machines**), it is still popular today in art colleges and with professional embroiderers for its speed, smoothness and efficiency.

It is best to use fairly strong threads on this machine, but by adjusting the tension, even some rayon threads can be used. Very large machine needles are available for relatively thick threads or difficult surfaces. Metallic threads and wool can wear out the tension mechanisms, and given that existing machines are now rather old, this is undesirable. However, most threads, even flosses, can be used on the bobbin using a **cable stitch**. The bobbin can also be **bypassed**.

IRON
This is an essential piece of equipment for the embroiderer.

Apart from the obvious necessity of starting off a piece of embroidery on a well-pressed flat piece of fabric, finishing it off in the same way may obviate the need for **stretching**. An iron is also used for **bonding**, vanishing Heataway or vanishing muslin, distressing surfaces such as Tyvek or plastics, fixing various dyes or taking wax out of the fibres in **encaustic colouring** – and much more besides. You don't necessarily need a good-quality iron for your embroidery room, as it might get spoilt, but to avoid the worst damage always have some **baking parchment** handy, and place anything remotely suspect between sheets of baking parchment before applying the iron. Work on a clean, soft fabric surface – but it doesn't have to be an ironing board: a large covered table may be more suitable for some work, so be flexible. However, a porous surface or steam table is advisable when pressing fabrics with moisture, which should be taken through the fabric and away, as when pressing wool with steam, for example.

ITALIAN QUILTING
The technique of working two parallel lines of stitching through two layers of fabric in order to introduce a cord through the backing fabric between the stitching, to raise the line on the front of the work. The two lines of stitching can obviously be done by machine.

Twin needles are often considered unsuitable for this technique as it is difficult to introduce the cord afterwards through the one thread of the bobbin on the back of the work. A similar effect can be achieved by threading a cord for **corded pintucking**, on a smaller scale. Or use a wide twin needle (4mm or 1/8 inch) and a loose bobbin tension to allow a quilting wool to be passed through the stitching.

The technique can be used on two pieces of see-through fabric and a coloured cord introduced for shadow work. Other dyed and manipulated fabrics could also be used as an interesting base for working Italian quilting.

Traditional Italian quilting designs can be found in books. It is often associated with **trapunto quilting**. Celtic designs can also work well as a base for this embroidery technique.

JEWELLERY
Many artists and designer–makers have experimented with embroidered jewellery, and there are a number of techniques that lend themselves to the creation of fine and interesting jewellery.

Vanishing fabrics are a good option for creating dynamic pieces that can be threaded to form earrings or necklaces. Choose **Solusheet** or **vanishing paper** for their firmness when vanished. Embroidery vanished in this way can also be sculpted, as these

Tiara, jewellery and a bag by Janice Lewis. Made with silks, chiffon, organza and metallic threads. Burnt cutwork and vanishing lace techniques.

vanishing fabrics leave a residue in the fabric which can be quite stiff.

Wires or metal shim can be incorporated into the embroidery to give more controllable forms if desired, though do be careful of hard or sharp edges that may rub against skin. Metals can be added to Soluweb for inclusion in embroidery. Objects can also be sandwiched in clear plastic with machine-stitched edges to created beads or individual pendants or earrings. See also picture on page 96.

JOG
On computerized machines, when the thread breaks in the middle of stitching a design, you can use the jog button to go forwards or backwards within the stitch count of the design before restarting the machine. There is also a button to jog the needle left or right to make

sure that it starts a design in the correct position on the fabric when it is held in the hoop.

JUMP STITCH
This is a zigzag or satin stitch made on a sewing machine without a swing needle. It was invented before swing needles were available on industrial machines, and was used for even longer by users of domestic machines. It involved moving the fabric, which is held in a hoop as for free motion embroidery, from side to side under the needle of the machine. With practice, and worked with the rhythm of the machine, jump stitch could be very accurate. It is often difficult to tell the difference between jump stitch worked on a domestic machine produced by the Singer workshops, and satin stitch produced at the same time on an Irish machine,

which produced a zigzag from 1908. Often the only difference is the width, as it was difficult to produce a stitch wider than 0.5cm ($^1/_4$ inch).

Today all domestic machines have a swing needle for zigzag, so we no longer need to use jump stitch. It is interesting, though, to try moving the fabric from side to side under the needle to produce a zigzag or satin stitch. Although an accurate stitch is very difficult, a more liberal interpretation of zigzag stitching can be obtained, especially when using a slow speed.

Jump stitch is also used in digitizing. It is used when there is a movement from one part of the design to another. A colour change could also be involved. The jump position represents the position of the first stitch in an outline. If a jump is not programmed then the automatic program will make it at

Worksheet of lace edges and insertions from Romanesque churches, worked on hot and cold water vanishing fabrics by the author.

the closest position possible to the last stitch of the previous outline. See also **shading stitch** and **tacking**.

KNITTED FABRICS

In order to embroider on knitted fabrics without distortion it is essential to use a **stabilizer** to support the work. Knitted fabrics can then be embroidered on using free motion embroidery or programmed embroidery without any of the problems that are usually involved in using an embroidery hoop.

KNITTING THREADS

Knitting threads and ribbons can be useful in embroidery, partly because they can be less costly than hand embroidery threads. There are some super threads available and they often find their way into sales – one or two balls may not be enough for

a jumper, but can be very useful to an embroiderer. Obviously they have a use as hand stitch threads but they can also be used to create hand-wound or machine-wrapped **cords**. They can be applied to the surface of embroidery as a cord or as padded satin stitch. If they are not too bobbly, uneven or prone to shredding, they can be hand-wound onto the bobbin of the machine and used for **cable stitch**.

LACE, ADDING

Bought or handmade lace can be added to embroidery, and if it is well integrated with stitching or even dye and paint, it will add a beautiful texture to the work. It can also be included in **reverse appliqué** for openwork, or it can be applied to vanishing fabric for incorporation into machine-made lace structures.

LACE EDGES

Lace edges can be added to any surface or fabric by first attaching a band of vanishing fabric to the edge of the fabric. The edge of the fabric can then be stitched over into the vanishing fabrics and a lace built up onto the vanishing fabric. Once the vanishing fabric is dissolved, the fabric will have a lace edging. The vanishing fabric band must be wide enough to be able to work comfortably in an embroidery hoop. Other considerations depend on the design used. The vanishing fabric band could be attached with machine stitching if this can be incorporated into the overall design, or it could be tacked (basted) into place. The edge could be straight, or the supporting fabric could be cut into interesting shapes to create a more informal edge. The best way to do this is to place the fabric and

89

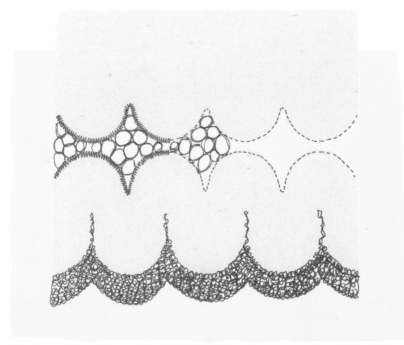

Insertions and lace edges worked with pink fabric, the yellow representing vanishing fabric.

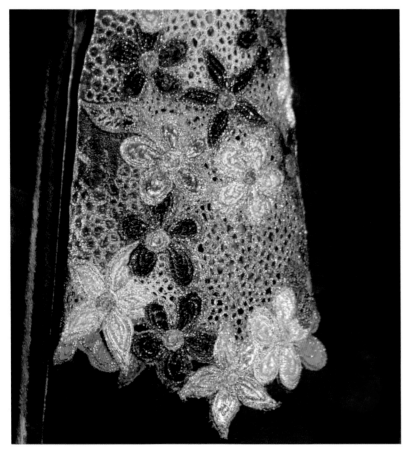

Detail of coat sleeve by Lesley George. Fabric and lace worked on vanishing fabric.

vanishing fabric together, stitch a straight stitch line of the desired edge shape, cut back the supporting fabric to this edge, then make the lace over this edge to bind the cut fabric to stop it fraying. This could be done with repeated rows of straight stitch, small circles over the edges, or satin stitch. Care should be taken in choosing a suitable **vanishing fabric**. See also **borders** and **insertions**.

LACE FILLINGS

Lace fillings in fabrics can be best made by stitching a piece of vanishing fabric behind the area where you wish to make a filling, with two rows of straight stitching. Now cut away the fabric in this area, leaving the vanishing fabric.
A lace structure can now be created on the vanishing fabric, but be careful to stitch into the fabric holding the vanishing fabric from time to time for security. Once the lace is completed, the fabric around the edge can be finished off with a satin stitch, rows of straight stitching, small circles, or some other securing and neatening stitching. The vanishing fabric can then be dissolved. The appropriate quality of vanishing fabric will depend on whether the fabric can be boiled or not, or whether the residual stiffness of cold water vanishing fabrics will cause a problem. See also **holes** and **insertions**.

LACE STRUCTURES IN FABRIC HOLES
See **holes**.

LACE TECHNIQUES

A useful starting point for lacy effects worked on vanishing fabric is to look at traditional lace-making techniques. This strategy was used in the 1880s for the production of the first 'guipure' laces. Using the patterns and structures of hand laces to inform you, you may find new and interesting ways of producing and expanding upon vanishing fabric lace techniques.

Go, go, go seek some other where. Close up of lace on dissolvable film (see also picture on page 50) by Carol Cann. Hand drawn and free motion embroidery. Photograph by Kevin Mead.

LACY EFFECTS

Any fabric created on vanishing fabric will have to hold together once the fabric has been dissolved. An underlying structure of a grid or circles will do this, but may not always be appropriate for the total design, so try to develop structures that are relevant to the final aspect of the work. Practising different patterns of stitches can be a useful start; you may find inspiration in traditional lace designs.

There are certain rules when stitching that are essential:

■ When stitching on a normal fabric, if two threads appear to touch on a given drawn line, this is sufficient. But on vanishing fabric if two threads are meant to touch it will be important for the whole structure of the fabric, so make sure that they do cross over, so that the work will hold together.

■ **Satin stitch** is only a closed zigzag, and with the fabric removed it will become a straight line. It is therefore necessary to work it over several rows of straight stitching so

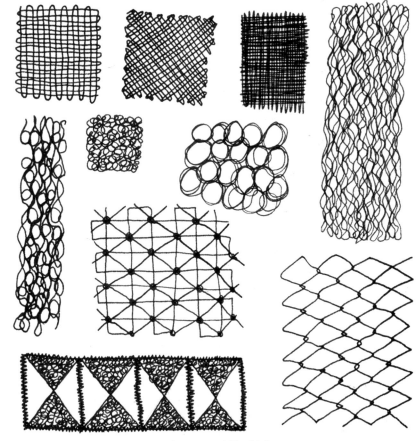

Stitch patterns suitable for creating laces on vanishing fabric.

91

that it holds together. Heavy areas of overlapping open zigzag can work, although there may be the occasional hole where the threads don't interlink.

■ Working with **tension techniques** needs careful thought and planning. Bear in mind that it is the position of the fabric between the looser tensions that allows the loops that are created to have a form. If the fabric is removed, the copious amounts of loose thread and loops will make for a disorganized tangle of threads and an unclear design. **Whip stitch**, or **whip stitch cord** and couched **cable stitch**, will work well and can be used as **gimp threads**, which are thicker threads used in lace making to pick out shape and stabilize a design. Any other tension techniques such as **feather stitch** can be worked on vanishing fabric if there is an existing surface of stitching or applied fabrics to hold it in place.

LAID STITCHES
Long stitches laid down side by side to create a surface. These can be produced by using the **tacking** (basting) facility available on some machines. Using **free motion embroidery** and working with a good rhythm, it is possible to create very long stitches of up to 3–4cm (1–1¹/₂ inches). If your machine does not have this facility, use a slow machine speed and a loose top tension to produce the longest stitches possible with free motion embroidery. These can be laid side by side to produce a sort of satin stitch, using a technique similar to **jump stitch**. Once you have put a quantity of laid stitches into place, you can stitch over them in places with other stitches to create textural effects. Laid stitches can also be made by programming very wide satin stitches into an embroidery machine, then working over these stitches with free motion embroidery. See **tacking (basting)** and picture on page 157 (bottom).

LAYERS
Layers add richness and depth to embroidery. Consider the following:

■ Layers of stitches, layers of fabrics, layers of appliqué.

■ Layers of see-through fabric, cut through, or burnt through with a soldering iron.

■ Layers of hand stitching with machine stitching on top.

■ Layers of machine stitching with hand stitching on top.

■ Layers of see-through fabrics used to create shadows, and new colours like layers of watercolour paint.

■ Layers of acrylic paint or gesso, to make textures.

■ Layers of stitched scrim or muslin with more stitching added.

■ Layers of bubbled plastic, burnt and destroyed.

■ Layers of stitched newspaper.

LEATHER
Leather can add a textural effect to work, and metallic kids have a traditional role in metal thread embroidery that can be exploited in machine embroidery. Leathers can also be stitched on in their own right as a base fabric, or used for bags, hats and other accessories. The traditional uses of leather are hard to break free of, and make it more difficult to be imaginative. Outside the more traditional embroidery uses, you might find jewellery, books, boxes, containers, hair pieces and clothing items made from leather, or it could be mixed with other patchwork or appliqué pieces.

Leather can mark easily when you are using a feed and a foot, so

Raku fired tile with layers of ceramic and layers of metallic thread embroidery worked on vanishing fabric, hand stitched into place. By the author.

use a **Teflon** or **roller foot** to prevent this. Special machine needles are available for leathers which have a dagger point and pierce the leather more easily. Stitch carefully to avoid stretching the fabric. If you have a choice of presser foot pressure, use a light pressure to avoid damage. Stitches should be large, to avoid creating too many perforations, which will change the nature of the leather (unless this is the effect you want).

Free motion embroidery can be worked onto leather without a hoop, but you may prefer to use a darning foot as the surface can lift quite badly. The fact that leather does not fray can be exploited, and it can be coloured and dyed.

LETTERS
More and more machines have letters incorporated as an option with the automatic stitches and patterns of the machine. There may be several font designs, and by using the memory of the machine, words and phrases can be put together.

Using the computer facilities on **embroidery machines** you can have fun with the letters available in the machine's own program, in the digitizing programs, or by scanning and incorporating your own lettering designs. The digitizing programs usually include a large number of font designs which can be enlarged, turned, mirrored, superimposed and otherwise adjusted in the program. Different filling stitches or satin stitches will create different effects.

Letters can make interesting decorative effects as individual motifs, repeat borders or all-over designs, and can sometimes end up having little to do with the letters themselves. See also **alphabet** and **writing freehand**.

LINEN
Linen is a strong fibre of plant origin (flax) used in fabrics for many traditional hand embroidery

Letterbox by the author. Grid and letters are worked on Solusheet vanishing fabric. The residue gives the stiffness to the box. The grid and letters were programmed on a Janome 10000 embroidery machine. The box is zigzagged together by machine.

techniques. Its strength and its ability to accept dyes, paints, heavy embroidery and heavy wear make it very suitable for hangings. It has a natural gum that will help it to retain its shape when it has been stretched once the embroidery has been completed.

Linen is a very expensive fabric to buy, but old, worn linen sheets are not! See picture on page 18.

LOCK STITCH
Small, compact stitches used on computerized motifs to secure the thread and prevent it unravelling. They are generally included at the start and finish of the design, at a change in stitch pattern, and at any colour change.

Many machines also have a button to make a lock stitch of

small stitches worked backwards and forwards and then on the spot, to tie off the thread; on most normal machines this is now a regular feature.

LOCK STITCH SEWING MACHINE
The lock stitch sewing machine uses a thread through the needle and a bobbin on the underside of the machine. The bobbin moves to and fro in order to pass the thread through the loop presented by the top thread as it passes through the needle plate.

The lock stitch sewing machine was developed between 1850 and 1860, culminating in 1872 with the invention of the take-up lever to create the perfectly tensioned stitch. Before this time machines could stitch a short length of straight stitching with a lock stitch, or chain stitch machines produced a single line of stitching with a single thread which could easily be unravelled. The lock stitch sewing machine is the sewing machine that we are familiar with today.

LONG STITCHES
Using the **tacking** (basting) facility available on some sewing machines, extremely long stitches can be made with feed and foot, or by using this method with free motion embroidery. For free motion embroidery it is best to use a slow speed and to be aware of the rhythm of the machine in order to produce the largest stitches and place them where you want them on the fabric. While the take-up lever is giving extra thread, and for the once or twice or three times that the needle does not enter the fabric, move with the excess thread to make your very long stitches.

By working with the rhythm of the machine, long stitches can be produced in your **free motion embroidery**. This can give a looser, sketchy feel to an embroidery, compared with using small short stitches which can better express fine details in the design and also rounded shapes. See also **laid stitches** and **tacking** (basting).

LOOPING FOOT
See **tailor's tacking foot**.

LOOPS
If you are experiencing unwanted loops above or below the fabric, this is due to incorrect tension. See **tension settings**. Extreme looping on the underside of the fabric is usually due to the presser foot not being put down, or the top tension not being correctly engaged, in which case put the presser foot down again to make it engage properly. This can be a recurrent problem on older sewing machines. See **feather stitch, moss stitch** and **tailor's tacking foot** for decorative uses.

LOWER TENSION
See **bobbin tension**.

MACHINE EMBROIDERY THREADS
There are many different threads on the market for machine embroidery, in all manner of fibres, twists, thicknesses, finishes and prices. In general they are cheaper per metre than ordinary sewing threads, which are strongly twisted for tensile strength and are usually available on smaller sized spools for home sewing purposes.

Machine embroidery threads have other advantages too:

■ Machine threads are specifically made for the purpose and are smoother and usually finer.

■ They generally have a looser twist than ordinary sewing threads, which makes them softer with a better spread; they cover areas more easily and make a better satin stitch. The lines of stitching will also appear less 'scratchy'.

■ They are more prone to breakage than normal sewing cottons, but this can be an advantage – the stronger threads are more likely to pull the needle and break it if they are caught, while the weaker thread will break first – still annoying, but less so.

■ A wider colour range is available in machine embroidery threads than in sewing threads, and there is a choice between **shiny threads** and **matt threads**. There are also **shaded threads** and **variegated threads**, as well as a huge variety of **metallic threads** to choose from.

■ The variety of thicknesses and finishes available can suit different purposes, from thick quilted lines to painterly areas of colour. Every embroiderer will have a favourite type and size that suits their style of work. Fine threads allow the mixing of colours, and several threads can

be passed through the needle at once if a thicker finish is required.

■ Very fine cheap thread is available in white, and sometimes black, on pre-wound bobbins for your machine. These can be useful and time-saving when you are sure that the colour, or lack of it, will not show or be of importance.

■ Cotton, rayon and polyester are the main fibres available, but you may also find silk, acrylic and nylon (often a see-through 'invisible' yarn).

■ A **vanishing thread** is available which can be useful for placing fabrics or for **marking** a design. It can also be used for **moss stitch**.

■ Different **embroidery machine** programs use different ranges of threads for their colours. Some can be programmed to accept a wider range of threads.

MACHINE MAINTENANCE
Today's sewing machines leave little for the user to do physically, as it is not possible to gain access to many of the moving parts. However, certain procedures should be carried out regularly. Always follow the cleaning and maintenance advice given in the instruction book. Before you do anything, disconnect the machine from the mains by removing the mains plug from the socket. Remove fluff and pieces of thread, which will collect under the stitch plate, around the hook, bobbin case and race. The hook, bobbin case and race need to be oiled about once a week. As well as these simple steps, your sewing machine specialist should carry out a regular check (where you bought the machine if possible).

Older models are often easier to maintain yourself, as moving parts are more accessible. Again refer to the instruction handbook provided if possible, but in general you should open upper and side covers, and carefully turn the machine onto

Cotton, acrylic, polyester and rayon machine embroidery threads.

its side to expose the underneath, then lightly oil all moving parts. These can be identified by moving the hand wheel. Always use a high-grade oil, recommended for use on sewing machines.

In general use, remove immediately any thread or the like that becomes wrapped around the wheel, motor, belt or bobbin winder, as this can be dangerous and impede the motor, and will shorten its life. Remember to replace used light bulbs, as it makes sewing easier on the eyes (this can be quite a fiddle, but is worth doing). Finally, needles need to be replaced frequently as they dull quickly, especially when sewing synthetics, paper, metal and other more unusual materials.

MACHINE NOISE

It's best to work in silence, or with background music if you prefer, but avoid using headphones when you are machine embroidering as it is essential to be aware of the noise that your machine is making.

■ Excessive noise probably means it's time for an oiling, or even a service.

■ Any squeaking should be oiled, but if it doesn't go away, a service will be required.

■ Regular clicks might indicate incorrect threading, the presser foot not being lowered, or the needle hitting the needle plate because it is slightly bent out of shape.

■ An excessive punching noise as the needle enters the fabric may be normal (what are you stitching on this time?), but if the fabric is normal, even if just a little heavily worked, the needle is probably blunt, so change it.

■ The machine may even block, and you will hear this before you see it. Is it that the fabric is too thick? Has the needle hit the hoop, or been bent and hit the needle plate? Are threads caught in the bobbin mechanism?

Listening to your machine and getting to know its noises will tell you a lot about its condition, and will warn you as soon as things start to go wrong.

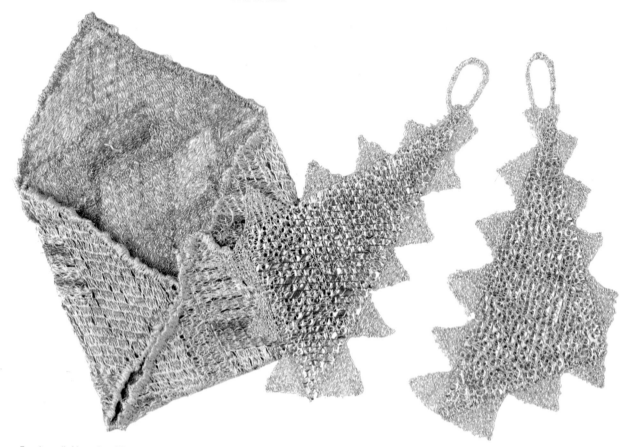

Envelope (left) made of free motion stitched metal mesh, following the lines of the mesh. The edges are satin stitched for security. Earrings (right) in metal shim with metal mesh applied, worked on vanishing fabric for the lace edges.

MAGIC FILM

This is a dissolvable film that disappears under a hot iron at 110°–130°C (230°–266°F) in 2–5 seconds. Protect the iron and the ironing board with a fine cotton cloth. For free motion embroidery it is best to use two layers of film and a ballpoint needle. Dissolved correctly it leaves no residue. The best use for this delicate fabric, which has a non-slip side, is for **topping** embroidery on computerized embroidery machines – it was invented for this purpose for industrial embroidery.

MANIPULATING FABRIC

See **fabric manipulation**.

MARKING

It is frequently necessary to mark your design on the fabric, or just to make one or two marks to centre a design. If you just need to make one or two points you can use a small stitch, or a water- or light-soluble marking pen. A light pencil mark may also be sufficient. Do be careful about not overusing a soluble marking pen as they can have an effect on the fabric, or sometimes return after disappearing, when ironed for example. Vanishing threads can also be used to mark the fabric as they will disappear in the wash after the stitching is finished. See also **transferring designs**.

MATT THREADS

Matt threads are dull, non-shiny threads, usually made of cotton, but they can also be polyester, or an acrylic/wool mix. Available in 30 or 50 thickness, they can create shadow against shiny threads, and act as a foil for their shine.

MESH

There are many different types of metal mesh that can be used for machine embroidery. They come in punched format – that is, a metal sheet that has had holes punched into it – or woven format, which may be diagonal or square. These are both available in different sizes, but if you can't buy a piece large enough you can always sew some pieces together. These elements can be applied to embroidery to give some glitz to a project. They can also be stitched into in their own right. The interest of stitching into metal mesh, or applying appliqué onto it, is that you have a malleable surface that can be shaped into any form. Mesh can therefore be useful for caskets, jewellery, or any other three-dimensional project, including stumpwork.

Be careful when stitching woven meshes. Try not to hit the threads as they may become unwoven and go into the bobbin race of the machine. As with any work on metal, the needle will become worn, so change it afterwards, or keep one especially for working only on metal.

METALLIC FABRICS

Many shiny fabrics in gold, silver, metallic and iridescent colours are now readily available, including metallic nets of different constructions, and sequinned fabrics. There are a number of specialist suppliers, including some used by theatrical designers, and around Christmas time it is possible to find a huge variety of such fabrics in any fabric shop.

Metallic fabrics are stitched easily, preferably with a ballpoint needle. They can be burned, holed or edged with a soldering iron (wear a mask and work in a well-ventilated space). They can be incorporated with other fabrics, just to offer a bit of shine to an embroidery, or worked with lots of stitching to integrate them. They may react badly to a hot iron or to being boiled, so be careful to choose a suitable **vanishing fabric** if you are going to incorporate them into vanishing fabric work. If you need to use an iron, place the fabric between a sandwich of **baking parchment** to prevent sticking. See **crystal strands**.

METALLIC POWDERS

Metallic powders are also known as bronze powders, and they are made by a number of different manufacturers. They can be held in a special binder (metallic or bronze binder), which is white but dries to a clear finish. Like fabric paint it is fixed by ironing. This binder can be diluted with water, so you can easily create anything from a full metallic gleam to a thin metallic wash. Pearl binder can also be used to give an iridescent finish. **PVA** can also be used, although it is advisable to add another coat of PVA only afterwards to be sure that the powders are held. The finish of these powders is superior to that of ready-mixed paints – less glitzy and more 'real'.

The powders are available in a wide range of gold, copper and silver which can be mixed together for an even broader spectrum of colours. They can also be mixed with other colour powders or fabric paints for a more subtle finish.

Once dry the work can be stitched into on the machine, though be careful that the powder is well incorporated into the binding agent and does not drop into the machine. See pictures on pages 49 and 70.

METALLIC THREAD HOLDER

A common name for a gadget that sits on top of the sewing machine held between the two spool holders where they are vertical. The thread holder ensures that the threads are taken off the top of the spools, thus preventing the thread from slipping down to the bottom of the spool and being caught around the spool holder. This can be a problem with metallic and rayon threads, so the thread holder is a useful device. See also **uncontrolled spool-off**.

METALLIC THREADS

There is now a wide variety of metallic threads available for the embroiderer, in almost any colour imaginable, and with varying degrees of metallic finish. The array of threads ranges from a metallic filament wrapped around a fine thread, to mixed metallic and non-metallic threads wrapping a coarser thread. Crochet-style yarns also come in all imaginable colours. The

Gold metallic powders worked onto felt, held in PVA medium (where brightest) rubbed into the surface and fixed with PVA afterwards (where dullest). Metallic transfer film has been added in small quantities using bonding powder. Stitching with metallic threads is in circles and satin stitch blocks with free motion embroidery.

surfaces each of these different threads can achieve are obviously different, as are the degrees of subtlety or glitz offered by their use.

The most important consideration for technical success when using metallic threads is needle size: if the needle is too small, the threads will shred and break. For the finest metallic threads, an 80 or 90 needle might do the job, but for the coarser wrapped and 'crochet' threads a 90 or 100 is a must, especially when stitching into difficult or more heavily stitched surfaces, although the use of the darning foot will help.

Metallic threads wear out needles quite badly and often quickly because the metallic filament overheats as it passes through the needle. An **embroidery** or **topstitch needle**, which has a larger hole size in relation to the size of the needle, will wear out less quickly.

Here are a few specific points about working with metallic threads:

■ **Colour spotting** can be particularly subtle when using metallic threads on the bobbin, or with the metal thread on top of the machine a light whip stitch bringing up a bobbin thread in colour will attenuate the metallic thread a little.

■ When working whip stitch or feather stitch with a metallic thread on the bobbin, it is necessary to use a looser bobbin tension and a tighter top tension than normal to achieve the same effects, because the metallic thread pulls through less easily.

■ If using a metallic thread on the top of the machine, be careful not to tighten the top tension too much as this will cause more wear on the thread and the needle as well as on the tension wheel.

■ Metallic threads that are too thick or textured to go through the needle might work well for **cable stitch**, so put them on the bobbin and work in reverse.

■ A thicker metallic thread on the bobbin for couched cable stitch, with a top thread in a colour, will create an *or nué* effect on the underside of the work. See **Opus Anglicanum**.

■ To create an 'Indian' handworked effect, work a couched cable stitch using an ordinary thread (particularly one with a good shine such as rayon pearl) on the bobbin and a a metallic thread on the top for the 'couching'.

METALLIC TRANSFER FILM
A fine metallic film available in different colours – gold, bronze, silver, pearl, and metallic colours – in various sheet sizes. It can be transferred onto fabric using a **bonding** process, either with **Bondaweb** or **bonding powder**. Tear out bits of adhesive webbing or sprinkle bonding glue onto the surface of the fabric; place the transfer film on top, metallic surface face upwards, and top with **baking parchment**. Now iron the surface. When you carefully pull off the transfer film, parts of it will be left behind, transferred to the surface. If you use a large piece of adhesive webbing you will have stuck down all of the film and have a bright, glitzy surface. However, the potential of this method is the subtlety of metallic finish that can be achieved. By using bonding powder, just small fragments of metal finish will appear here and there, giving brighter spots to the work. Try using this on areas where you have included metallic powders, to see the difference in the gold colours. The transfer film can be used again and again, and as it gradually wears out it will leave less and less metallic behind on the surface, so it becomes more and more subtle. It can be stitched into – a fine ballpoint is the best, but use a fine needle to stop it falling away from the fabric. On the other hand if you have added very little to the surface you won't want to destroy

its brilliant effect by stitching over it, so use **crazy stitch**, **vermicelli** or 'drunken wiggle' to stitch around it rather than destroy it. See pictures on pages 97 and 172.

METAL SHIM
Fine metal shim can be bought from specialist suppliers, or for a less expensive solution try using the inside of tomato purée tubes. The metal can be sewn with a foot in place, but you might prefer to use a roller foot, or simply free motion. Use a heavyweight backing, interfacing or Solusheet to prevent the thread being caught in the sharp edges as the metal is stitched. Use a large, robust embroidery needle (this will protect the threads better) and keep the needle **only** for working on metal as it will blunt very quickly. If the shine is too great, more stitching will help to knock it back in the design, or try shoe polish, paints and other media. Brass or copper shims colour nicely by being held in a flame (use tongs and oven gloves). Slow heating produces the best results. Metal shim can also be embossed with any object that can make a mark, such as a worn-out ballpoint pen, a screwdriver, or an embossing tool. Place a piece of wood underneath the metal shim to avoid marking the table surface while you work.

Work on ways of integrating the metal into the surface of the embroidery so that it has a role to play. If it must sit on the surface, make it part of a **metal thread embroidery**. For inspiration, look at metal thread embroidery designs that incorporate metallic kid. To integrate the metal shim you may need to use heavy stitching, or place see-through fabrics over it, or vanishing laces. Make sure that you can work it into the surface so that it is part of the design of the embroidery. Metal shim can also be stitched to Soluweb to create a lace structure around it. This could be useful for box making or **jewellery**. See pictures on pages 49, 96 and 157.

METAL THREAD EMBROIDERY

Metal thread embroidery is traditionally the use of precious metal alloys or synthetic equivalents, alone or as the majority of the work but with various other non-metal working threads. It is found throughout history, and there is an enormous quantity of hand threads that can be applied by machine, or that can be used on the bobbin for cable stitch.

Precious metals are an expression of great wealth and opulence. Rich textiles are reserved for festive occasions, and costly metals are only used on everyday garments where society demands that status is reflected in dress. There is still a use for rich handmade goldwork in banner making, church work, or court dress and military costume, and metal thread embroidery created by machine can fit into this tradition, or reflect its opulence, particularly in dress for special occasions or in church work.

Autumn Leaves by Rosemarie Brewer. Different metal embroidery techniques including vanishing lace and embroidered metal shim.

Metal thread embroidery can respond to the tradition of this opulence either in a positive or a critical way, in the manner in which the embroidery is conceived, worked and displayed. Metal thread embroidery techniques can also be used with other embroidery techniques. See picture on page 44 for applied Japanese gold.

METAL WIRE
See **wire**.

MIRROR GLASS
Shisha work is an Indian technique that is worked by hand and incorporates pieces of mineral glass or mirrors into an embroidered surface by working stitches over the mirror to form a lacing framework and then buttonhole stitching onto these threads. Cut-out circles or other shapes can also be made from obsolete CDs.

Small mirrors can be added to machine embroidery using machine embroidery techniques:

■ With a great deal of care, mirrors can be stitched down with a free motion **feather stitch**. The needle must enter the fabric closely around the circumference of the mirror and the top thread must be much tighter than the bobbin tension so that long loops are formed over the mirror, keeping it in place. Practise first with large sequins, which won't break the needle if you hit them.

■ Make **eyelets** in the fabric to be used slightly smaller than the mirror you wish to trap. Then make a sandwich of the fabric with the eyelets and a backing fabric, with the mirrors underneath the eyelet holes. For ease of work they may be glued to the backing fabric in the right place. A running machine stitch around the outside of each piece of glass will hold it into place. If worked from the back you

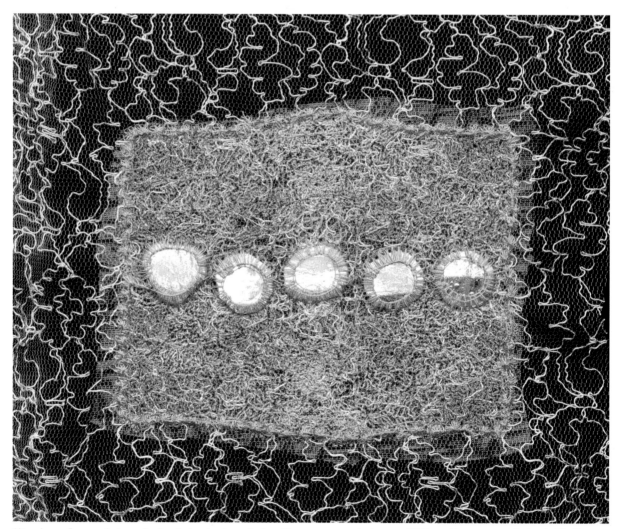

Mirror Image. From a photograph of canicular clouds worked on Sfumato program by Janome 10000 machine on net with dissolvable film used as a stabilizer. The shisha mirror glass is applied using feather stitch in circles.

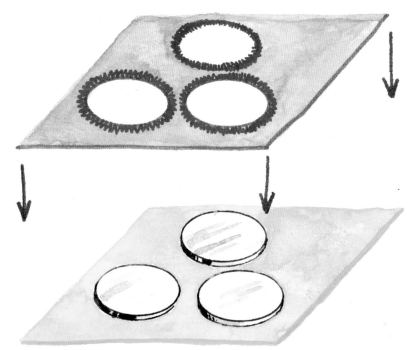

Eyelets on the top fabric are lined up with the mirror glass glued to the backing fabric. Stitching can be added to hold the two layers together. If cable stitching is worked from the wrong side of the embroidery, the stuck-down pieces of glass can be seen and avoided. The cable stitch can add an 'Indian' feel to the work.

will be able to see the mirror so as not to hit it. As you are working from the back you could try a couched **cable stitch.**

■ Using a long free motion stitch either by stitching slowly and dragging the fabric, or by using the tacking (basting) facility on the machine in which the machine skips every other, or often more, stitches (see long stitch), stitch across the glass until it is secured into place.

Note that all these methods could be used to incorporate sequins, bits of metal, ceramic or any other material that is too hard to stitch into.

MIRROR IMAGE
This is the image of a design one would see reflected in a mirror. Most electronic machines include this facility for the **automatic patterns and stitches** available. All computerized embroidery machines have this facility for the automatic patterns and the computerized

motifs. You will also find this facility available on **customizing** programs. It's a useful way of moving a presented image away from the ordinary, and can produce some interesting effects when used with **letters,** for example.

Mirror imaging can also be a way of designing **border** motifs for your embroidery. To see whether a design will work as a mirrored image, simply put a small mirror against the design and draw the result, or work with tracing paper and photocopies. You can also scan the design of your choice and use the design facilities in paintbox programs on a computer.

MISSED STITCHES
If the machine is missing stitches there can be several simple causes, which are easily remedied.

■ If working with **free motion embroidery,** or computerized machine embroidery, the most common cause of missed stitches is

that the fabric is not taut enough in the hoop. See **hoop** and **stabilizer** for more details and remedies.

■ Check on the quality of the needle. It is essential to use the best-quality needles in your machine for all your work, but especially for machine embroidery. They are more finely made and the difference in price will be repaid, not only because good-quality needles break less often, but also because they are better aligned. The machine will need less tuning and fewer repairs for realignment of needles.

■ Even a good-quality needle may become blunt or damaged, especially if you have been sewing through paper or metal, or using metallic thread. So changing your needle for a new one may be all that is necessary to eliminate the missed stitches. Some machine manufacturers recommend changing your needle after every eight hours of sewing.

■ If you have tried all the above, rethread the machine and check that the bobbin is correctly threaded. Try changing the thread, just to be certain the problem persists. At this point you may consider that there is a problem with the alignment of the machine. Has it got seriously blocked recently? When was the last time you had it serviced? You may need to take it in to your dealer for further assessment.

MIXED MEDIA
The accomplishment of skills beyond the core disciplines has long been a teaching objective in creating textiles. As the idea of what art is, what it may represent, or what it can consist of, has changed and expanded in our fast, consumer-driven world, so the disciplines of embroidery and textile art have changed too. It is no longer considered essential to spend hundreds of hours painstakingly stitching, and this skill is no longer

Unfolding Word by Angie Hughes, detail of the picture on page 8. Recycled paper, waxed paper, cork, copper foil, wire, cocktail sticks, and metallic thread; free motion embroidery using a swing needle. The cocktail sticks are machine wrapped to make little frames for the letters. There is some cross stitch and some machine cording. The side squares are joined to each other by carefully spaced machine lines.

valued either. Other quicker methods of production and reproduction can be used to express what needs to be expressed. Thus we find that we are not only including other surfaces in our embroidery such as metal, plastic, wood, ceramics or plaster, but also other representational media such as paint, photographic or computer-generated media. The inclusion of anything in a piece of work (even the first stitch!) must be considered, and must have a reason, if we are to avoid gimmick and kitsch.

Embroidery has become one of the areas that is subject to the art/craft debate. We as embroiderers and textile artists can make use of this debate so long as we maintain the essential vision that good art is not only well made, but must also have a conceptual content. The jury is still out on whether we can accept 100% concept with no actual representation of object or craft content (the word 'craft' here being used to denote any act of skilled making); but there is a certain awareness that even in the most representative of art, a minimal conceptual content is required to carry the work. The conceptual content of the work could be the expression of deeply held political or important beliefs, or a response to particular or everyday events, but it can also be *joie de vivre*, sadness or some other emotion, or a response to space and colour. The importance is that it is there, central to the work, and perceptible to the viewer.

MOLA WORK

A traditional hand stitch reverse appliqué technique created by the San Blas Kuna Indians, involving several layers of fabric tacked (basted) together in a design. Lines are gradually cut into the layers of fabrics, which are then hemstitched to reveal fine lines of the coloured fabric beneath.

On the sewing machine the technique can be translated into

This slashed embroidery by Lynda Grattidge is an example of mola embroidery.

layers of different-coloured fabric tacked (basted) together. Straight stitch lines create a design, and the layers can be slashed through on either side to reveal the colour. Edges can be neatened with satin stitch, other free stitching, or left to fray a little. See also **burnt cutwork**.

MOSS STITCH
A stitch of small, apparently unconnected loops of thread sitting on the surface of the embroidery. It is produced on a Cornely machine by turning the hook in the opposite direction to that used for chain stitch. Moss stitch is a very unstable stitch and can easily be undone if one of the loops is caught. For this reason, the reverse of the work should be bonded or glued to hold the stitches in place.

Moss stitch can be worked on an ordinary domestic machine. Set the machine up with tensions as for a **heavy whip stitch** and work haphazardly in large stitches over the surface of the embroidery. Now carefully pull out the top thread; cut it in places to pull out small lengths at a time if necessary, so as not to disturb or pull on the loops. The result is the same as Cornely moss stitch. Again the back of the work should be bonded or glued to prevent the stitches from unravelling – a spot of glue on the back of each or most of the stitches will do. Use PVA medium, as this

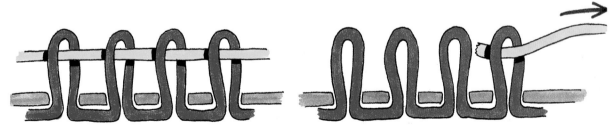

Moss stitch loops created using a heavy whip stitch or feather stitch tension. The yellow top thread will be pulled out, but a vanishing thread can be used instead, which can be washed out when the work is finished. Glue can be applied on the back once the fabric is dry.

won't show. The larger the **whip stitch** or **feather stitch**, the greater will be the loop produced. Closer stitching will produce a greater concentration of loops. Vanishing thread can be used as the top thread, to be vanished in cold water rather than being pulled out. This makes the process very easy indeed, and greater quantities of stitching can be put down onto the surface. The vanishing thread is quite strong, but use a loose bottom tension rather than a top tension that is too tight. See picture on page 36.

MOTIF

A motif in textile work is generally considered to be the design itself, particularly where it is placed on a plain background fabric. Traditional motifs of birds and flowers strewn over the surface of Jacobean counterpanes are an example which to some extent can be replicated by using motifs available on computerized embroidery machines. The motif in art terms can also mean the central interest or driving force of a figurative work. See also **spot motif**.

MOUNTING

Before mounting any work that is puckered or out of shape (and is not meant to be so), it should be **stretched** flat to improve its appearance.

If you are mounting a piece of work that will be framed, it is best to pin it in place first, using dressmaker's pins to fix it to the sides of the card. Then stitch or glue the work in place. Start at the centre of opposite sides, and work towards the corners, pinning as often as necessary, but at least at every 2–3cm ($^3/_4$–1 inch). Any straight vertical or horizontal lines or fabric grain should be perfectly parallel to the corresponding side. Once the work is pinned into place, stick down the corner (see diagram opposite), and then the sides can be held down onto strips of double-sided sticky tape. For a large or stiff

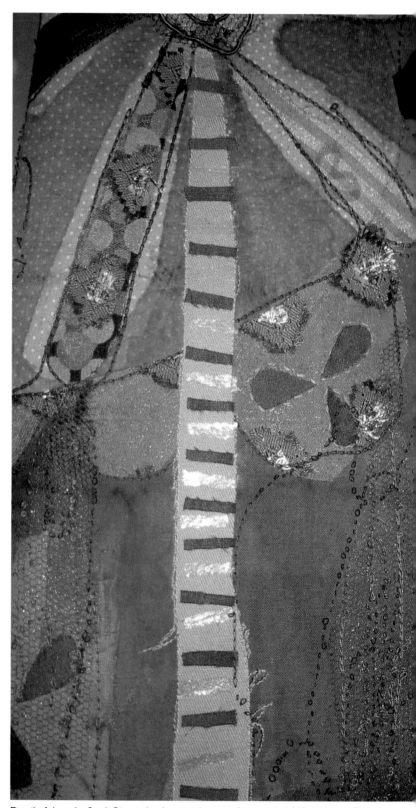

Detail of dress by Sarah Birtwistle, showing the use of moss stitch. Worked on a Cornely machine. The full piece is shown on page 38.

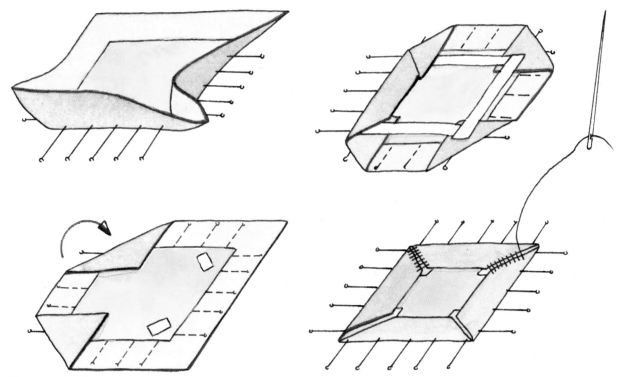

Mounting embroidery over card.

piece of embroidery you can use carpet-quality double-sided tape. To achieve good corners, oversew them afterwards on the back of the work. The finished piece can then be mounted and framed.

MULTIHEAD MACHINES

The multihead embroidery machine is the most modern and widely used industrial embroidery machine. It was first developed before World War II, but it only became popular in the 1970s and then in much wider use in the 1980s and 1990s.

Today the embroidery produced on these machines is designed and **digitized** (translated into stitch), using advanced software. The information is either downloaded onto a disk which is put into the machine, or it is transferred by cable, i.e. the computer itself is attached to the machine.

The machines themselves can have up to 36 stitching heads and as many as 20 needles (although 9–12 is more normal) on each head.

These machines can therefore produce very accurately embroidered lengths of fabric or be used to stitch directly onto garments and accessories. With the introduction of the multihead machine, embroidery has become much less expensive and is now an everyday decorative feature on all sorts of items.

With the takeover of Cornely by a Japanese multihead manufacturer in the 1980s, a Cornely-type chain stitch work is now produced on one particular type of multihead machine.

MULTIPLE SPOOL HOLDER

A platform, generally free-standing, used behind or at the side of the machine for holding a quantity of spools ready for threading onto the machine. It is particularly used for computerized machine embroidery where the colours will be selected and prepared in advance, but can also be a good device to use as a support for threads to prevent **uncontrolled spool-off**.

MULTITHREADED NEEDLE

A needle can be threaded with as many threads as will go through the eye, and as many as your thread-holding equipment will hold. Embroidery and topstitch needles have larger eyes that can more easily accept several threads.

The threads can be treated as one, and taken down one side of the tension wheel, or they may be treated in two groups and separated on each side of the tension wheel.

If a darning foot is used with more than one thread through the needle, this helps its passage through the fabric, and avoids thread breakage.

The obvious advantage of using two or three threads through the needle at once is that an area can be filled in more rapidly. Another advantage is in colour, where several close shades of one colour can add a subtle nuance to the work. It is also a more subtle way of using shaded or variegated threads: by placing a shaded thread

Olive Trees by the author. Two reds, of a very close hue, are threaded through the needle for the tree trunks. A variegated with a plain thread are used for the hill, the grass and the road.

with a solid-coloured thread that shares one of its colours, the changes in colour will be less obvious.

The thickness of a line for an outline or for a quilting pattern can also be increased but still using finer threads. This is especially useful if you have yet to invest in a larger variety of threads of different thicknesses and colours.

MUSLIN

There are various types of cotton muslin, scrim and cheesecloth cotton on the market. They come in a range of stiffnesses, and some are dyed (although it is a very easy fabric to dye yourself).

Muslin offers an interesting surface for machine embroidery as it is very easily manipulated by stitching, and can offer a distressed or airy, misty look. Bits can be added or holes pulled or manipulated in the surface, with your hands or machine stitches, to create **pulled work**. It can be used on its own, or be added to other work: **bonded**, painted with **dyes** or **acrylic paint**, pleated by pulling threads, heavily or lightly stitched.

Muslin can offer endless surfaces and experiments and can provide a response to foggy rubbed-out drawings as well as heavily painted surfaces. It also has the added

advantage of being inexpensive, easily available and safe to use.

In its simplest form it is probably best used in a hoop, as it is otherwise difficult to stitch and will 'manipulate' perhaps a little more than desired. You can use any needle, any thread, any stitch and any technique. See also **vanishing muslin**, and picture on page 36.

NAPPY LINER

One way of applying texture to a ground is to apply nappy (diaper) liners using a **hot air tool** or **iron**. The liner can be coloured first before melting into the surface of the fabric, and the process can be repeated to add more layers and more colours. Different fabrics respond in different ways, and so do different nappies (diapers) so you will need to experiment to find surfaces that appeal to you. This is a good base material to use to represent peeling stucco walls and organic forms, too. Embroidering through the melted, textured surface is easiest with an embroidery or

The Sea Bag by Lesley George. Strips of fabric are laid down and stitched freely or with a stitch pattern. A variety of threads – textural hand threads, knitting yarns and so on – are stitched over this to make an even richer texture. Beads are added by hand. Machine-wrapped threads make the drawstring, with tassels made from machine embroidery threads.

topstitch needle to protect the thread, and you may prefer to use a darning foot to keep the surface from being pulled up with the needle and the threads wearing unnecessarily.

NEEDLE BREAKAGE

The most frequent reason for needle breakage is that the needle has hit something hard. This sounds obvious, but it is not always apparent. If you are stitching down wire, beads, wood or other hard objects, the broken needle may not surprise you, and perhaps you need to be a little more careful or stitch a little slower. Maybe you have got just a little too close to the hoop – again it's necessary always to pay close attention.

If you can't see the immediate reason, it may be that the fabric was pulled along with the needle in it, causing the needle to hit the cover plate. Another frequent fault for novices is holding on too tightly to the threads as you started off, causing the needle to hit the cover plate. This can be avoided by putting the needle in the work before starting. If the work has been pulled with the needle in it, or the needle hits a hard surface, it may just bend in the first instance and break later. Do be careful – your machine won't appreciate working with a bent needle, which can cause it to go out of alignment.

If the needle is a cheap one (in which case you shouldn't be using it in the first place!) or if it's faulty and worn (from stitching with metallic threads, or on metallic surfaces or paper for instance), then it will break more easily. The needle can simply break because there are too many layers of fabric or stitching to go through.

NEEDLEMADE LACE

Handmade needlemade lace **slips** and three-dimensional items are frequently employed in **raised embroidery** or **stumpwork**. These items can easily be made on

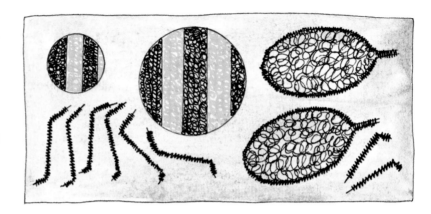

Needlemade lace on vanishing fabric to construct a stumpwork bee. The wings have wire stitched around the edges and the legs and antennae are stitched over wire. The finished bee can be seen on page 156.

vanishing fabric with small **circles** or **granite stitch** to resemble fine needlemade lace, although other filling stitches could be used. Wire may be included for sculpting, but as cold water vanishing fabrics can leave a residue that can be sculpted, this is not always essential. Starch or **PVA medium** can also be used. Different flowers, leaves, butterflies and fine clothing are often made in needlemade lace, and they can all be achieved by machine.

NEEDLE PLATE

This is the plate covering the bobbin mechanism under the needle. The hole or throat under the needle will be of a width suitable to accept the **swing** of the needle, the largest available **stitch width** on the machine – between 4 and 12mm

(¹/₄–¹/₂ inch). There will be two or more elongated holes for the **feed dog** (sometimes up to seven), and there may be a small hole for threading a cord through for **corded pintucking**. The needle plate will have a **cover plate** to cover the feed dog for **free motion embroidery** if the feed dog cannot be lowered.

NEEDLES

The choice of needle is important for successful machine embroidery. A wide variety of sizes and types are available. As a general rule, it is best to choose the finest suitable needle so as to avoid visible holes in the fabric – for this reason an 80 is good for most sewing. Certain threads require a larger needle (90 or 100) in order to run through smoothly without fear of breaking or shredding the thread – this is particularly true for **metallic threads**. Some hand embroidery threads can be used through the needle, but may require an even bigger needle of 110 to 130 (available from specialist suppliers). An **embroidery needle** has a bigger eye relative to the size of the needle, so the thread is less likely to shred, and embroidery needles can also help prevent needle damage when using metallic threads. If the embroidery is heavily worked or layered, larger needles can also prevent shredding and breaking. A **topstitch needle** has an even bigger eye, which helps to avoid thread breakage on difficult or heavy surfaces, and is particularly recommended for metallic threads.

The nature of the fabric dictates the type of point on the needle. A sharp needle is good for most uses – but see **ballpoint needle** for when it is best to use this type. Leather needles, with their dagger shape, are essential for **leather** and

also useful on some harder plastics. Advice is given throughout this book under individual fabric types; if no specific advice is given on the best needle to use, then a sharp needle will be fine.

Wing needles are for specialist embroidery techniques such as imitation drawn thread work – your handbook will guide you on their specific use with certain automatic stitches, and you can use them for pulled work techniques. **Spring needles** can be used instead of a darning foot.

The quality of the needle is paramount. Always buy the best available. Cheap needles are not as finely honed as expensive ones, so they break, wear and bend more easily. They can cause misalignment in the machine, missed stitches, poor tension control and difficulty with tension techniques. Some machine companies have their own needles because their sizing needs to be very precise, so follow advice if your machine requires special

needles. Good-quality needles break and wear less, so in the end they actually cost less.

NEEDLE THREADER
Different needle-threading devices are available on most modern machines. In a well-lit workspace you may have no problems threading your machine, but for some embroiderers such a gadget may not seem a luxury. If it encourages you to change the thread colour in your needle a little more often to create more interesting work, it can only be a good thing! It may take a little time to get used to the needle threader on a new machine, but the effort is worth it in the long run.

NEGATIVE SHAPES
The shapes left blank by the motif in the design. These can be as important to the success of the design or composition as the main image, so they should always be taken into consideration.

Kissing Fishes, a mirrored border design showing the importance of negative shapes in a design.

NETS

The most widely available coloured nets are machine-made hexagonal-based nylon tuile. The variety of colours available is enormous, and these fabrics are incredibly cheap.

These nets are, however, virtually impossible to dye in the home (although they can be painted) so choose the colours you need and layer them together to create the impression of additional colours.

There are many net-type fabrics available in nylon or natural fibre, made for the curtain industry, and metallic nets are also available in specialist shops (or around Christmas for evening wear). These are available in gold, silver or multicolours, in squares, diamonds and hexagonal shapes.

NETS AS FABRICS IN THEIR OWN RIGHT
In order to work on the larger open-structured nets it is necessary to put the fabric in a hoop and work in small stitches across the holes to create a surface that will firm up the overall structure; alternatively, work them on top of a dissolvable film.

The firmer hexagonal nets can be stitched freely with the fabric in a hoop, or without a hoop but with a **darning foot**. They can be particularly interesting for embroidery as the structure of the net gives a slightly haphazard result to a design. For nylon nets use a ballpoint needle. The choice of bobbin thread is important as it will show a little on the finished piece of work. A greater amount of colour can be added by using a different bobbin colour, or extra texture can be added with **tension techniques**.

NETS USED WITH OTHER FABRICS
Stitched or not, nets can be applied to other fabrics to build up textural interest, or, with delicate nylon nets, to build up colour. Paint or dye can be added to the surface or they may be used in conjunction with other nets or laces and coloured in the mass with fabric paint or acrylic to build up a textured surface for further stitching. If using nylon nets, a ballpoint needle is best. They can be applied to the background fabric with **Bondaweb** or **spray bonding glue** (use **baking parchment** to avoid contact with the iron) to hold them in position before stitching. Equally, a darning foot and a cocktail stick for holding the pieces of net in place while stitching can also be useful.

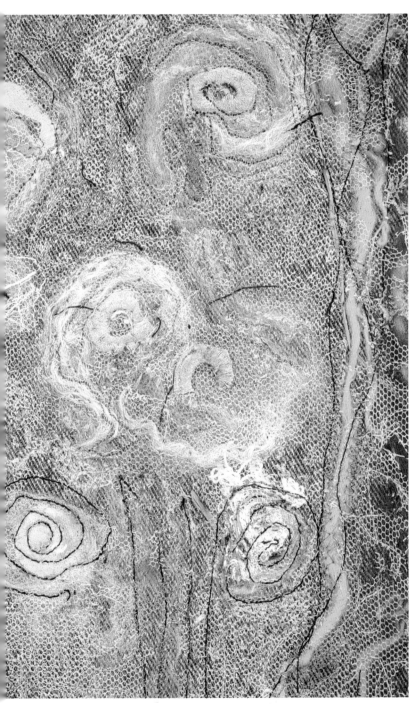

Sunflowers on Net by Mary Lawrence. Free stitching and burning through layers with incorporated threads.

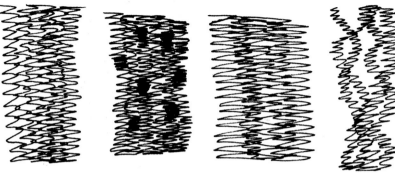

Stitch patterns for free motion embroidery with open zigzag.

Many nets, particularly nylon tuile, can also be distressed using a **hot air tool,** or cut with a **soldering iron** – though remember to use a protective mask if you are using this technique.

OIL

After around eight hours of intensive stitching, or at the very least once a week, a little good-quality machine oil should be placed in the bobbin race. Let the machine run for a few seconds afterwards without threading it up, then do a few stitches on waste fabric first. Most modern machines don't allow access to any other parts of the mechanism for oiling. Some manufacturers guarantee that their machines don't need oiling – check with your supplier. See also **machine maintenance.**

OPEN DARNING FOOT

The open darning foot is a metal foot with a horseshoe shape, open at the front. Its spring mechanism allows it to hold the embroidery at the point of entry of the needle, but it moves up again in between points of needle entry to allow easy movement of the fabric. It holds the fabric just as well as a completely circular foot, but has much better visibility. This foot is very useful for **free motion embroidery** when the surfaces you are working on require the use of a darning foot. An alternative is the plastic see-through foot. The open embroidery or see-through foot improves visibility to such a degree that it rarely causes a problem except when stitching backwards over an existing line. They are known by several names – open toe foot, free motion embroidery foot – so persist when trying to find one to fit your particular machine.

OPEN TOE FOOT
See **open darning foot.**

OPENWORK

Openwork refers to embroidery techniques in which areas of fabric are cut out to leave small holes or larger open areas against solid fabric or built-up areas of lace and stitching. Small holes are easily formed in fabrics using **eyelet** techniques or **buttonholes.**

Traditional openwork techniques include **cutwork,** Richelieu, Renaissance and reticella, where progressively less and less fabric is left to hold a lace structure that is more and more elaborate. These techniques are traditionally worked in white or cream to create the maximum contrast of textural effect. The traditional designs of openwork are a useful starting point for technical samples and design paperwork which can lead to finished designs.

It is easy to copy all openwork techniques using vanishing fabric techniques with machine embroidery, once the technique of reconstructing lace within a structure of solid fabric that has been cut into holes has been understood. It is a small step to move on to create your own versions of **cutwork** and lace to create delicate ephemeral structures.

For techniques see **cutwork, free eyelets, holes, lacy effects.**

OPEN ZIGZAG

A closed zigzag is **satin stitch.** Working with a foot on and the feed dog up, stitch width can be selected and the stitch length set at greater than 0.5mm, to create an open zigzag. According to the settings you employ, the openness of the zigzag can be selected, as well as the width of the stitches. With free motion embroidery, the width can be set on the machine. The openness of the zigzag will depend on the movement of the hoop in relation to the speed of the sewing machine.

If you are working with the foot on, you can use the backwards and forwards motion of the machine to use open zigzag as a filling. It may also be used for **appliqué,** for **applying thread, cord and ribbon** and for **overlock** edges in cases where an overlock stitch is not available.

In **free motion embroidery,** an open zigzag can be used to create texture and fillings in a number of ways. By varying the movement of the hoop the zigzag can be more or less open, and even blocks of satin stitch may be included here and there. If you are working fillings, you might try changing the width of the stitch for a variety of textures. Working an open zigzag on different surfaces provides different results, notably on muslin, linen scrim and canvas, where the threads are pulled together and holes created, or on felt where it can pull and manipulate the fabric.

OPUS ANGLICANUM

Opus Anglicanum is the famous English metal thread embroidery of the Middle Ages. It was first copied from Byzantine textiles in the 6th

Le Pull et La Mini-jupe de Margot by Fanny Viollet. The pullover is worked on the newspaper *Le Monde*, torn into strips and put onto a transparent vinyl support before being stitched with a free motion open zigzag in a shaded thread. 'The newspaper is destined to be thrown away after it has served its use as an intermediary between the outside world and me. But I find it difficult to throw away old newspapers, I've never finished with all the details. I also have difficulty throwing away old pullovers.' The mini-skirt is worked similarly, with white thread in straight and zigzag stitching, on paper from the envelopes of bank correspondence. The inside of these envelopes is printed in such a way that the contents of the letters stay confidential, as the envelopes are opaque. 'It is this desire to hide from the eyes of the curious that I played with here. The miniskirt also has the function of dressing the owner and hiding the essential.'

century AD, and by the 10th century the techniques employed had become finer and more sophisticated. The examples that remain are almost entirely church pieces, though there is a good chance that it did move into secular circles. There are examples of Opus Anglicanum in many good museums – for example the Victoria & Albert Museum in London and the Metropolitan Museum of Art in New York – and this early embroidery, with its way of narrating stories and, especially, drawing figures and faces with fine lines can be useful points of study for any embroiderer, including the machine embroiderer.

Or nué was used in Opus Anglicanum as a method of shading. Different coloured threads couch down heavier gold threads with different intervals of stitching. This technique could be explored using **colour spotting** or **cable stitch**.

ORGANDIE/ORGANZA

A see-through fabric usually in white in cotton (organdie) or silk (organza), which is frequently used for delicate **whitework**, especially on the industrial machine embroidery of the late nineteenth century. This fabric can also be used for **shadow work** and any related technique. Hung in space, these fabrics are ethereal and work well as diffusers of light. They are readily dyed (painting the surface ruins their translucency) and easy to stitch on.

Coloured and printed versions are available in abundance these days for the home decoration market, as are synthetic organdies in nylon or polyester. These react particularly well to burning with a soldering iron and being layered onto other fabrics, or to other layers of organdie.

OUTLINES

Outline stitch is a running stitch used on computerized machine embroidery to surround the outside of a design to finish it off.

It can also be a useful way of **transferring a design** in **free motion embroidery**. It can be used where a great deal of accuracy is required in the design transfer, or where the use of a pencil (which can create a permanent mark) or vanishing pen (which may have an effect on the fibres) seems inappropriate. This technique requires the use of tracing paper. See **transferring designs**.

OVERLOCK

The act of stitching over the edge of a fabric to prevent it from fraying, so that it will wash and wear better, particularly in garment making or household furnishings. There are usually several suitable stitches included in the automatic patterns and stitches of modern machines. If not, a zigzag stitch will work, if perhaps not quite as well or as elegantly. The **cut and sew foot** offers the possibility of overlocking on an ordinary domestic machine

OVERLOCK MACHINES

A special machine for overlocking, often with a choice of overlocking options, or even **faggoting** possibilities. The machine will cut the fabric just before overlocking it, to provide a beautifully finished seam edge.

OVERSTITCHING

Stitching back over an area with different techniques or different colours can give an interesting effect (see **worker stitches, building up surfaces, integrating** and **colour circle**). Overstitching an edge can be an interesting way of finishing off a piece. See **wrapped edges**.

PADDED SATIN STITCH

In hand stitching a satin stitch can be padded with a cord, or with felt in different cut-out shapes, to create a raised effect. A satin stitch can also be padded or raised in machine embroidery. A cord, string, roll of felt or wool can be tacked (basted), pinned or held in place while a satin stitch is worked over it, either with

Narbonne by the author. An outline drawing was scanned into the Janome customizer program and worked on papyrus backed with Vilene on the embroidery machine. It's best to trace in pen onto tracing paper for the cleanest scanned image. For the programming, the order of stitching for the lines was indicated in order to avoid too many jumps.

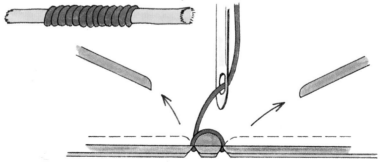

Padded satin stitch over a cord (top). Satin stitch over a foam padding that splits as it is being stitched (bottom). This technique is used particularly in computerized embroidery designs.

free motion **embroidery** or by using the feed dog, foot and a set stitch. The stitching could be left as an open zigzag, allowing the padding to show through for a textured effect.

A special padding exists for computerized machine embroidery. This foam cuts as the machine sews the outline stitching. The excess can then be removed and the machine will stitch a satin stitch over the padding. Special designs are available for this method of embroidery.

PADDING

Padding can be added to embroidery in the form of padded **appliqué** from the front of the work, or **trapunto** or **Italian quilting** where the padding is introduced

from the back of the work. For padded appliqué, pre-cut pieces of felt or quilt wadding are introduced under the shape before it is applied. See **raised appliqué.**

A padded **satin stitch** introduces a small amount of padding to the front of the work underneath the satin stitch, to raise it from the surface. Cords or wool can be used with normal satin stitch.

PAINT

See **acrylic paint, dyes, ink, paint, pastels, watercolour.**

PAINTING STITCHING

The base ground for an embroidery – fabric, paper, plastic or whatever else you use – can be painted with **acrylic paints, paint dyes** or **ink.**

Fantasy Towers by Julie O'Brien. Padded appliqué and trapunto quilting. Machine and hand embroidery. Procion dyes, cotton wadding, polyester filling. The embroidery is mounted on driftwood that has been treated with liming wax coloured with pigment.

Empty Shrine by the author. Old lace applied to linen ground with PVA and acrylic paint. The areas without lace are worked over with an open free motion zigzag. The work is repainted. 'The Empty Shrine series result from a visit to Angers to see the Apocalypse tapestries (14th century) and the 1950s reply by Jean Lurçat. The next-door exhibition space was taken up by a late 20th-century tapestry artist, again devoted to meditations on God. On leaving the exhibition an empty shrine in a wall caught my attention.'

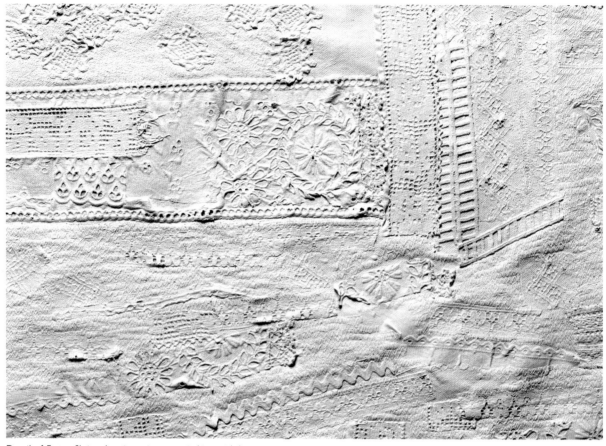

Detail of *Empty Shrine* showing paint overstitching with lace.

Once the stitching itself has been worked, that can also be painted, with thick or thin layers, to create a texture and homogenize the whole surface.

PAPER

All paper – whether it is handmade or bought, wrapping paper, newspaper, magazines, tracing paper or other finds – can be stitched with the machine in free motion embroidery or using automatic stitches or patterns, but some types will stand up to the treatment better than others. As the stitching creates perforations in the paper, the closer the stitching, the more likely it is that the paper will tear. The more malleable the paper, the less likely it is to tear; thicker papers and handmade papers, particularly cloth-based ones, are particularly resilient. Using larger

stitches decreases this tendency – even the crispest paper can be stitched onto if a foot and feed are used with large straight stitches. Avoid satin stitch: instead use an open zigzag. When using a foot and feed dog, a Teflon or roller foot may be preferable to avoid marking the paper. Intense stitching on papers can create a distressed effect on the surface – this is particularly interesting on newspaper, using a slightly open, wide zigzag, and working repeated rows of stitching; the paper starts to tear so it is only the stitching that holds it together.

When working with **free motion embroidery** the paper can be pulled up by the needle, causing thread wear during the stitching process, so use a **darning foot**. As papers are generally quite stiff they do not require a hoop for free embroidery.

More intense stitching can be

worked onto a paper surface if it is first applied to a fabric. Choose something lightweight such as habutai silk – otherwise the delicate quality that can be achieved by stitching on paper will be spoilt.

The perforations themselves can be used to good effect. Using an unthreaded needle, stitch decorative **automatic stitches** onto a firm paper surface to leave a pattern of holes.

If paper is stitched to a fabric surface using small stitches, the excess paper can be torn away on one side of the stitching, leaving appliquéd shapes in selected areas.

All papers and foils wear needles badly. Use a topstitch or embroidery needle to avoid excessive wearing of the threads. Once you have completed the embroidery, either throw the needle away as it will be blunt, or keep it just for using for embroidery on paper.

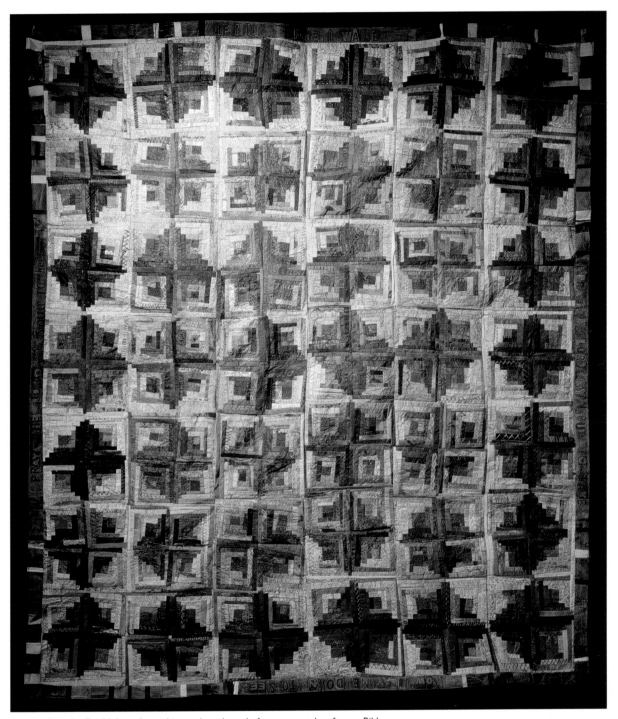

Down to Sleep by Cas Holmes. Log cabin patchwork made from pages taken from a Bible.

PASTELS

Pastel crayons can be used to subtly colour a fabric. Soft pastels need water added to them in order to brush them into the surface and to avoid excessive dust, once you have added enough colour. Oil pastels require turpentine. Neo-pastels, which are a little like oil pastels but dissolve in water, are an excellent colouring medium for fabric; any drawing marks can be left as they are not dusty. See also **encaustic colouring**. Pastels can be used on **Bondaweb** and applied to fabric.

PATCH

See **patchwork, slip.**

PATCHWORK

This is the traditional technique of hand patching fabrics together to form designs. Old fabrics were used for aesthetic reasons or simply for the sake of economy. This fact seems almost to have been forgotten in the elaborate designs of today. Many patchwork techniques are based on the simple seaming together of cloth in straight lines, most notably in Seminole patchwork, Amish quilts and the Log Cabin style; but there are other methods of strip patchwork and patchwork-based squares. All such techniques can be interpreted by machining the seams together, rather than hand stitching them, which is laborious, and often less secure. A special 0.5cm (¹/₄ inch) seam foot is available for machine patchwork with a guide that allows you to sew a perfect 0.5cm (¹/₄ inch) seam, and a **rotary cutter** makes the accurate cutting of multiple shapes much easier and quicker.

Seminole Indians in North America devised the form of strip patchwork now known as Seminole in the late 19th century when trading with newly-arrived settlers made sewing machines available to them. Strips of plain, brightly coloured fabrics are first stitched together, then cut and reassembled into different designs. The reassembling process can become quite involved.

Offset or angled to give different effects, this style can make beautiful borders for other designs. About one third of the area of the fabric will be lost during the cutting, seaming and reassembling process.

This technique is at the base of many strip patchwork techniques. A **rotary cutter** will help considerably in the accurate cutting required for the success of this technique.

Appliqué details can be added to machine-made patchwork, and quilting may be done by machine instead of by hand. Some embroidery machines have a special **quilting stitch** that looks a little like hand stitching.

PATTERNS

See **all-over designs, automatic patterns and stitches, borders, mirror image, negative shapes.**

PEARLS AND PIPING FOOT

A beading foot is available for some machines that allows the stitching into place of pre-strung beads up to 4mm (¹/₈ inch) in diameter. It can also be used to stitch over a piping or other cord.

PELMET VILENE

This very firm non-woven fabric can be used for construction techniques for items such as boxes

Patchwork by Rebecca Franks, while a student at Manchester Metropolitan University. Based on squares which have been worked with satin stitch to add additional colour and texture. Inspired by Amish quilts.

Embroidery with woven pelmet Vilene strips, by Roma Edge.

and books. It is also a pleasant surface to stitch onto. As it is firm, and doesn't need to be placed in an embroidery hoop for free motion embroidery, it can be used as a base for the creation of other surfaces, using paint, bonding or other techniques, and then stitched into with layers of embroidery, as heavy as required.

PHOTOCOPYING AND PRINTING

Poor-quality (non-laser) photocopies or newspaper printing can be transferred to fabric using solvents such as trichlorethylene or bonding agents. Fabrics can also be prepared to receive inkjet printing from a computer printer, which opens up the possibilities for photoprinting

Books by Frances Pickering. Pelmet Vilene is particularly useful for construction in book and box making, because it gives a more tactile finish than covered card.

Déchirures (Torn) by Pascale Doire. 'Conscious of the role of image in our society I use different magazines and transfer their inks onto different pieces of frayed fabric that represent the passage of time. I fix the fragility of an instant and the examples become mirrors for some people or decorative objects for others, or simply the hidden expression of my experience.'

Déchirures by Pascale Doire (detail).

onto fabric. Used wisely, these techniques can add another quality to a surface before embroidery. It is used by some people to apply an image to a surface that will simply be covered in embroidery afterwards. The ethereal nature of some of the images created by these methods offers other choices, and less stitching may allow the actual image to speak for itself.

PICTURES

An obvious opening for machine embroidery is the creation of pictures, which allow free rein to the creative spirit. By picture we probably mean a two-dimensional object, usually hung in a frame on a wall, depicting a more or less realistic image, or at least an image based on a motif taken from reality. The depicting of the motif is the essential essence of the work, and not the technical processes involved. For this reason, the technical processes should be subordinate to the image in the making of the work, the most important aspect of the work being the successful rendition of the chosen motif or image.

The chosen image for a picture may come from photographic or magazine sources, or from your own drawings. Whatever the source, it is worth going through the process of drawing the original image so that you are aware of how it can be constructed, the colours and textures that can be used, and of any compositional difficulties that need to be ironed out. Sampling is always important in order to find the best way of interpreting an image in such a way as to leave the image to speak for itself. Once you have decided how the picture is to be worked, consider how you are going to present it before embarking on the project, in order to avoid framing and mounting difficulties later on.

There are many ways of framing and mounting work and these should be appropriate to the image and technique used.

PIECED WORK

Different ways in which pieced work can be created include the following :

■ Pieces of fabric held together with stitching to make a patchwork.

■ Pieces of fabric stitched to a surface, creating a fabric with inherent textures.

■ Pieces of fabric attached to vanishing fabric, or held between two layers of dissolvable film, and stitched together.

See **crazy patchwork, creating fabrics, patchwork** for more information on pieced work.

PINTUCKS

Pintucking is an old decorative technique, most often used on fine lawn, consisting of seaming together the fabric into pleats. These are generally fine, but can be up to 0.5cm (¹/₄ inch) deep. Obviously these pleats can be made by sewing a machine line, but simpler still is the use of the machine's **twin needle** for pintucking.

Twin needles are available in different widths from 1.6 to 4mm (up to ¹/₈ inch). The wider the needle used, the wider or more developed the pintuck, although the very wide needles do not work well on fine fabrics. For best results use a grooved pintucking foot. This should be selected as follows: 3

groove – heavy fabrics; 5 groove – medium fabrics; 7 groove – fine to medium fabrics; 9 groove – very fine fabrics such as lawn and silk. A tighter top and bottom tension will cause a greater pleating of the pintuck, but don't go too tight: it can be annoying if the top threads break too often.

You can experiment with placing the pintucks side by side using the grooves to guide you, or further apart by using the **quilting guide**. Try doing them at different angles or on the **bias** of the fabric. Placing coloured fabrics underneath and cutting through the pintuck can add another dimension, or try working smocking or other hand techniques into the pintucks or pintucking into

Patchwork on vanishing fabric, by Mireille Vallet. The pieces of fabric were held between two pieces of dissolvable film and stitched with free motion embroidery.

crazy patchwork or layered appliqué. Pintucks offer a simple and interesting method of fabric manipulation that can become quite enthralling. See also **corded pintucks** and picture on page 14.

PIPING CORD

Piping cord is a twisted cord, usually made from cotton, available in a number of different sizes. It can be enveloped in fabric and used to pipe the edges of cushions or other textiles. To envelop it within a fabric, the fabric is usually cut on the bias to allow the easing of any corners, and the cord is held tightly in place by stitching up to the cord with a **zipper foot**. The piping cord can then be placed within a seam. If the twist on the cord is more than required, the cord may be placed within a fine layer of quilt wadding or Vilene within the fabric.

Piping cords can also be wrapped with a satin stitch. Guide the piping cord under the needle, keeping it in place under a **darning foot**. Use a large enough satin stitch so that the needle goes into the machine on either side of the piping cord so that it is completely wrapped. See **wrapping cords**; and the diagram on page 21, which shows layers of piping cord and wrapping cords.

PLASTIC AND POLYTHENE

All manner of surfaces can be machined into, painted and stitched together. **Crazy patchwork** is a useful method: various materials can be appliquéd, heat-treated, cut and holed with a soldering iron (always do so in a ventilated area and wear a mask), and included in your embroidery. Materials can range from yoghurt cartons to shopping bags, plastic film to old blow-up toys. Experiment with the best needle to use for your chosen surface. A fine ballpoint needle will work well on plastic food wrap, but you will need something sturdier for stitching into a yoghurt carton, and leather or PVC point needles can be useful for cutting through plastic.

The breaking of threads on more rigid plastics can be avoided by using a larger needle size or a backing. It is best to keep the needles you use with any such materials separate, as they will become too blunt for normal use. When using clear plastics remember that the bobbin thread will show too. For all plastics the machine marks will be permanent, so think ahead enough so that you can avoid unpicking.

There are many different types of polythene and plastic and many experiments can be done to see what surfaces can be achieved. Experiments in the creation of different surface qualities are quite pointless if they don't lead to mature, thoughtful, considered work, or at the very least to interesting surfaces for stitch experimentation. Remember that nothing is really new – I wrote my

Cut pintucks in felt by Lynda Mennell while a student at Manchester Metropolitan University.

La Nouvelle Robe d'Eté de Gabrielle by Fanny Viollet. Bits of yoghurt-pot lids and other plastic food wrappings embroidered, with free motion embroidery in curved lines of straight stitch, onto a base of transparent vinyl. 'All these elements are destined to be thrown away, but have, however, a very high power of seduction during their short existence, as well as their technological sophistication. I'm only reusing this vocation of seduction.'

and their use in the piece of work, are there to say something quite specific.

POLYESTER THREADS

Polyester threads have been around for a long time in the sewing industry as a reliable strong thread. Their appearance in the world of embroidery is more recent, but their strength makes them particularly suitable for embroidery machines. A wonderfully wide colour range is now available, as well as a variety of different thicknesses.

POLYSTYRENE TILE

This is a very useful piece of sewing equipment because it can be easily and accurately pinned into with ordinary dressmaker's pins. It can also be immersed in boiling water. These two properties mean that it is very useful when making vanishing fabric lace, which can be pinned out on the surface of the tile to keep its shape, character and open quality. This can be done once the fabric has been vanished or before the work is immersed in water (boiling or cold) and the work will thus keep the size and shape intended. On heavily and evenly worked pieces this is not really necessary, and such pieces can be dried under a weight such as a book or board. On very lacy or unevenly worked pieces of embroidery, pinning out can be useful, especially where there are open areas and heavily worked areas in the same piece, where pins can be used wherever necessary to keep the piece intact.

PORTRAITS

Real, imaginary, or self-portraits are an excellent source for expressive embroidery, and many different styles and techniques can be adopted. To make figures and portraits work in machine embroidery you need good source material, preferably personal drawings, so that you have already understood the image. Look at other textile ways of interpreting

1982 thesis on a little-known Italian abstract expressionist called Burri who spent the 1960s burning huge sheets of polythene! The originality lies in how you use the work rather than just the surfaces or materials you use. Gimmicks in your embroidery are all very well, but they must make sense. Perhaps the material integrates totally into a surface where it offers the right textural appearance for the work. Or your reasons may be conceptual – perhaps the origins of the plastic,

Portraits by Michele Dendy, while a student at Goldsmiths College, University of London. Worked on the Irish machine.

portrait images, for example Opus Anglicanum, with its use of stitch direction, can be a helpful source. Learning about stitch direction through some quick samples by machine or hand can be useful. Look at painted images for ideas about colour and paintstroke directions, as these might help inform stitch directions.

Computer programs exist that design from photographs for an embroidery machine. A certain amount of manipulation in a paint program will probably give better results than just asking the program to work on the photo as it stands. The results could be improved upon with free motion embroidery afterwards, making the image your own rather than simply being 'programmed'. Such programs can also work from a scanned drawing.

PRESSER FOOT

The presser foot is attached behind the needle of the machine, and

Super Model by Michele Dendy.

holds the fabric down on the bed of the machine on each side of the needle. There are many different styles of presser foot, each having a specific function for different types of sewing or embroidery.

Your machine's handbook will tell you the uses for the different feet provided with the machine, and it should be possible to get hold of a leaflet giving information about other feet, should you wish to acquire them.

Many modern computerized machines indicate which is the best foot to use for the type of stitching that you have set.

The presser foot lever must always be in the down position for sewing, even if you are not using a foot (for free motion embroidery), as the top tension is not engaged until the lever is down. Again some computerized machines will remind you, others do it for you, and some even flatly refuse to start unless the lever is down.

For different types of feet see **gathering, darning foot, embroidery foot, open darning foot, open toe foot, pintucks, zipper foot.**

PRESSER FOOT PRESSURE

Many machines allow you to alter the pressure on the presser foot. On some older machines this isn't possible, but it may be worth looking at your machine handbook. Reducing the foot pressure will help prevent puckering when stitching on fine fabrics or stitching curves. It can also be useful on thick fabrics where there is a change in bulk as you stitch over seams.

Many of the latest machines have a choice in presser foot pressures – the handbook will guide you in the best way to use this technical improvement for ordinary sewing and automatic patterns or computerized embroidery. This choice is, however, often made by the machine as it senses the depth of the fabric and adjusts the pressure itself, so you may not even have to worry about it.

PRE-WOUND BOBBINS

Pre-wound bobbins are of fine, cheap cotton thread and are available in black or white. Many people find them an invaluable time-saver. Whether to use them or not is a matter of choice, but in many circumstances the colour of the bobbin thread can be important, for example for openwork, work on vanishing fabric, or when using tension techniques, so do consider the options carefully.

PROBLEMS

See **bird's nest, hoop, missed stitches, needle breakage, tension settings, thread breakage, uncontrolled spool-off.**

PROGRAMMING

On modern computerized machines there are facilities for programming the different available stitches and patterns into a memory directly on the machine. Stitches can be flipped, mirrored or **elongated** and programmed in a desired order for your embroidery.

On computerized domestic embroidery machines there are elaborate programs that require hooping up the fabric for a large embroidery that may be up to 15 × 35cm (6 × 14 inches), or larger still if designs are combined and the hoop is moved as required. Again designs are provided within the machine that can be changed and **customized** to suit you within the programs available on the machine. The only barrier to the sizes available is the movement of the sewing arm attached to the machine.

Such machines can also be programmed from your computer using **customizing** or **digitizing** programs which are specially created for the purpose. Many programs now available can be read by different machines, as the basic technology and programming is the same for all of them.

Using these programs you can create your own designs and ask the computerized embroidery machine

to recreate the design for you. This sounds incredibly easy, but as with any artwork, when dealing with a computer you have to be precise in your request, and understand the fullness of the task you are asking the machine to perform. Using a scanner to copy your drawings into a digitizing program is easier than drawing directly into the program, unless you have a graphic tablet, and you will quickly learn what kind of design works best. This said, the interest in this technology for the creative artist is to ask it to go beyond the somewhat industrial designs that are provided with the machines or on the available disks or cards. By programming your own designs it is possible to get results that are not quite so industrial, or that can form a base for free motion stitching. Designs can also be programmed in that will look good on a pre-treated surface (either dyed or bonded), or as cutwork or appliqué designs.

When programming you can include stops for colour changes within the program – don't be lazy and leave these out, as they will be necessary when stitching. Many different fills for areas and lines are available on the digitizing programs, so try to find something that suits your design, instead of leaving it to the program to choose automatically. One of my favourites is the satin stitch – on the Janome I can make a bigger and more beautiful satin stitch than I can create with free motion embroidery, and the flattening of such areas is interesting when the work is based solely on colour and composition.

The most important point when programming your machine is to experiment with the programming tools, and be prepared to redraw your designs when there is a problem to resolve. Do try things that have never been tried before – the technology is new, and no one has yet gone to the end of the programming possibilities, so trying new things may well give valid and interesting results. Even when embroideries don't work out as hoped or expected, they can always be used as a colour and texture base and reworked with free motion embroidery.

PROGRAMS

Programs are now available to enable you to **customize** or **digitize designs** on your computer for use on your embroidery machine. Once the designs are created they are formatted in such a way that the embroidery machine will be able to understand them. They can be sent direct by cable, if your machine and computer are close together in the same room, or using a CD-ROM, **disk, ATA CP card**, or reader/writer box (depending on your computer system).

Each computerized embroidery machine has its own programs that can be added later, or bought with the machine as part of a package. To a large extent, the quality of the work done by the machine will depend on the quality and ease of use of the program available. Existing programs for other machines may be adaptable for your machine, so if you find an easier or more suitable program elsewhere, and are willing to pay for the extras it offers, this may be a cheaper alternative to changing your computerized machine.

Additional programs are also available on the Internet. The Embird with Sfumato programs are particularly useful for interpreting drawings or photographic sources for creative embroiderers. The stitches created resemble **free motion embroidery** stitching, so additional free motion stitching can be added and easily integrated into the whole. However, things are developing and changing all the time, so keeping up to date is essential. Most importantly, keep looking until you find a program that suits your work, rather than working to suit the programs you have.

PUFFING
See **gathering**.

PUFF PAINT
Puff paints are like fabric paints, but a puffing agent is included which will puff up when heated. The puffing agent, which can be bought separately, is composed of tiny plastic bubbles that expand when heated, creating the raised surface. To make your own puff paint, mix 100–150g (4–5 oz) with a cup of fabric paint (or experiment with quantities as you go along for a greater or lesser degree of puffing). The paint can be painted, silk-screened or stencilled.

Consider the texture of the fabric when using puff paints, as a very textured fabric will have a tendency to break up the created texture of the puff paint. A smooth fabric works best, and any fabric can be used providing that it can stand treatment from the **hot air tool** or iron that is necessary to expand the puff paint. If the paint expands too much, bubbling off the surface of

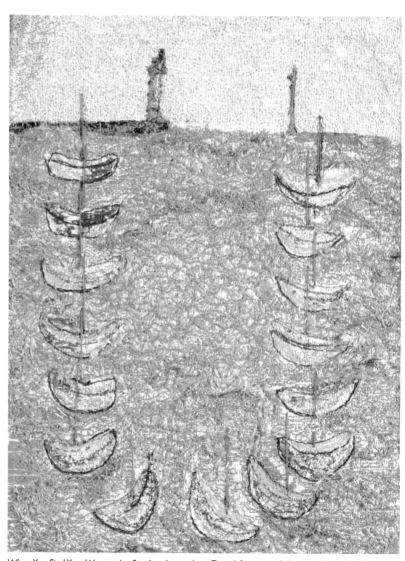

When You Find Your Way to the Sea by the author. Detail from worksheet with embroidery worked on Janome computerized image after Sfumato program, from a scan of a watercolour. Pieces of plastic film, with threads trapped and stitched in circles to create bubbles, are integrated into the surface with vermicelli stitch. Straight stitch details are added to the boats and hand-stitched masts.

Wisteria by the author. Worked on scrim in successive layers of free motion zigzag and satin stitching, which pulls holes in the fabric's surface.

Stitch pattern ideas for pulled work on evenweave fabrics or scrim.

the cloth, too much medium has been used, or too much heat.

Objects, glitter or other colour can be added to the puff paint as it dries, and these will become embedded into the surface during the puffing process. The surface can also be painted or dyed after being expanded. When a high concentration of puffing agent is included, it is easiest to stitch into the areas that haven't been painted, increasing the effect of the raised surface. **Long stitches** could also be used over the raised areas. See **Xpandaprint** and picture on page 49.

PULLED WORK

Pulled work is achieved by working in tight stitches on an openweave or evenweave fabric, pulling the threads together to create holes in a given pattern. Traditional pulled work effects can be achieved with automatic stitches and patterns and a relatively tight tension on top and bottom with the feed dog up and using a normal presser foot. How tight the tension will have to be to create pulled work effects will depend on the firmness of the fabric, and the starch dressing present in it. Starch can be added to finely woven cotton fabrics to maintain them. Zigzag, four-sided stitch and a host of other automatic stitches can all produce interesting results when worked carefully and evenly, taking into account the weave of the fabric in relation to the size of the stitch. Pulled work can be created on traditional evenweave fabric or on scrims or muslin, or even on canvas (but don't use a lockweave canvas).

You can also create pulled work effects with free motion embroidery using zigzag or satin stitches to pull the fabric together. Working over the surface again and again, pulling the threads together can create an interesting surface. See also **scrim**.

PVA MEDIUM

There are times when bonding techniques will be inadequate, in which case the best thing is to use PVA medium as a glue. It can be used to stick small bits of fabric to a surface, or to incorporate large pieces together into a homogenous surface. Place glue behind a piece of work with moss stitch, so that it doesn't unravel. Glue can be added to acrylic paint to increase its adhesive qualities. Colour or metallic powders can be added to glue to coat fabrics, papers or plastics. If you wish to stretch the final work and keep it flat afterwards, a coating of diluted glue on the reverse side can help a piece to keep its shape and form after stretching, particularly if it is large or unruly. Use glue to sculpt a piece of embroidery into a three-dimensional shape that will keep its form. And finally, use glue to mount a piece of work firmly onto paper or card when the work is ready to be shown (although double-sided tape is also useful for this). For all these techniques use PVA medium, which is white but dries clear, leaving a slightly shiny surface that never discolours.

Pandora's Box by the author. Spray-dyed background with hand-painted gold fabric paint surround. The box is an applied envelope that can be opened to read the message within, or to add your own message. The box is made of pulled work scrim over silk satin. The 'tassels' are stained porcelain. Pandora is quilted. The circles in the surrounding area are worked before the quilting process with a tight tension to manipulate the fabric into 'bubbles'.

QUILTING

Quilting is produced by stitching through a sandwich of two fabrics with **batting** or **wadding** in the middle. Stitching lines and contours worked on this sandwich change the surface, which will reflect light in different ways. The strong stitch produced by machine quilting is harder in appearance than the traditional running stitch worked by hand, although for those who prefer this appearance there are now computerized machines with a large flat bed which are able to stitch a lookalike **quilting stitch**.

The backing fabric should be of a heavier weight and quite firm so that the effect of the quilted or sculpted surface comes to the front of the work. It is not necessary to use an embroidery hoop for quilting, but a darning foot will be necessary to hold down the springy surface as the needle makes its stitch, or use a spring needle on lighter fabrics.

The three layers of fabric should be carefully tacked (basted) together at regular intervals before stitching begins so that small pleats and tucks don't appear during the stitching process. Any work required on the top fabric, such as dyeing or appliqué, should be done beforehand as it will be difficult once you have started quilting. Quilt wadding, especially synthetic wadding, should not be ironed as this will flatten it.

Designs can be linear, or you may outline existing shapes or flatten areas with stitching, allowing others to remain raised. Stitch length will have an effect – the larger the stitches the less obvious the quilting effect will be. All types of free motion stitches are useful, from **straight stitch** and **satin stitch** to **granite stitch** and **vermicelli**.

There are different types of quilt wadding on the market, available in silk, cotton, wool or synthetic fabrics. Each has its own particular properties. See **quilt wadding**.

QUILTING FOOT

A larger, see-through plastic version of a darning foot, which really flattens the quilt wadding around the needle for a good-quality stitch in free motion embroidery.

QUILTING GLOVES

Soft cotton gloves with points of non-slip rubber on the palms and fingers to hold fabrics onto the surface of the machine. They are very useful for easy movement with any relatively firm work (not only quilting) when not using a hoop but with a darning foot. Because you are not obliged to press down hard, or hold a fold of fabric in order to move the work, they allow a greater relaxation in the muscles of the arms and shoulders and can really help when working on projects without a hoop. Open the fingers of both hands and just place them on the embroidery – the gloves will almost 'stick' to the surface and allow it to be guided easily.

QUILTING GUIDE

A simple metal bar with an open L-shape at the end. The bar fits into a hole provided on the back of some feet. The leg part of the device touches the fabric on the right-hand side of the needle, at a set distance from the needle – use the screw on

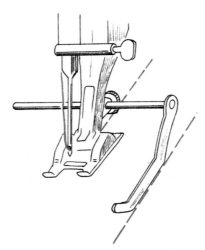

The quilting guide can be lined up with a previous row of stitching to create equidistant rows.

the back of the foot to adjust the length of the bar. This is a very useful method for creating equidistant lines of stitching, which need not necessarily be straight.

QUILTING STITCH

Some of the latest machines now produce a stitch for quilting that resembles a hand running stitch. The effect of the gaps that a running stitch creates are made by using a transparent thread on the top, which picks up and drags the coloured bobbin thread every other stitch. The transparent top thread forms a transparent stitch in between coloured stitches. This is useful if you do a lot of this kind of work and prefer not to have the harshness of the solid machine line.

QUILT WADDING

The quilt wadding most readily available is synthetic polyester, available in a number of thicknesses. A ballpoint needle should be used to stitch through this fabric, and a darning foot if working with free motion embroidery. It does not have good drape or insulation qualities.

Cotton wadding provides a better drape and insulation, but it can be heavy in use and it lacks the springy bounce of synthetic wadding.

Domette and **silk wadding** both have excellent drape and insulation qualities, are easily stitched and are not heavy to wear. They may seem a little thin for some uses, though several layers could be used. They are rather expensive.

Each project will have its own best choice of quilt wadding.

Quilt wadding, particularly if it is synthetic, should not be ironed.

RAISED APPLIQUÉ

An applied piece of fabric is padded to raise it above the existing surface. The applied piece of fabric should be lighter in weight than the background fabric so that the padding pushes the applied piece outwards. The fabric can be pinned to the surface of the work over a piece of foam or wadding, or stitched on three sides then stuffed. Additional stitching can be added in order to sculpt the padded area.

The technique of raised appliqué can also be used with see-through fabrics, nets or plastic, where found objects, leaves, buttons, feathers, beads, etc. can be trapped between the two layers. Again the piece to be appliquéd can be pinned over the objects, or stitched on three sides and then the pieces slipped in.

Trapping objects can be interesting in between two pieces of see-through fabric, as in **shadow work,** or with transparent **plastic**.

RAISED EMBROIDERY

Raised embroidery is another name for **stumpwork**. Raised effects can also be achieved with **padding, puff paint** or **Softsculpt**.

RAYON ACETATE

Rayon acetate, also known as artificial silk, is a fabric created from cellulose fibres. It is silky with attractive drape qualities.

The fibre was useful in the **guipure lace** industry because it could be dissolved away in acetone. This allowed for cotton or silk stitching to be used to create a lace structure that would be left after the fabric had been dissolved. This was a much cheaper option than the existing processes at the time, which involved stitching in cotton on silk (or vice versa) before dissolving it. Although it can still be used to create vanishing laces, dissolving the fibre is a smelly and unpleasant process. Rayon acetate has the same qualities as hot water dissolvable fabric, which is much simpler and more pleasant to use.

RAYON THREADS

Made from a cellulose fibre, rayon threads are produced by many different manufacturers, notably Madeira in Germany, and Natesh (among others) in India. Their

Padded Squares by Liz Maidment. Raised appliqué squares of padded silk on a silk ground.

quality varies enormously, in terms of the way they stay on the reel (some are particularly prone to **uncontrolled spool-off**), the tensile strength, the amount of twist, and thickness. Colour ranges differ too, and all makes have a range of shaded and variegated threads which will seduce you if they happen to fit in with your colour schemes. We all have our favourite threads – there

are some we like because they are easier to use, and others because they have a superb shine and the colours available suit us. Each embroiderer will find the threads that best suit their own work and their own sewing machine.

RECYCLING

Recycling old objects can have a conceptual impact on textile art.

La Nouvelle Robe d'Eté de Gabrielle by Fanny Viollet. Detail of the picture on page 121.

Old worn-out items of clothing, cast-offs, rubbish and printed paper, for example, all had a meaning in a former life that can be carried forward into the new work.

Recycling old or unfinished pieces of embroidery or samples into new pieces, bags or parts of wearables can often create new ideas. Bits and pieces of old embroideries that are considered unsuccessful could be integrated into new embroideries.

REPEAT MOTIF
A design or motif may repeat itself. Repeats can be worked in exactly the same way as the first motif, or mirrored or reversed. **Borders** or **edges** or an **all-over design** can be designed using repeat motifs. See drawings on pages 20 and 108.

REVERSE APPLIQUÉ
Reverse appliqué involves applying a piece of fabric to the back of the work, stitching around it, then cutting the top fabric to reveal the fabric underneath.

Choose a piece of fabric larger than the finished piece, in the desired colour and texture. This should be pinned or tacked (basted) into place behind the main fabric.

(Bonding is unsuitable as once it has been stitched the top fabric must be separated from the applied fabric and cut away).

The required shape should then be stitched around with a normal machine stitch or free motion embroidery. Two lines of stitching will hold the work better and prevent fraying. The top fabric is then cut away. To separate the two, rub them between your thumb and forefinger, snip into the separated top fabric, and cut down to the corners. The fabric can now be folded back to these corners and cut away.

The edge can be finished off with a neat satin stitch that covers the lines of stitching and enters just into the applied fabric, and just into the main fabric on the other side of the straight stitching. Other free motion embroidery techniques can be used to create an edge that is a little less formal. Any remaining fabric on the reverse side can be trimmed back if it is likely to show or to hinder further stitching.

An embroidery machine can be programmed to produce reverse appliqué or appliqué. Bought programs are also available.
This technique can also be used to create a type of **mola work** or for **lace** insertions.

REVERSE STITCHING

Most machines have a knob or button that allows the **feed dog** to move the work backwards instead of forwards. The obvious use for this technique in sewing is to reinforce seams, but it can also be used as a **lock stitch** or **holding stitch** if your machine doesn't have this as a separate facility. Working with a presser foot and feed dog, and forward and backward stitching over **applied fabrics** or **crazy patchwork** can create an interesting effect of movement. Also, the evenness of the stitching is generally superior to that which most **free motion stitching** can achieve.

Working a reverse appliqué design.

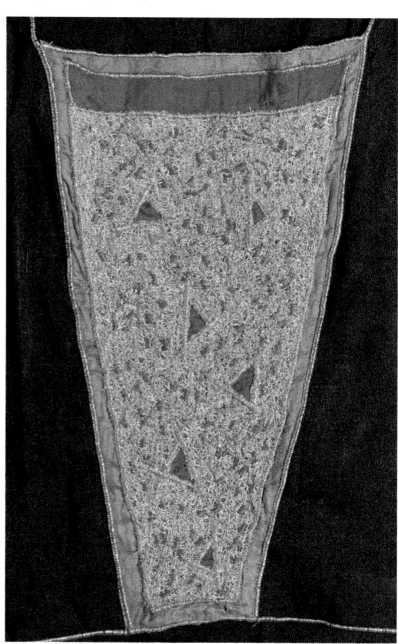

Panel with reverse appliqué worked in pulled work on scrim over silk satin. The scrim is cut away in some areas and the edges satin stitched, revealing the satin underneath.

RIBBONS

Many fine ribbons can be wound onto the bobbin and used with **cable stitch** and a bypassed tension or with the **bobbin tension** screw considerably loosened. See also **applying thread, cord and ribbon**.

ROLLER FOOT

A presser foot supported on two metal grooved rollers that roll along the fabric as they hold it down during stitching. This can be useful with fabrics where an ordinary foot would leave marks, such as velvet, leather, plastic or paper.

ROTARY CUTTING

This is a useful method for cutting fabric to the same dimensions speedily and accurately. It is used particularly in patchwork techniques where many pieces of fabric of exactly the same dimension are required, but it can also be useful in appliqué, or for cutting up tiny bits of fabric to apply to a surface, to create a multicoloured image. The basic equipment is a large plastic score-resistant cutting board, and a circular blade. The boards are available in a range of sizes and will virtually last a lifetime, so buy the biggest you can afford – it will also be useful for cutting card mounts. The rotary cutter itself is a circular blade set in a handle with a safety lock. It is also available in a range of sizes – a large one is practical. If you wish to cut accurate shapes for patchwork you will also need a large clear plastic ruler, with a straight, non-bevelled edge. These come in a variety of sizes, are wide, and are marked with diagonals as well as squares and measures to ensure accurate cutting of a variety of shapes. A bias square is also helpful for cutting patchwork pieces. With a little practice you will be able to cut through many layers of fabric at a time, and each one will be the same size and shape. This method can be used to cut out any patchwork pieces based on straight lines for machine patchwork. See **appliqué** and **patchwork**.

ROTATING

Used for embroidery machines, this technique allows the computer program, or the sewing machine itself, to rotate the design exactly to the required angle. The final embroidery can then be sewn at an angle or simply moved through 90° to be horizontal instead of vertical or vice versa.

This technique allows a better use of the hooped area, where there is a greater allowance of length than width, and also allows movement of different designs within the hoop space, so that they fit together more accurately.

RUFFLER FOOT
See **gathering**.

RUG CANVAS

Rug canvas is available in sizes of around 2 threads per cm (5 threads to the inch). It is possible to completely cover the threads of rug canvas with a satin stitch, thus producing a firm embroidered grid. This could be added to an embroidery, or used as a base for further work. To cover the threads, use an ordinary or embroidery foot with a satin stitch setting and the feed dog in place. Any additional stitching can be added with free motion embroidery and a darning foot; a hoop is not required as the surface is firm, although stitching into the holes will be considerably easier than stitching into the grid itself. Hand stitches could also be worked into this surface.

RUNNING STITCH

A single line of stitches (or even just one stitch) between two points. This can be used as an outline stitch or to create fine detail in **free motion** or **computerized embroidery**. In free motion embroidery running stitch is frequently used to create filling stitches and **colouring in**.

SAMPLES

Samples are very important in all embroidery. In order to improve your techniques, and to try things out for their appropriateness for projects, it is necessary to sample different ideas and new techniques. Unless you need to present them for exam purposes, the best use of samples is to keep them in a file for future reference. Ringbound plastic pockets are useful, as you can add new samples to the appropriate place in the file. On a sheet of paper on the back of the sample, write down how it was created, how you ended up using the technique or might envisage using the technique, and any difficulties encountered. Follow-up work should be placed in the next space in the ring binder. However, when engaged on a project it is worth putting the relevant samples on your workboard in front of your workspace. (Just in case that sounds like the luxury of a professional embroiderer, there must be somewhere in the house where you can put a small table with a machine on it that can be your workspace – mine was in the living room for years!)

Samples will build up into a body of work, information and expertise so that, in time, less and less sampling will be required for new projects as you have more and more information at hand. However, trying out new techniques and ideas in new ways from time to time doesn't do any of us any harm, although we should always keep our focus firmly fixed on our own personal agenda and our individual goals of expression.

SATIN STITCH

Satin stitch is achieved by setting the **stitch width** control to a zigzag – you can usually choose between 4 and 6mm – and setting a minimum **stitch length**. To create a satin stitch with the feed dog up and a foot on, choose an **embroidery foot** with an open wide groove to accept the

Park at St Remy by the author on a Janome 10000. Worked on the digitizer program from a scanned pen drawing, filling in with satin stitch.

satin stitch. Next select a stitch length of about 0.5mm (¼ inch) and gradually reduce it without pulling the fabric or pushing it through the machine. The machine should be able to work on its own and not get stuck on the stitching. If the machine does get stuck, the stitch length is too short. The fabric should go evenly through the

machine with a close enough zigzag to form a satin stitch.

A machine embroidery thread without much twist produces a much better result than heavily twisted sewing cotton. See also **appliqué** and **curves.**

For a free motion embroidery satin stitch the principle is the same and will be helped by holding the

hoop correctly. The thumbs push against the middle fingers to go forwards, the middle fingers push against the thumbs to go backwards. With a good control and a slow hoop movement you will create a good free satin stitch without having to pass back over it (this is undesirable as it can look untidy). See also **jump stitch, swing needle, zigzag.**

SATIN STITCH BLOCKS

Stitching blocks with satin stitch in different directions can produce wonderful textures. Small ones with a tiny width of stitch worked almost on the spot create a **French knot** effect or **seed stitch**; a longer version with a narrow stitch may make a **bullion knot**. Use a wider or very wide stitch on the spot for **bead stitch**, or medium stitches in a block.

The blocks may be more or less the same, or blocks of different sizes may be worked together in the same area. However, just as you would not work one single hand stitch on an embroidery and then change to a different stitch, you should be aware that the work will be more unified if collections of blocks are the same size, rather than all different.

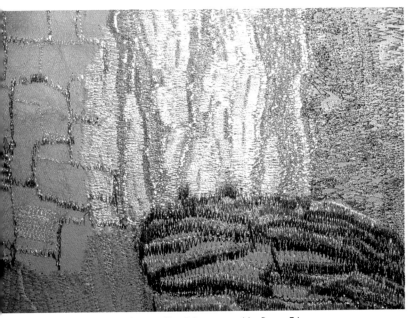

Free motion satin stitch and zigzag. Detail from a panel by Roma Edge.

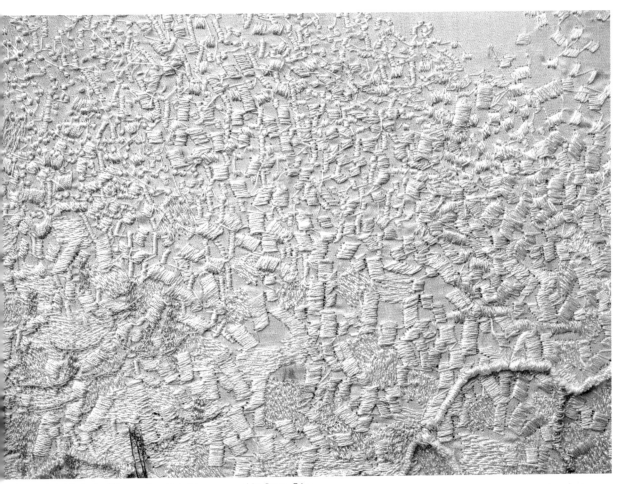

Satin stitch blocks in different sizes. Detail from a panel by Roma Edge.

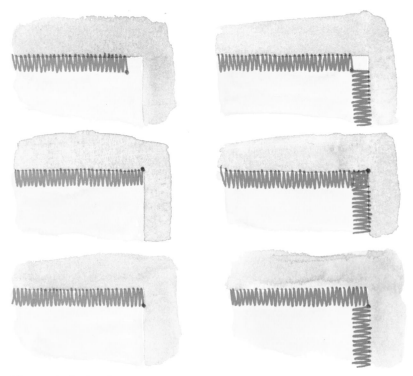

Three methods of working a corner appliqué in satin stitch. The point shows the position of the needle. In the first two methods the needle stays in the fabric and the work pivots around it. In the third position the needle needs to be adjusted after the work has been pivoted. It goes into the same hole as before but with the zigzag now forming to the left and not the right – the fabric will have to be moved slightly under the foot.

minute division on a clock face. Continue the process until the flower is finished, always being careful not to pull against the central hole or to move the hoop while stitching, or the flower will be spoiled. As a variation a second flower can be made on the inside of the first one in a narrower satin stitch or a different colour. The stitch width can be changed after each petal to give the impression of a flower viewed from the side in perspective, but be careful to re-centre the needle after changing the stitch width. Your own experiments will yield a variety of daisy-type flowers. Even if you don't particularly want daisies in your work, producing one is not a bad exercise for mastering machine control. Of course, with a programmable machine you can ask it to do this for you.

SATIN STITCH EDGES
See **edges** and **scalloped edges**.

SATIN STITCH PATTERNS
Different satin stitch patterns are available on many machines; sometimes they can be elongated or mirrored to create other motifs. On machines with a memory there are sometimes different parts of a satin stitch motif that can be put together: different starts, middles and endings will create different lengths of motif. These can be stitched with a presser foot and a feed dog, but are also effective in free motion embroidery, where they can be bent, turned over or manipulated to create flowing leaves or waves. See **elongating forms.**

SATIN STITCH CORNERS
Stitching a corner in satin stitch, whether you are using a feed dog and a foot, or working free motion embroidery, requires attention, and you will need to decide in advance the stitching effect you wish to achieve. See the diagram above.

SATIN STITCH DAISIES
Working with free motion embroidery and the fabric in a hoop, start with the widest stitch

width setting. Keeping the hoop absolutely still, work between four and 12 stitches, finishing with the needle at one side; this will become the centre of the flower. Turn the work carefully (always in the same direction, clockwise or anticlockwise), being careful not to pull on the central hole and enlarge it. Then work the same number of stitches again, finishing in the centre. Turn the work the same amount as before – imagine a five- or ten-

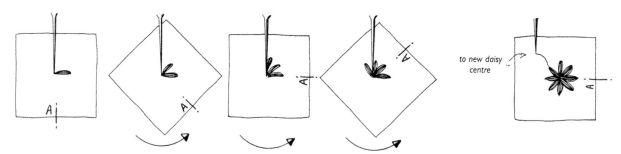

Satin stitch daisies worked with free motion embroidery. Each petal is stitched on the spot.

Automatic satin stitch patterns. Detail of patchwork panel by Rebecca Franks, while a student at Manchester Metropolitan University.

SATIN STITCH TENSION

To create a **correct tension setting** for satin stitch, where the bottom thread is not pulled through to the top of the machine and the threads lie smoothly without pleating the fabric, it is necessary to change the top tension. This may be done automatically by your machine (see **automatic tensions**), or there is often a buttonhole symbol on the tension wheel at about 3 which indicates the best setting for satin stitch and buttonholes.

SCALLOPED EDGES

Stitch a straight stitch edge to represent the scallops – there may be an automatic stitch on your machine to do this for you. Cut back to this edge, then satin stitch over it as in the diagram. On finer fabrics it may be worth putting Stitch and Tear or a vanishing fabric such as Solusheet along the edge to support the edge and the stitching as you go.

Many computerized machines include a selection of scalloped edges, so you can machine them first and then cut up to the edge. A soldering iron can be used to finish off any fraying on many fabrics.

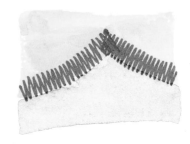

Stitching a scalloped edge with satin stitch. A better result is achieved if the satin stitch is worked over an already cut edge. It can be held and supported with Stitch and Tear or vanishing fabric.

SCANNERS

A scanner is used to transfer a design from the original paperwork to the computer program that will rework it (with your help) into an embroidery design for an embroidery machine. Although many early embroidery machines do not carry this option, or require their own scanner, the embroidery programs now available can work with a normal scanned image. If you do not have your own scanner, you can go to a graphics shop to have a design scanned and put onto a floppy disk in bitmap format. This can then be read into a customizer or digitizer program for development into a design. If you have your own scanner, scan your design into a program so that you can save it in bitmap format. Some programs, such as Paint, will give you the option of playing with the image afterwards, adding different textural and colour techniques. Unfortunately most of these added qualities, while working well with the original drawing, may prove problematic when you are trying to turn the design into an embroidery. Too much texture and colour will be read in individual pixels (the

point of colour that forms on a screen) and your embroidery machine will create a pointillist embroidery for you – not unpleasant, but try cutting all the joining threads! Experience will tell you which drawings and designs will scan the best for use as embroideries, but it is worth experimenting, as surprising results can be achieved, and it's only through experimentation that we can be truly creative. As a free motion embroiderer you can always rework any 'failed' images.

For line drawings, black pen on tracing paper gives the best definition when scanning, and the paint or embroidery programs will allow you to tidy up imported line drawings if necessary. Some embroidery programs include their own paint programs so that the imported image can be improved specifically for the embroidery program being used.

SCHIFFLI MACHINE

The Schiffli is a successor to the first ever industrial embroidery machine (the hand stitch embroidery machine) and was first used in the 1860s. Today there are only a few

manufacturers worldwide still producing embroidery using the Schiffli, as the computerized multihead has become much more advanced and accessible, although sample Schifflis can still be found at a few educational establishments. The Schiffli machine works by having the fabric on a large frame with a roller top and bottom, enabling several metres of fabric to be held at one time. It is this frame that moves to produce the stitch length required. Originally, like the hand stitch machine, it was controlled by a pantograph, but the more recent versions are controlled by computer. The needles move backwards and forwards, piercing the fabric to make a lock stitch, with a bobbin on the other side. The bobbin is boat-shaped – hence the name Schiffli, which in German means a small boat. The needles need to be re-threaded with different colours if more than one colour is to be used in the design, and the colour order of the work is defined accordingly. It is this inconvenience that has led to the machine's demise in the face of competition from the multihead machines. The largest machines are approximately 19 metres (21 yards) long and contain 1,416 needles. The embroidered fabric can be cut up into trimmings, motifs or garment parts, after it has been removed from the machine.

SCRIM

A fabric made from linen, available in white, ecru or natural, and sometimes even dyed or shot (i.e. with different warp and weft thread colours) versions. It has an open woven structure of varying densities, and is more or less starched depending on the origins of the fabric. If the scrim you have is too rigid it can be washed and boiled, and it can also be dyed or painted. It can be stitched on with automatic stitches and the foot in place, and will give interesting **pulled work** effects.

A scanned photograph is reworked in a Balarad paint program to provide a starting point for a computerized embroidery (pictured on page 179) working with a Sfumato program.

Detail of *Shroud Poem* (poem by George Mackay Brown, permission granted), worked by Angie Hughes. Handprinted poem, covered in scrim and pinned to Stitch and Tear. Machine-wrapped pearl threads. Free machining over the lettering.

Place in a hoop for free motion embroidery, with stitches based on wide or narrow zigzag or satin stitch that will work over a number of threads, and pull and manipulate the fabric into holes. Many colours can be added in layers to the holed surface, filling it in to a greater or lesser degree.

If you start with elongated figures of eight using a medium stitch width in the direction of the threads (warp or weft), this will start to pull the fabric into holes. Additional layers of stitching in a wider or narrower zigzag will add more colour and texture. It's possible to get fairly precise results, but lines will never be totally exact, and this is the charm of stitching on this surface, which makes 'Impressionism' almost inevitable: using different colours, stitch widths, density of zigzag and satin stitch, different movements of the hoop – straight lines, circles, 'drunken wiggle' with a zigzag stitch or perhaps the occasional straight stitch – an impression of an image begins to emerge. Bits of thread and offcuts of fabric can also be added.

As the work gets heavier you may need to use an embroidery needle for its larger eye size, or a larger needle than the usual 80 to be able to pass through the heavy areas of embroidery more comfortably, or you may have to use a **darning foot.**

For even more freedom and unpredictability, try stitching the same kinds of structure onto cotton muslin instead of scrim.

For a textural surface, try working on scrim with heavy zigzag to create a pulled work texture, then cutting the resulting piece out and applying it to another fabric to be embroidered again. See also pictures on pages 85, 125 and 130.

SCULPTURE

A precise definition of sculpture is hard to make these days. However, if we wish to define art in a space, textiles and embroidery can offer an interesting response.

Projects based on creating a soft version of a real life object, which itself is hard or soft, are still popular. Flowers, fruit and vegetables are probably the top favourites, but any edibles can and do receive this treatment, and the ensuing work can even be conceptual – addressing our relationships with food in a world that pushes us to consume as much as possible, while staying top-model thin! An installation by Stacey Bloom including real and constructed fabric food posed numerous questions about these relationships.

Sculpture in space also implies installations (permanent or temporary), mobiles and earthworks.

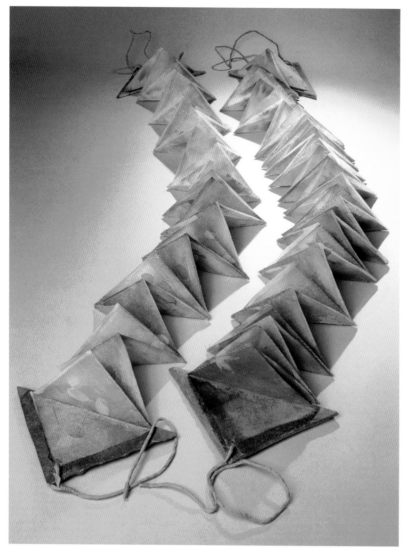

Slate-leaf book by Cas Holmes. Photograph by Peter Greenhalf, courtesy of the Crafts Council, from the 'On Paper' exhibition. 'I continue to develop my techniques working in both gallery and non-gallery spaces. I like to use discarded items, waste material no longer considered useful. Recycled materials have a history. These I break down, tear and cut until they are reassembled to create something more meaningful. Fragments and layers mark the passage of time, rituals of making (cutting paper, gathering materials, machining, sewing) acting as part of the narrative of the work.'

Stitch and textiles have much to offer us in these areas of art production.

As pure sculpture in mobiles or installations, textiles can pose questions about relationships with space and light, as well as form and colour. Installations can also be made that may question or remark upon the place of women, or political or everyday events, that can be all the more effective because of the textile content.

Mixed media works with a textile content have a significant role to play in putting textile and embroidery into the art arena.

The secret behind the success of such works is the same as for all art: good ideas, good research, good design, and good craftsmanship in the execution of the work.

SEAMS
A seam is the joining together of two pieces of fabric. The join can be hidden on the inside of the work, disguised with embroidery or overstitching, or decorated with faggoting or run and fell stitched seams, where the edges are turned into a second row of stitching. Extra layers can be added within the seam for decorative effects – perhaps a piping or cord. The join can be left on the exterior and decorated or frayed.

Seams joining two different fabrics together can occur in many decorative pieces, wall hangings, patchworks or garments and are therefore an essential element of many textile constructions, with a history of meaning and implication in their choice and making.

SEED STITCH
Traditionally this consists of three tiny zigzag stitches worked over each other. They can be used close together for an effect similar to hand seeding stitch or small French knots.

SERGER
See overlock.

SEWING ACROSS SPACE
See holes and lace fillings.

SHADED THREADS
Shaded threads are embroidery or machine embroidery threads that change from tints (gradations of a colour towards white) to shades (gradations of a colour towards black) within the same colour. They can be useful to supply a greater variation of colour when embroidering without constantly changing the thread. They should be used carefully, however, or ugly stripes can appear and the use of these threads can become a little too obvious. By watching the thread as it reaches the needle, the embroidery can be manoeuvred so that the lighter or darker part of the thread appears in the right place and works to shade or highlight the

object being embroidered. Another way of integrating them into the work is to use them in a needle with a plain thread at the same time. More colours (and thread) are stitched, but it means that the obviousness is avoided. See **multithreaded needle, variegated threads,** and the picture on page 154.

SHADING
To create effects of shading on an object try **colour spotting, shading stitch, shaded thread.** Use the complementary colour in small quantities (see **colour circle**), or work a **crazy stitch** in a darker or bluer shade into small **circles** or **granite stitch.** Layer see-through fabrics, or work stitching over a darker-coloured background. Use dark blue or black outlines for a post-Impressionist or Expressionist effect. Use shaded threads, paying attention to the colour changes.

SHADING STITCH
Available on some machines, this automatic stitch is an uneven satin stitch, uneven either on one side, or both. It can be used with free motion embroidery and gives an unusual zigzag or satin stitch that is rather freer than usual.

SHADOW WORK
All embroidery that features stitching, appliqué or wadding showing through a translucent ground may be classed as shadow work. Traditionally it is worked in neat bands of herringbone stitch on organdie, producing an outline like backstitch on the right side. White on white or pastel shades are traditionally used, which can be appliquéd using this stitch.

For every traditional technique there are a multitude of ways that the technique may be interpreted for modern machine embroidery. The essential quality of shadow work is that it's light and translucent. Using any translucent fabric as a base, other fabrics and stitches can be added to create shadow work. These should be lightweight, and traditionally translucent also, though this is not essential.

Layers of different fabrics can be pinned together, a design stitched, and areas can then be cut away to create a design. Suitable fabrics could include **organza, organdie, chiffon, muslin, net,** shot **organdie,** and so on. Threads or **tops** in silk or cotton could be added to the design. The work could be dyed after embroidery to create a unified piece, or the elements and layers incorporated could be of different toning or contrasting colours. If areas are to be cut away to reveal layers underneath after stitching it is best not to use a **bonding** glue. If the fabric is to be left as a whole,

Vines, Olives and Cypress Trees by the author. Worked on hot water vanishing fabric from a soft pastel drawing.

Shadow work by Eileen Whipps. Machine embroidery on organza.

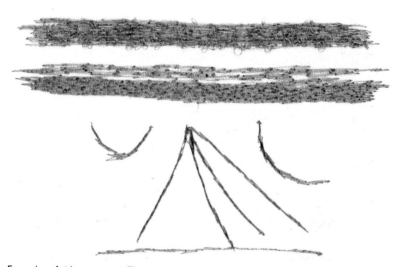

Examples of sideways zigzag. The top example uses feather stitch.

bonding could help to hold everything together for the stitching process. Simple line stitching, straight or undulating, will probably work best to allow the delicacy of the fabrics to play their part in the design. If the edges are to form part of the design, a corded **whip stitch** over a firm top thread such as number 12 pearl cotton or buttonhole twist will hold the edge against fraying. This can be stitched in a hoop, allowing for undulating shapes, then cut very neatly close to the stitching. The edge produced is quite firm on lightweight fabrics.

SHINY THREADS

Machine embroidery threads that have a sheen are generally synthetic, and usually rayon or polyester in origin, although silk machine embroidery threads do exist. The interest in these threads is the quality of light reflection that they give, reflecting light differently if stitched at different angles or with different **fillings**. There are a number of different qualities, thicknesses and twists available. Note that the greater the **twist** the stronger the thread, but also the less will be the effect of sheen. Many of the very shiny rayon threads are of Indian origin – if you find a cheap source it's worth checking out the thread quality before investing heavily. Very cheap threads may not be dye-fast, are sometimes poorly wound onto the bobbins which can cause difficulty with **thread breakage**, and they may be weak – again leading to a certain amount of thread breakage – so try them first.

Shiny threads can also create an interest in a surface texture when used with **matt threads**. See also **floss threads**.

SHISHA

See **mirror glass**.

SIDEWAYS ZIGZAG

This is a technique working with free motion embroidery and a large width of stitch, working from side to side across the machine rather than backwards and forwards. The result is akin to a handworked stem stitch or split stitch if worked carefully. Otherwise it makes an interesting filling, particularly useful for water. On scrim it makes an interesting surface.

SILICONE SPRAY

A useful, easy-to-use product for oiling the workings of the machine. The spray can be applied to the workings of the bobbin race, or to the inside of the machine when necessary. Note that a hard-working machine needs weekly oiling. There is a school of thought which says that silicone spray is better than oil in the long term as it avoids a build-up of oil. But more recent thought says that you can get a build-up of silicone, which is also undesirable. The best thing is to ask your own individual machine supplier – it's always best to be in agreement with the person who is going to repair your machine!

SILK

The only natural filament yarn is created by silkworms. Silk has a natural sheen even in its rawest form. From fine chiffon and habutai silk, to thicker satins or coarse raw silks, these are beautiful fabrics to stitch on and have a wonderful drape quality as well as natural warmth. They dye easily, and are strong to stitch on. For fine weights and satins it is best to use a fine ballpoint needle to avoid snagging the yarn.

For heavy embroidery, noil (raw) silk can be very useful as it has a lot of natural gum which will help the fabric to hold its proper shape after **stretching**.

SILK PAINTS

Silk paints are meant to be used on animal fibres such as wool (or wool **felt**) and **silk**, where they achieve their best results. They can also be used on other fabrics, on paper and on **Tyvek**. Most silk paints available

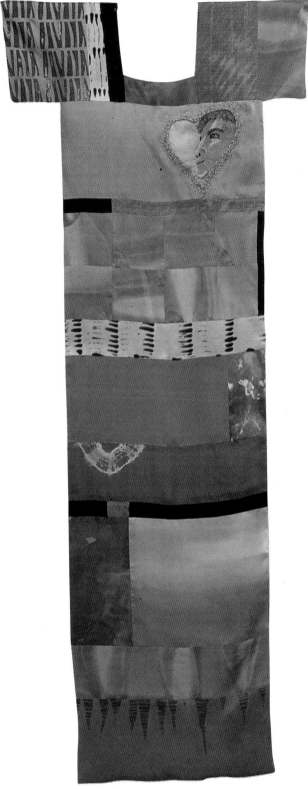

She Left Her Heart Behind by Diana Parkes. Hand-dyed silks, piecing, machine stitching and beading. Abstract rendering of garment portions.

Detail of *She Left Her Heart Behind* by Diana Parkes.

same direction as the first layer. The whole should be placed between layers of **baking parchment** for ironing to set the bonding glue. Leaves, threads and other objects can be trapped between the layers.

Silk papers can also be bought and stitched on, as for **paper**. They accept a reasonable amount of stitching without falling apart. For a sample using cotton tops and linen, see picture on page 18.

SILK WADDING

Silk wadding is available from specialist suppliers. Used in quilting it has a good draping quality and provides warmth – much more than synthetic wadding, so it is useful too in garment making.

Silk wadding is also an interesting fabric to use in its own right. It can be dyed, wetted and ironed to resemble felt and can then be pulled and manipulated just like felt, with the added advantage of a quilted surface. Silk wadding is a matted surface like felt, but thicker than any commercially available felt. It becomes more felt-like and more stable to stitch on if it is treated to damp heat and then ironed. It also has a delicate sheen, unlike wool felt.

If you are worried about whether it will take the amount of stitching you plan to put on it, it can be backed with a fine habutai silk, which will not ruin its draping qualities. It is best used without a **hoop** (which would cause hoop burn), but do use a darning foot. It can be stitched on to flatten the surface, leaving the unstitched areas raised – any type of stitching is suitable. Stitching firm repeated lines can pull it out of shape and undermine its integrity, with interesting effects. Threads and fabrics can be applied to the silk, or the silk may be applied to other surfaces. The best appliqué method is probably to work fairly heavily over the edges of the applied pieces so that the fabrics become integrated through stitching.

these days can be fixed with ironing (much easier than steaming or chemical methods). There is a whole panoply of equipment and products that can go along with silk painting to prevent the dyes from running (gutta comes in clear, coloured and metallic versions) or to create interesting marks (try salt), which can be useful for background fabrics or for pieces to cut up.

Some experience is required to achieve good silk painting with gutta and well-defined edges, but the machine can be very useful for 'repairing' or hiding the damage if paint should 'spill' outside of the desired area of the fabric.

SILK PAPER

So-called silk paper (which is handmade) is a cross between paper and felt, made with different silk tops and binding agents. It can be a very attractive surface to stitch on. If the result you achieve is too fine, you can place it on habutai **silk** or **dissolvable film** for stitching. It can be used to create beautiful **openwork** effects. A quick, delicate version can also be made using **bonding powder**. Pull the silk tops in one direction, sprinkle with bonding powder, cross this with silk tops going at right-angles, add another sprinkle of bonding glue, and a final layer of silk tops in the

SIMPLE INSERTIONS
See **faggoting, insertions, lace fillings, reverse appliqué**.

SINGER WORKSHOPS
'The embroideresses who worked in the London Embroidery Department of the Singer Sewing Machine Company must be given full credit for all the pioneer work they did for art or free embroidery worked on the sewing and embroidery machines'

(Christine Risley, in *Machine Embroidery, A Complete Guide*, 1973).

Techniques worked with a beauty and precision were perfected in the Singer workshops between the years of 1889 and 1962. The work was done on domestic and Irish machines to create many forms of lace, appliqué and pictures. The workshops produced work for sale and commissions, and prestige pieces for exhibitions. They also taught individuals or teachers for colleges and shops, and worked closely with artist embroiderers. The Singer workshops had held a formidable role in the development of the use of the machine and in the increased interest in machine embroidery throughout this important period of modern embroidery history. The major books on the subject were published by Singer themselves: *Singer Instructions for Art Embroidery* in 1911 and *Singer Machine Embroidery* by Dorothy Benson, published in 1946.

SKETCHBOOK
A sketchbook is an essential piece of equipment for any embroiderer. Try to carry a sketchbook with you at all times and a pencil case with a good collection of coloured pencils or other useful mark-making materials. Glue in a stick may also be useful for keeping found objects or creating quick collages. You never know when you are going to find interesting views, details or ideas that you may want to record.

Over time you will find your preferred paper and method of recording. Strong pencils or fibre-tipped pens, or a small watercolour palette, might do. The paper in the sketchbook must be suitable to your medium – and do you prefer a bound book or a ring file? Make

A collection of sketchbooks with drawings in coloured pencils, pastel and watercolour.

sure that you can fit the sketchbook and pencil case or box into your regular bag, so that carrying it becomes a habit.

When you are able to travel around in a car, you can be a little more extravagant, and perhaps carry around a larger sketchbook and a greater choice of materials and colours.

A sketchbook may be just a record of things you see that you will develop at a later date in a different book or on worksheets, but it can also be an ideas book where recorded information starts to be written down, or ideas drawn. If you've never kept a sketchbook, the idea can seem a little intimidating at first, but remember that no one else has to see it!

Regular drawing and observation really does pay off – your paperwork and embroidery will inevitably get better if you keep at it (not just for a week – keep it up for a whole year and you will appreciate the improvement).

To help you consider how to lay out or keep a sketchbook, have a look at other people's sketchbooks at degree or City and Guilds shows. Look also at travel sketchbooks from practising or famous artists. This is a popular book publishing genre at the moment, so there is a lot of material around.

SLIPS

Slips are separately made motifs or figures applied to the ground after the stitching has been finished. They were used in **Opus Anglicanum** embroidery when the work was on a difficult ground such as velvet, and again in **stumpwork**. They are frequently used in ceremonial embroidery, where it is useful to create intricate motifs first, before applying them to the background.

They can be used in machine embroidery too. By creating an object on a separate piece of fabric (or a vanishing lace piece) and adding it afterwards, it may be easier to place it on top of existing work, rather than machining it on top of the work directly. If the piece of work is large, separate intricate motifs may be more easily worked as slips.

Slips can also be created using motifs on computerized machines, then cut out and added to existing work and even worked into again.

Slips worked on a computerized embroidery machine are used on this fun narrative embroidery by Amanda Toiley, worked while a student at Manchester Metropolitan University.

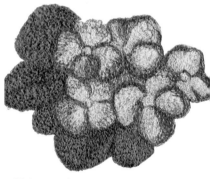

Hydrangea slip made on hot water vanishing fabric. The area to be embroidered was first covered with small circles in appropriate colours. The final embroidery followed the movements and colours of a coloured pencil drawing.

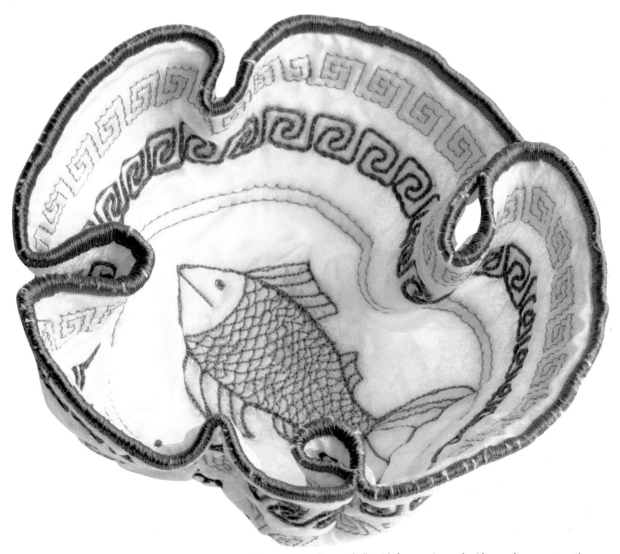

Fishy Dishy by the author. A sandwich of Softsculpt bonded between two layers of silk, with free motion embroidery and some automatic stitching with cable stitch. The edge was satin stitched twice. The whole piece was then put in an oven to soften the Softsculpt before the bowl shape was formed using a ceramic bowl.

SMOCKING

Smocking is a traditional hand stitch technique where fabric previously gathered into small regular pleats is held together with surface stitching. The result 'gives' as if it has been elasticated.

Smocking machines can do the time-consuming gathering of the pleats for you. They can be purchased or even hired.

To create a similar effect on a sewing machine, fine shirring elastic can be hand-wound onto the bobbin to gather the fabric. The

tighter the elastic is wound onto the bobbin, the greater will be the gathering. You can experiment with rows of straight stitching or use the smocking-like stitches from the **automatic patterns** on the machine. The technique can also be used as a fabric manipulation technique, creating interesting gathered surfaces that have little to do with smocking. Gathered surfaces could also be dyed, and then the gathering undone after the dyeing process, a little like tie-dye but with a different level of precision.

It is also interesting to hand smock **pintucks**, or haphazardly machine pleat or smock surfaces in **fabric manipulation**.

SOFTSCULPT

Softsculpt is a thermoplastic foam which can be embossed or moulded if heated with an iron under baking parchment or in the oven. Directions for use are usually included when buying a sample packet. It is available in black and white and in two thicknesses. The thicker version is best used for

145

making embossed surfaces to be applied to another surface, or used to print with. The finer version will easily take on different shapes when moulded, so vessels and other manipulated forms can be made.

Softsculpt can be machine stitched, as it remains soft and won't damage the needle, but it is best to use a backing, as its non-slip properties make it difficult to work with and to move around freely on the bed of the machine. Lower the feed dog, use a darning foot or no foot at all, and a ballpoint needle – and make sure you stitch slowly. You can reinforce any images that are embossed in the Softsculpt by stitching into the already flattened areas. The foam may be covered with chiffon for a more 'fabric' quality finish, or may even be sandwiched between fabrics before being formed when it is used for sculptured forms or vessels. When doing this choose a fabric that will withstand heat and bear in mind that heat times may need to be increased from the usual 1–1½ to 2 minutes at 150°C (300°F/Gas Mark 2). Oven gloves can be used if necessary, but the foam itself cools rapidly. Once hot it is necessary to form it within the following 10 seconds, so have everything you need ready at hand. If you don't like the result you can put it back into the oven where it will regain its original shape, and you can then repeat the process.

SOFT SCULPTURE

Creating three-dimensional objects using padded stuffed textiles with embroidery where appropriate. Machine embroidery lends itself to working in relief, in three dimensions. It will stiffen a fabric by virtue of heavy stitching alone, and if the direction of this stitching is also considered the fabric can be manipulated by the stitching to take on certain shapes. Objects can be quite heavy, made with layers of fabric stuffed with quilt wadding; or very lightweight, created in lace on vanishing fabric. Any shape or form required, realistic or not, can be created in relief or become a completely free-standing work.

Should any sculptured object require stiffening to hold its form for the nature of the design, consider the design of the stitching, and using **quilt wadding, adhesive webbing** between two layers of fabric, **pelmet Vilene, starch, PVA medium** or **wire**.

Long Tall Silly. Soft sculpture vessel by Pauline Hann (photo Bruce Pert). This 3D vessel is one of a series, in which vessels are symbolic devices to store precious memories. This one reflects the exotic fauna and flora of the Caribbean. The form is worked on pelmet Vilene and machine appliquéd with silks, many hand painted and embellished.

Creating sculptures from natural objects is fairly simple, is usually successful, and generally causes delight in an audience. The most important aspect of this type of work, if it is to be a success, is the study of the real object in detail in order to be able to reproduce it exactly. Make use of photographs, but also drawings, and take the object apart so that you fully understand it before embarking on your sculpture. Most shapes can be constructed with a bit of preparation, and a model can be made in calico to get an idea of how to cut out the necessary shapes.

Hard objects made in soft materials can also pose questions about our relationship with the world. The artist Claes Oldenburg spent a great deal of the 1970s addressing these issues, along with those of scale. Soft sculpture has always had a conceptual as well as a humorous content, and one must be aware of this past in order to create successful pieces in soft sculpture.

Sculpture can also be non-figurative, and in this case you will need a lot of design work (in the form of worksheets or sketchbooks) to arrive at particular shapes and forms that work in three dimensions. See also **sculpture, stumpwork, three dimensions.**

SOFTWARE
The programs used to program an embroidery machine or allow its connection to a computer are the software, as opposed to the **hardware**, which consists of the products themselves: computer, scanner, etc.

Programs exist for customizing or changing existing computer designs ('customizing') or for making your own individual and unique designs based on your drawings or design material ('digitizing').

SOLDERING IRON
The soldering iron has become one of those indispensable tools to the modern embroiderer. I recall the horror on my tutors' faces in the early 1980s as I set about burning my embroideries with matches, with a water spray handy, over a stainless steel sink. Soldering irons

Sunrise. Unfinished embroidery by the author showing different uses of a fine-tipped soldering iron. Layers of polyester organdie are added to acrylic felt. In some areas, by moving the soldering iron slowly, cuts and incisions are made. In other areas the soldering iron was slashed quickly over the surface to solder the layers together. Straight stitch with a normal tension, whip stitch and heavy whip stitch are used. For the heavy whip stitch in the foreground the work is moved unevenly under the needle to create occasional bobbles.

certainly do add a precision to an otherwise fairly dodgy process!

Soldering irons are available with heads of varying sizes and shapes. The finest are probably the most useful for embroidery. They will burn natural fibres, but melt synthetic ones, and burn holes in plastics, at the same time preventing any edges from fraying. The success with which this is achieved depends on the nature of the fibre and the thickness of the fabric, so experiment with the fabrics you intend to use. A slow movement will cut and make holes; quicker slashing movements can cause fabrics to meld together – layers of see-through fabrics onto an acrylic felt background, for example.

Small pieces can be cut out that will not fray, holes or lines can be drawn, and cutwork and lacy effects made in the fabric which could be layered through to other surfaces. The edges can be cut and sealed with the soldering iron. Holes can be bored in plastic for stitching.

The easiest way to cut out fabric with a soldering iron is to place the fabric on an old piece of plywood and just draw the required shapes fairly quickly. When the fabric is pulled off the wood, it will be cut to those shapes.

For any technique of distressing or treating fabric, the creation does not end with the technique – otherwise it's easy to fall into the same patterns of production that you have seen elsewhere, and the technique just becomes another gimmick. So use the technique with stitching and your own design ideas, to make it your own.

Note that when using a soldering iron with any fibre or plastic you should do it in a well-ventilated area and use a mask. See also **burning, burnt cutwork, candling, hot air tool**.

SOLUSHEET

A non-woven dissolvable sheet, a little like Vilene, that is very easy to stitch on and hoop up – but follow the same procedure as for dissolvable film for correct hooping. It can be stitched with an ordinary needle and has no difficulty with any type of stitching, however heavy this may become. Such a wonderful fabric inevitably has a downside, which is that it leaves a strong starch residue when it is vanished, although using hand-hot water and washing in fabric softener can help a lot. For some work this starchiness may prove an advantage. See also pictures on pages 63 and 93.

SOLUWEB

A weblike structure, sticky when heated. It resembles, in a more delicate version, the webbing part of Bondaweb without the backing paper. It sticks two fabrics together using heat from an iron – useful in **appliqué** (use **baking parchment** if you are ironing initially to just one surface), but it is soluble in cold water. If the surfaces are stuck together they remain so, but can be pulled apart when wet, and repositioned (perhaps just once).

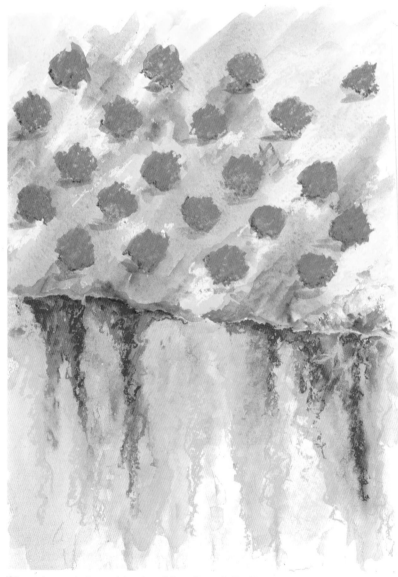

Watercolour and oil pastel drawing of *Roussillon with Olive Trees*.

A sandwich can be made between chiffon (try using old scarves) or organdie, using Soluweb's bonding qualities. The fact that it is destroyed by washing removes the old problem with Bondaweb, where it remains clearly visible if it is used between layers of fine fabric or chiffon. Soluweb cannot be stitched into in its own right, so for more stability when creating lacy structures a sandwich can be made: first a layer of Solusheet, then a layer of Soluweb, followed by the fabrics and threads that you wish to incorporate, and then a final layer of Soluweb, followed by a layer of baking parchment. Iron the whole sandwich together using the wool setting on the iron – too hot and it will melt, too cold and it won't stick. This surface can now be stitched into with or without a hoop. This is a useful technique where it is imperative that the fabrics and threads in the sandwich stay in position (otherwise you can simply place the bits between a sandwich of dissolvable film). Soluweb also makes an good **stabilizer** or **topping.**

SPOOL
A term variously used to describe the thread carrier, made in plastic, cardboard or wood, on which the thread is wound. It is then placed on the top of the machine for the thread to pass through the needle. See also **bobbin** and **cotton reel.**

SPOT MOTIF
See **slips.**

SPRAY BONDING GLUE
505 is a temporary fabric adhesive that comes in the form of an aerosol. It is colourless, odourless, and doesn't contain CFCs. When sprayed onto fabric, the fabric can then be cut into pieces and attached to a surface or backing fabric simply by using the pressure of your fingers. The fabric pieces can be repositioned a number of times by lifting them and replacing using finger pressure. When you like the result, the work may be stitched by hand or machine. The glue is only temporary, so stitching is essential. It can be washed off small areas, or a large area can be dry-cleaned if you wish to eliminate the spray glue.

This is a very useful product for **appliqué**, particularly where very small pieces of fabric are used to build up the colour.

606 works in a similar way, but by ironing the work once you are happy with the arrangement of the bonded pieces, the bonding becomes permanent.

SPRING NEEDLE
A needle wrapped around with a spring, that holds down bouncy fabric in a similar way to using a darning foot, but without the inconvenience of the darning foot – that is to say, you have better visibility and there is no problem with bumpy surfaces such as **Tyvek** or dimensional or puff paint. It can be used in **quilting,** and with **paper**

Roussillon with Olive Trees by the author. Worked on Solusheet, with the fabric pieces held between a sandwich of Soluweb. Straight stitched on the machine with straight lines, 'drunken wiggle' and fleece stitch (with whip stitch – see detail on page 65). The shadows of the olive trees are worked with a wide satin stitch.

and **canvas**. It's worth a try using a spring needle with any surface where a darning foot is recommended, but they don't always work as well as a darning foot. They are also relatively expensive, so beware on surfaces that are hard on needles.

SQUARES

Squares are all the same shape, but come in many different forms:

■ Squares for machine patchwork of the same or different sizes.

■ Squares of straight or satin stitch in different directions for a textural effect in a filling.

■ Squares of embroidery all the same size for a theme in a collective exhibition of work by different embroiderers, so that the exhibition remains coherent.

STABILIZER

A material used to protect or prevent the distortion of the fabric during the process of embroidery, most particularly on embroidery machines but it can be useful elsewhere too. The stabilizer may be in the form of a firmer fabric tacked (basted) or bonded into place. **Vilene, Stitch and Tear** or **Totally Stable** can be placed or bonded behind the fabric for added support and removed afterwards. **Soluweb** is lightweight and bonds to the underside of a fabric and makes stitching easier and more exact. It can then be dissolved after stitching. It can also be used as a **topping**.

Most fabrics need some firm backing added for machine embroidery stitching when using programmed designs if the fabric is not to be distorted during stitching and the design ruined. For computerized embroidery, an iron-on stabilizer can be the best choice, particularly when using a stretch fabric, as it will not have any give in it, unlike some interfacings. For heavily embroidered areas, several layers of stabilizer can be used if necessary. These can be torn or cut back to the stitched area when the work is finished. 'Totally Stable' is excellent for this.

Vanishing muslin was frequently used as a backing for commercial embroidery on the **Irish machine** so that the work was stiff enough to be hand held instead of being put into a hoop. Vanishing muslin (Heataway) can be dissolved with a hot iron once the embroidery

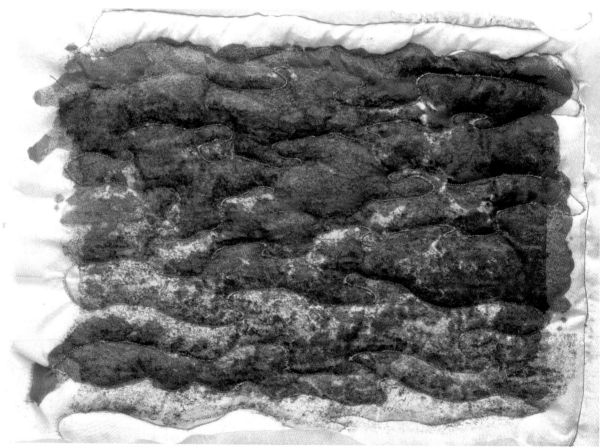

In this sample piece, worked on silk, two layers of Bondaweb are fused onto the surface, one coloured with pink ink, one with blue. Stippling is worked over the quilted surface.

process is finished, without leaving a residue in the fibres. This can be done from the back onto a soft surface to avoid damaging the embroidery. This process can be useful for free motion embroidery if you are worried about hoop burn (the marks left by the hoop on some fabrics after the hoop's removal).

When working on fine or see-through fabrics or nets on an embroidery machine it is preferable to use a dissolvable film as the stabilizer where necessary. If the stitching is to be heavily worked, use two layers.

Stabilizers are available in many weights, sizes and styles and it's worth having a collection available for your use, particularly if you do a lot of embroidery using computerized designs. See also **topping**.

STARCH

Laundry starch can be used to stiffen surfaces and hold interesting sculptural shapes, but it is not permanent to atmospheric humidity. Some wallpaper pastes have a similar base and can be used for stiffening – they may be particularly useful on the back of a piece of work that needs **stretching** back into shape after it has been stitched. The starch can be pasted on the back of the finished work if there isn't enough natural starch in the fibres to help hold the final shape.

STEM STITCH

See **sideways zigzag**.

STIFFENING FABRICS

See **acrylic paint, dissolvable film, gesso, PVA medium, stabilizer, starch, Vilene**.

STIPPLING

This is a little like **vermicelli stitch** in that it works backwards and forwards in a wiggling movement, but on a much larger and more open scale. It is associated with quilting on patchwork or appliqué quilts as a freer way of quilting all the layers together.

STITCH AND TEAR

Stitch and Tear (Stitch 'n' Tear) is a papery material which can be used as a backing or stabilizer behind an embroidery to help hold the fabric during the stitching process, and to prevent the fabric from puckering or stretching. The Stitch and Tear can then be torn back to the stitching and will remain only under the stitched areas for firmness. It can be used with free motion embroidery or automatic stitches if a particularly flat, non-puckered finish is essential. It is also useful for working over edges, and for stitching on knit fabrics. For computerized embroidery some sort of **stabilizer** is essential for all stitching, and this is just one such product that may be useful, according to the use and fabric you have in mind. The fact that it can easily be removed from areas that are not stitched makes it a particularly attractive option.

STITCH DENSITY

This refers to the density or closeness of the stitches in a design on an embroidery machine. The stitch density can be set within the digitizing program. Once a design has been programmed and sent to the machine, the number of stitches in the embroidery (stitch count) will normally be determined. The design will have been sent to the machine at 100% of its design size. In the machine it is usually possible to change this size to between 80% and 120% and there will still be enough stitches to cover the fabric, but the density of the stitching will be greater or lesser. If you need to enlarge or reduce the design by more than this percentage it will be necessary to go back to the computer to adjust the design, and the quantity of stitches used will be changed. The stitch density may change in a design according to the percentage of the design size used. The result will also vary according to the thickness of the threads used. This should be taken into account when reducing the size of a design (and so increasing stitch density) or enlarging a design (and so reducing stitch density).

Certain machines are now capable of recalculating the stitch count required to maintain the stitch density, within the machine itself. The designs can thus be greatly enlarged or reduced without these problems.

From a design point of view, the fact that the stitch count stays the same when enlarging or reducing a design can be interesting. In the picture on page 35 the colour circle was designed and then enlarged to 120%. As the stitch count stayed the same, the density of the stitches became quite open, allowing for the design to be worked twice, and for the colours of the first passage to have a pronounced effect on the colours of the second passage.

STITCH LENGTH

A knob or button on the machine will set the stitch length to between 0 and 5mm (up to $1/4$ inch), or sometimes longer for **tacking (basting) stitches**. This adjusts the movement of the feed dog and the length of the stitching as the fabric progresses under the needle.

The stitch length for **free motion embroidery** is governed by the movement that you make with the fabric under the needle relative to the machine speed.

See **free motion embroidery** and **straight stitch**.

STITCH-OUT

A test piece of computerized embroidery worked as a sample to make sure that the fabric and threads chosen, as well as the **stitch density,** will work for the design. It is important to always do this to ensure that you are not disappointed with the final embroidery, particularly if using a pre-made garment that could be spoilt. Note that the stitch-out embroidery should be done on the same or similar fabric as the final

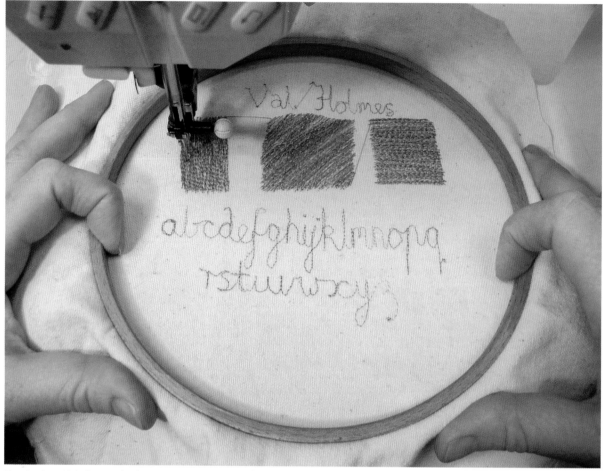

Exercise in straight lines to familiarize oneself with the position of the hoop, always held with the same top, bottom, left and right positions and working in straight stitching: vertical lines, horizontal lines, lines at 45°, writing freehand. Shown with the correct hand position on the hoop under the machine while stitching the work.

piece to ensure that the result will be the same.

These stitch-out samples could be filed in a sample file with your remarks for future information and use, or they could be the base for another embroidery or slip.

STITCH WIDTH

All modern machines have a **swing needle** which allows the needle to go from side to side, as well as the feed system that will make the work go forwards and backwards. There will be buttons or a dial that govern the width of the stitch, which can go from 0 to 4, 6 or 9mm (between 0 and ³/₈ inch). The number on the dial represents the width in millimetres. The swing needle is required for

zigzag and **satin stitch**, but also for any **automatic stitches** and patterns. You can change the widths on the dial as you are stitching in order to grade a satin stitch. For a successful large stitch width you may have to adjust the tension if your machine does not do this for you automatically. For more information see **swing needle** and **satin stitch**.

STRAIGHT STITCH

All sewing machines produce a straight stitch on their simplest setting (i.e. without touching it when you switch it on), using the feed dog and an ordinary sewing foot. The length of the straight stitch available varies, but is usually up to 4mm. The numbers marked

on the dial or screen represent the length in millimetres.

Many sewing machines now have automatic tension controls, and even sensors for the depth of the fabric under the foot, and they will set the tension automatically for you, bearing in mind the stitch length you have chosen (or that the machine has chosen) and the fabric being used. These controls can be overridden, or you may need to set them yourself on your machine.

The normal tension on the machine, set when it left the factory, should do for most normal sewing. This will either be a stronger mark between a + and – sign, or it will be number 5. For larger stitches or on finer fabrics you may need to reduce the top tension to avoid puckering. To make sure that both the top and bobbin tension are equal, see **correct tensions**.

Rows of ordinary straight stitch can be used to influence the colour of a fabric, or change its surface texture in the way the light is reflected, particularly if the tensions are a little tight and the fabric is allowed to pucker. Machines generally offer the option, with the aid of a knob or button, to work backwards and forwards while doing straight stitch with foot and feed dog in place.

Straight stitch can also be worked with **free motion embroidery** without a foot or feed dog. You are now the guide of the machine, and can decide on the stitch length and direction. As a starting point with free motion embroidery, it is a good idea to start by attempting **fillings** with a straight stitch. With the fabric in a hoop and using a correct hand position, draw rows of straight stitch side by side to fill in the fabric vertically, horizontally, and then at 45° in both directions. This really helps you to get the hang of moving the hoop while keeping it always in the same position (top, bottom, left, right). Then try drawing simple objects with a straight stitch. Short stitches are easier to create more or less the same size, and the fabric being pulled through the needle is less, so you are less likely to pull and bend the needle, which might cause it to hit the cover plate and break. However, with practice you can create longer stitches by moving with the rhythm of the machine: start off with a slow machine speed and gradually increase the speed. You will decide for yourself which you prefer – the delicate accuracy of small stitching which can be placed just so, or large stitches that create a movement and vitality with perhaps a sketchy finish.

See **straight stitch fillings** and **colouring in** for other ideas for free motion straight stitch.

STRAIGHT STITCH FILLINGS
COMPUTERIZED EMBROIDERY

A series of running stitches used to cover large areas. Different fill patterns can be created when altering the angle, length and repeat sequence used to create the stitches. Most design programs include a wide variety to choose from which can be placed in the areas to be stitched on the program, usually using the paint pot filling technique – that is, the area to be filled has to be defined within closed lines.

The stitches can be flat (weave stitches) or form a textured design (embossed stitches) for a **decorative fill**. As a general rule, stitching weave stitches is much less bothersome than embossed stitches where the thread seems more likely

A collection of straight stitch fillings in weave stitch and embossed stitches on a computerized (Janome) machine.

Free motion straight stitch fillings. Square: straight stitch blocks in different directions with a variegated shiny rayon thread. Diamond: weave stitch with a variegated thread. Fillings: worked in small circles or granite stitch. Apples: worked with variegated thread and following the form of the circular shape. Star: straight line diagonal filling using a variegated thread. Arch: 'drunken wiggle' in variegated thread. Circle: vermicelli stitch.

relation to the design of the embroidery or the original drawing. Note that some fillings cover the entire ground easily, such as **encroaching satin stitch**, **weave stitch** or straight lines, while others will leave part of the ground showing through, such as '**drunken wiggle**', **vermicelli** or **encroaching circles**. This must also be born in mind in relation to the required result and whether the background is already coloured, or will require colouring or dyeing.

STRETCH FABRIC
Stretch fabric requires special working conditions when sewing if it is not going to be pulled out of shape, although if you wish to manipulate it, just tug it as you are sewing and have a good time experimenting – every stretch fabric will behave slightly differently. Trying to keep stretch fabric in shape is probably more difficult. Always use a ballpoint or stretch fabric needle for sewing to avoid snags in the fabric and difficulty in needle penetration. To avoid stretching on an area of embroidery, whether freehand or computerized, put a firm backing fabric or **stabilizer** behind the work before starting. It will be best if the backing fabric is ironed on or bonded to the fabric, as the glue of the stabilizer will protect the fabric from stretching or puckering.

STRETCHING
Before embroidery can be made up into the intended object or for any presentation, it may be necessary to stretch it back into shape. There are exceptions, such as vanishing fabric work that was pinned out before vanishing the fabric, or laid flat under a weight to dry; embroidery on felt or other fabric where the stitching has been done deliberately in such a way as to manipulate the fabric, and pull it out of shape; or stitching on plastics and leathers and other delicate surfaces that will not benefit from the stretching process.

to break because of the constant changes in machine speed. Slowing the machine speed, thus reducing the stitch count in the design, can help. Any program or machine will give details and images of the fillings available on your machine programs.

FREE MOTION EMBROIDERY
There are an enormous number of filling stitches that can be used for colouring in areas of free motion embroidery. When working, try to choose filling stitches that have a suitable texture for the area that you are filling or **colouring in**, in

However, most embroidery will benefit from being stretched. Any puckering or work that is grossly misshapen can be dealt with at this stage, and the final work, even if it is only a small sample, will look much better afterwards.

Hand or machine stitched embroidery is usually stretched by dampening the work, then pinning it out on a board and leaving it to dry naturally. Once dry, any natural gums or starch in the fabric will help the final piece to retain its shape. It is for this reason that for an important piece of work a natural fibre ground is preferable. If there is not enough natural gum in the fibres, the puckers may come back after stretching, although starch or a light coating of PVA medium on the back of the work can help this. Stretch the work with the stitching face down, wait until it is thoroughly dry, then add starch, wallpaper paste or PVA to the back of the fabric. Note that if the embroidery is not thoroughly dry, these products can bleed through to the front.

Stretching an embroidery, making sure the edges are straight and using a cord as a guide.

TO STRETCH AN EMBROIDERY
Embroidery can be stretched using the following step-by-step method:

1. Use a plywood board and cover it with a thin blanket or old flannelette sheet.

2. Dampen the embroidery with a garden spray – not too much at first: if there are stubborn wrinkles you can add more water later.

3. Place the embroidery face up on the board so that you will be able to see the result of your stretching. Secure the centre of each of the sides with good-quality drawing pins, making sure that the work is taut.

4. Now work outwards from those pins, always pinning opposite sides, and stretching the work as you go, until it is completely stretched and pucker-free.

5. Allow the work to dry naturally, away from direct heat.

TO STRETCH A LARGE PIECE TO A PARTICULAR SHAPE
Firstly, follow Steps 1 and 2 above.

3. Place the embroidery on the board, face up. Stretch a thick, easily visible thread over the embroidery to represent the desired finished sides. Attach this thread to drawing pins placed at the corners of the work. The pins should not go through the fabric, as you will need to pull it. Where the threads cross, check that you have accurate right angles.

4. Start at a corner, and pin one side to line up with the string. Then start on the adjoining sides. If this method is to work, you will have to deal with any problems as they arise. Sometimes it is necessary to put a few pins in the opposite side, or finish a corner. You may need to pin out the work, then go back to an area and work on it again. Re-dampen as often as necessary.

5. The larger the piece, the stronger the drawing pins will need to be; you may need to use carpet tacks.

No pins should be placed too close to the work, as they may rust and cause stains. If this is likely, use stainless steel tacks.

6. If the work is in danger of not retaining its shape, allow it to dry, unpin it, flip it over and stretch it again, face down. Now you can treat the back of the work with starch or glue to hold its shape.

OTHER POINTS TO NOTE

■ Embroidered garment pieces can be treated in the same way. Make templates of the shapes required.

■ For **dyed** or **painted** fabrics, where you are not sure about the fastness of the colours used, lightly dampen the backing blanket and not the embroidery.

■ For **quilted** or **built-up surfaces,** be very careful not to flatten the work. The backing layer (only) of quilts can be stretched to avoid this.

■ For layers of fabrics, if the puckering is unsightly and stretching the pieces all together doesn't seem to be effective, try stretching each layer individually. Pin the bottom layer as close to the embroidery as possible, then the next layer just outside this line, and then the next. Separating the piece into the supporting layer and then the rest may be sufficient.

■ Stretching **canvas work** requires special attention. Work as if stretching a large piece to a given shape, but with the embroidery face down. Canvas work can go badly out of shape and glue will almost certainly need to be applied afterwards to help it to hold its shape. It may need to be very damp to get it back into shape – allow it to dry naturally, then apply glue to the back. If you are using wallpaper paste, be careful to avoid any areas of appliqué.

■ On some embroideries certain lines in the design may need to be straight – contours of windows or other building details, grids, etc. If they are not straight once the work is stretched, put pins into the centre of the work to try to bring these into shape, at the same time trying not to spoil the overall shape of the embroidery piece.

■ If you have a large piece worked on cold water vanishing fabric – you can't dampen it! However, you should be able to stretch it on a plywood board, putting the pins very carefully into the work itself. Once stretched it can be sprayed hard with water – even using a garden hose – to vanish the fabric. Leave to dry on the board.

STUMPWORK
A 17th-century embroidery technique, also known as raised work, that is still popular today. It is based on three-dimensional embroidery in relief, usually of natural objects and figures. Many embroidery techniques are included, as the stumpwork piece was frequently the 'pièce de resistance' of a long education in embroidery.

Stumpwork bee. See diagram on page 107.

The most popular technique, and the one that is most frequently associated with stumpwork, is needlemade lace.

Lace objects can be made on the machine that resembles these original stumpwork pieces, using vanishing fabrics, particularly any cold water vanishing fabric, as it leaves a residue in the fibres. A **granite stitch** or small **circles** recreate the effect of needlemade lace rather well, and the edges of any object could have florist's wire incorporated within a satin stitch to add firmness and the possibility of sculpting the piece of embroidery. More considered stitching might give a more realistic appearance, for example leaves could be stitched to give a smoother appearance, with a reference to the veins found on leaves included in the stitching. **Raised appliqué** and **padded satin stitch** are also used in stumpwork. See also **needlemade lace, soft sculpture, three dimensions, wire.**

SWING NEEDLE
The ability of the needle to move from side to side as well as up and down in order to produce a **zigzag** or **satin stitch**. It is also essential for any decorative stitches produced on the machine using the feed dog and foot.

The first machine capable of producing a zigzag was invented in 1882, but the production of a machine on a commercial basis dates from 1908 with the Singer 107 class (**Irish**) trade machine. By 1913 this swing needle machine, with a zigzag of 12.5mm, was largely available to the embroidery industry and used in training colleges.

The first swing needle machines available for the domestic market date from the late 1950s and were manufactured by Bernina. The numbers on the stitch width dial refer to the number of millimetres that the stitch covers. Generally you can find from 4 to 6mm ($^1/_8$ to $^1/_4$ inch) on simple machines. Widths of up to 9mm ($^3/_8$ inch) are available on some computerized machines under specific conditions of operation. Tension becomes a problem that needs to be well understood with these larger zigzags, as it has to be set quite loosely if the fabric is not to pleat.

The hole in the needle plate will also correspond to the 'bite' or width of zigzag stitch available on the machine.

TACKING (BASTING)

Many machines offer the option of making large tacking (basting) stitches of 1cm (³/₈ inch) long or more. Some use a technique whereby the take-up arm goes up and down with the normal rhythm of the machine (thus feeding through the thread) but the needle only goes into the fabric to form the stitch every second, third or fourth stitch. Used with normal feed and a foot in place, this gives long tacking stitches that are easily undone for use in normal sewing. With free motion embroidery the extra length available with these stitches can be used to produce long decorative

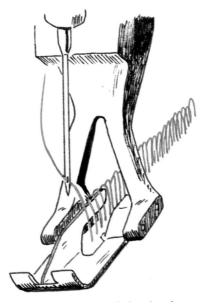

An open zigzag over a tailor's tacking foot can be used to add loops as texture to an embroidery

stitches for a difference in texture. Extra-wide satin stitches can be created by using the **jump stitch** technique of moving the fabric in the hoop from side to side with the rhythm of the machine. Your machine handbook will tell you if your machine has this facility. See also **fringing** and **laid stitches**.

TAILOR'S TACKING FOOT

Known as the tailor's tacking, basting or fringe foot, this foot has a raised bar at the front for the thread to go over (it is used with an open or closed zigzag). It produces large loops that can be left as they are or they can be glued from the back and cut to make a fringe (or tailor's tacking!). Used with a large open zigzag, this can offer another layer of texture to an embroidery. A satin stitch makes a dense fringe.

TEFLON FOOT

A presser foot with a Teflon finish, available for some machines. It glides easily over the fabric and is therefore useful for sewing fabrics that might otherwise be marked by a foot, such as leather, plastic or velvet.

TEMPLATES

Templates can be bought or made for patchwork, giving the correct shape and size for the finished patch. It is necessary to add on the seam allowance. This method is most particularly used for hand patchwork where stiff paper templates can be used for each patch (for example hexagonal patchwork), but making your own templates for machine patchwork or appliqué can also be useful.

Templates are used in computerized machine embroidery to aid in the placement of the fabric in the embroidery hoop, and the placement of the hoop on a ready-made garment if this is where the embroidery is to be placed. Templates in clear or opaque plastic or paper may be provided with the hoop or with a purchased embroidery design. You can make

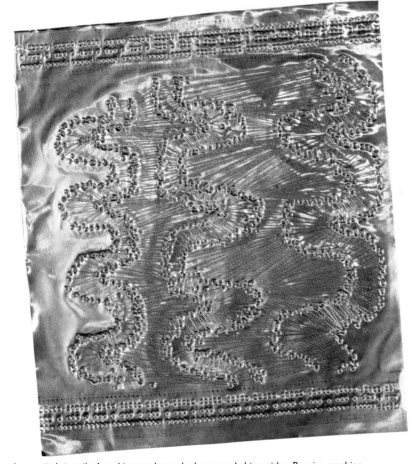

Jump stitch in tailor's tacking mode worked on metal shim with a Bernina machine.

your own template for a design that has no template, or that you have made yourself, by stitching it onto a test **stitch-out** first and making a paper template from that, or by printing off a template from your computer program.

TENSION SETTINGS

See **automatic tensions, bobbin tension – correct, straight stitch, satin stitch – tension, tension techniques**.

TENSION TECHNIQUES

Tension techniques can literally add another dimension to machine embroidery. By increasing the top tension or loosening the bobbin tension, the bobbin thread is pulled through to the top of the fabric to varying degrees. This can be effective for creating textures or adding more colours to the work.

Tension techniques can be used with ordinary stitching and automatic patterns, free motion embroidery and even computerized embroidery, to good effect.

The top tension is governed by a tension wheel that can be either numbered or marked from plus to minus. On a computerized machine, you will have to override the automatic tension and reset it on the computer panel. Your handbook will tell you how to do this. For ordinary free motion embroidery you may well have set the top tension on 3 or on the buttonhole mark that is often displayed on the tension wheel. This shows the best position for satin stitch and it also works well for free motion embroidery. You may also adjust a machine with automatic tensions if you find that the bobbin thread is pulled through when trying to stitch

normally with free motion embroidery. The normal tension will be 5 or where there is a thick mark. If the top tension is increased, the top thread will pull the bobbin thread through to the surface of the fabric. It is easiest to do this with a cotton or firmly twisted rayon or polyester thread to prevent excessive thread breakage.

Quite a few tension effects can be achieved by gradually tightening the top tension, including **colour spotting** and a light **whip stitch**. However, when the tension is very tight, the top thread may break more often, and certain delicate threads will break frequently. To increase the effects of the change in tension, you can start to loosen the bobbin tension, which will make it easier for the top thread to pull the bobbin thread through the fabric. It is important to keep a tighter

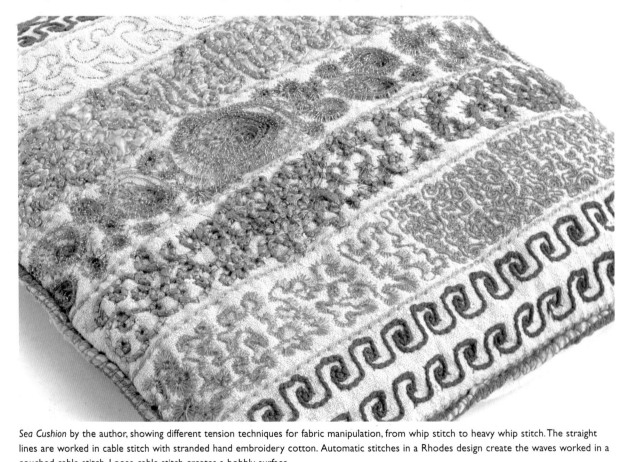

Sea Cushion by the author, showing different tension techniques for fabric manipulation, from whip stitch to heavy whip stitch. The straight lines are worked in cable stitch with stranded hand embroidery cotton. Automatic stitches in a Rhodes design create the waves worked in a couched cable stitch. Loose cable stitch creates a bobbly surface.

tension when loosening the bobbin tension: if both tensions are loose the thread won't know where to go and the threads may break.

You can experiment with altering the top tension anywhere on the plus side (more than 5) of the tension wheel to find different effects and see at what point, if any, there is unacceptable thread breakage.

With the top tension set on 6, you can start to adjust the **bobbin tension**. A screw on the side of the bobbin case adjusts the bobbin tension spring, whether the bobbin is horizontal or vertical. You may wish to note the original position of the screw, particularly on a horizontal case. Many horizontal cases can be pulled out of the machine and suspended just like vertical bobbin cases to reset them correctly; see **bobbin tension – correct** and **horizontal bobbin race**.

To loosen the bobbin tension for tension techniques simply loosen the screw in an anti-clockwise direction. If you are not sure how to do this, check in your handbook. It is best to loosen the screw over a surface (your stretched fabric in a hoop will be ideal) as the screws are generally very small and easily lost if they should spring out. However, you are unlikely to unscrew it to this degree until you start to do **cable stitch**.

To start off, unscrew the screw by just 'ten minutes' on the 'clock' and progress in this fashion to get an idea of the different results. At each change, suspend the bobbin case (if it comes easily out of the machine) to see what effect it is having on the flow of the bobbin thread, and check the result on the embroidery.

There are a few other criteria that can have an effect on the given results:

■ If the fabric is very stiff or layered, the bobbin thread will be more difficult to pull through, so a looser bobbin tension and tighter top tension will be necessary to achieve the same results as on a lightweight fabric.

■ If you are using metallic threads, they pull through the fabric with more difficulty, so again the tensions will have to be adjusted more than usual.

■ The speed of your stitching will also have an effect. A faster machine speed will produce a lesser degree of whip or feather stitch, but a greater degree of bobbles in loose cable stitching. Using different tensions you will be able to achieve **cable stitch, colour spotting, feather stitch, moss stitch, whip stitch** and **whip stitch cord**.

On some sewing machines the bobbin tension can be bypassed completely, if wished. See **bobbin tension – bypassing**.

TEXTURE
For various textures, experiment with the following:

■ Texture in stitching: **satin stitch, satin stitch blocks, straight stitch fillings, zigzag fillings.**

■ Texture with tension techniques: **cable stitch, feather stitch, whip stitch, whip stitch cord.**

Venice by Katherine Harris. A beautifully textured piece with fabric, found and dyed fabrics, paper and metal.

■ Texture in the surfaces chosen to work on: **felt, knitted fabrics, leather, muslin, net, plastic, scrim.**

■ Texture in the way the surface is treated: **Bondaweb, fabric manipulation, heat treated fabrics, nappy liner, paint, puff paint, quilting, Softsculpt, Tyvek.**

■ Texture in things added to the surface: **appliqué, applying cords, beads, metal shim, metal wires, scrim,** and other fabrics.

■ Texture in the way the surface is worked together: **integrating, building up surfaces, worker stitches.**

THREAD BREAKAGE

There are many causes of thread breakage, particularly in machine embroidery, and therefore many remedies:

■ If the top thread breaks when starting off, you may be holding the top thread too tightly for those first few stitches. Holding the bobbin thread firmly, allow a little give in the top thread. If you have difficulty in mastering this, start off with the needle in the work, and hold the threads firmly. This can also cause the needle to break on the first stitch, as the needle will hit the cover plate. More recent machines are less fussy about the threads being held, or may have a cutter that retains them.

■ If the thread breaks straight away, with the noise apparently coming from the bobbin area, the thread is almost certainly not in the take-up lever/arm on the top of the machine, so check this, or just rethread the machine.

■ The top thread (and the needle) breaks more easily if the stitches are very large, simply because you are pulling the machine along faster to make the larger stitches. If you pull when the needle is not in the correct position, you will break the thread or needle. Practise stitching smaller

stitches by increasing the machine speed and moving the work more slowly. If you wish to make larger stitches, you can gradually master this as the sound and the rhythm of the machine become more familiar. Putting on the darning foot can help, as the rhythm of the machine becomes more apparent.

■ If the thread breaks or frays on the top of the machine while stitching, it may be that the top tension is too tight. If you wish to maintain a tight top tension, try using a stronger thread, or change to a **topstitch needle** or **embroidery needle.**

■ If the thread you are using is particularly delicate (a cheap rayon or floss, or a metallic thread) it may require a slightly looser tension, or change to a bigger needle or an embroidery needle.

■ If the top thread seems to be getting caught in the bobbin, it could be that you have overloosened the top thread – or have you put the foot down? If the foot is down, but the machine behaves as if it is not, put it down again firmly – this can happen from time to time.

Thread breakage may be caused by incorrect threading. If it happens repeatedly, it's usually better to rethread and start again rather than trying to spot the error. Check that the bobbin is assembled correctly.

■ If your design needs a particular thread that insists on fraying and breaking, using the **darning foot** and an **embroidery needle** can improve your chances of getting a good result.

■ If you have tried all of the above, including changing the needle (was it a cheap one, bent or worn?) then it may be that the machine is out of alignment – in which case it's time for a service.

THREADING A MACHINE

It may seem obvious, but correct threading of the machine is vital if

it is to work properly – and it's astonishingly easy to get it wrong. There will be a guide through to a top tension wheel, a lower hook, a take-up arm which pulls up excess thread once the stitch has formed, then one or two hooks as it takes the thread down with the needle. Your handbook will guide you on features specific to your machine.

The most frequent cause of repeated thread breakage immediately you start stitching is that the thread has missed the take-up arm. If you have just threaded up your machine and it doesn't seem to be stitching correctly, you can look to see what is wrong, but there is a good chance it will escape your notice. It's a good idea to just rethread the machine even if you can't see the fault – it's amazing how many times it can be missed.

For threading two threads (twin needle or two threads at once in the needle), put one thread on each side of the tension wheel if possible. For three threads this is not possible, so place two on one side, one the other. If you need extra spool holders these can be bought to fit at the back of the machine, or wind some bobbins and use those if you haven't enough space for more than two spools. When using two or more threads through the needle it is worth using a **topstitch needle** or **embroidery needle** to prevent excessive thread wear.

THREADS

See **hand embroidery threads, machine embroidery threads, matt threads, metallic threads, shiny threads, thread thickness, variegated threads.**

THREAD TENSION

See **correct tension** and **tension techniques.**

THREAD THICKNESS

Thread thickness is given in numbers. For machine embroidery threads the most usual is from 50 (the finest) to 30, although both thicker and finer threads do exist.

Although this is a standard measurement in theory, in practice it tends not to be, and a number 30 thread from one manufacturer will be similar but may not be identical to the number 30 made by someone else. For most machine embroidery this will not be important. Where it might cause problems is in computerized embroidery when using a design with a high **stitch density** and changing from one make to another – so do be aware of the problem.

If you have a range of fine machine embroidery threads and wish to produce a thicker stitch for a particular embroidery, you can easily double or treble the thickness by putting two or three threads through the needle at once as a **multithreaded needle.**

Other thicker threads can also be used for machine embroidery. Using a 100 or 110 needle, a number 12 pearl cotton can be used on top of the machine, and even a number 8 can be used with number 120 or 130 needles. Such large needles are more difficult to come by.

Embroidery needles for machines have a slightly larger eye for their size, so thicker threads have less difficulty passing through them.

Topstitch needles have an even bigger eye.

If you wish to use even thicker threads for your machine embroidery, you will have to put them on the bobbin and use **cable stitch.**

THREAD TIE-OFF
Many machines now have a facility for automatic thread tie-off, or a holding stitch for use with normal sewing, computerized designs and automatic stitches. This usually involves a small backwards movement and several stitches on the spot to secure the threads, which can then be cut off (or are automatically cut) without any danger of unravelling.

For free motion embroidery you can employ a similar method of starting with a small circle virtually on the spot, which will secure the threads when starting, so that you can cut them immediately. When jumping from one area to another, or changing the top thread, you can generally cut the top thread to the fabric, leave the bobbin thread attached, and the work will not come undone. This only becomes problematic when using very large stitches or wide satin stitches, where you may want to take more precautions. You can tie off the threads correctly, with a little stitching on the spot or by passing them through to the back of the work and tying them off, particularly if the piece of work is important.

THREE DIMENSIONS
See **bags, boxes, jewellery, raised work, Softsculpt, soft sculpture, stumpwork.**

THREE-STEP ZIGZAG
This is an **automatic stitch** working a **zigzag** with a wide stitch in three steps or small stitches. There is also a two-step zigzag. The three-step zigzag is made for working on stretch fabrics and applying elastic, as it will give without breaking. With careful control you can use it to create a lace on vanishing fabric.

A three-step zigzag can be used to make a delicate lace on vanishing fabric.

TOP FEED

The feed on all machines is from the underside of the machine with the use of the **feed dog**, which is two or more series of teeth that rotate backwards and forwards in such a way as to make the fabric move along as it is stitched. The problem is that in some instances this does not give enough pull. If the fabrics are heavyweight or slip easily, or you have to match a plaid across a seam, or you are working with quilting, leather or plastic, it is useful to have a top feed. This is a feed that works on the foot and feeds the top fabric as well as the bottom one. On some machines, an additional pull-down device attaches to the foot to help the feeding motion; for other machines you may require a **walking foot**.

TOPPING

This is the term for a stabilizer used on top of the fabric during the embroidery process to protect the fabric and the stitches. When stitching on a pile fabric such as velvet, towelling, or fabrics that have been treated with **dimensional fabric paint** or other relief material, the stitching can become lost in the surface. If this is not the desired effect, a topping stabilizer can be used during the stitching process to prevent the stitching from embedding into the surface. The most usual form would be a cold water vanishing fabric which will sit on the surface during stitching, and can be washed away afterwards. A topping can be used for free motion embroidery or computer machine embroidery.

TOPS: COTTON, SILK, WOOL

Fine threads, carded or uncarded, provided for spinning and weaving, but which can also be used for felt- and paper-making. They can be dyed and included in embroideries for a textural effect, and included in **lace** or fabrics created on vanishing fabrics. Layered with binding agents or bonding powder, they can make a non-woven fabric surface which can also be stitched into. See picture on page 18, and also **trapunto quilting**.

TOPSTITCH NEEDLE

This type of needle has a larger and longer eye relative to its length, which allows two or three threads to be passed through the needle at once, with less danger of shredding. They cause less wear on metallic threads and can also take thicker, woolly machine threads. This protection is particularly useful when working on difficult fabric surfaces or heavy embroidery. However, the needles themselves seem a little more fragile because of the size of the thread hole, but the large hole does also make them easier to thread.

TOTALLY STABLE

A paper-type **stabilizer** that can be ironed onto the fabric for computerized embroidery, or even free motion embroidery or decorative stitching, if required. Two layers can be applied if the work is to be very heavy. It does give a totally stable surface for the machine embroidery that is very unlikely to pucker or pull out of shape when stitched.

TRANSFER DYES

Transfer dyes are painted or drawn (some are available in the form of wax crayons) onto a paper surface, then transferred to the fabric using a hot iron.

These dyes are intended for synthetic fabrics or fabrics with a percentage of synthetic content. The colours may seem bright when you paint them onto the paper, then pale when transferred to the fabric. Differences in the brightness of the transfer will vary according to the paper used for the original painting (between a normal paper, greaseproof or tracing paper) and the quantity of synthetic in the fabric, as well as its surface quality. A painting can be used more than once, giving paler results on reuse.

As the transfer dyes are transparent, different layers can be overlaid.

By stitching in just one synthetic colour on a fabric, then using transfer dyes to colour the whole, interesting results can be obtained, especially if the nature of the thread is different to the fabric: the colours will be taken up differently according to the fibres used.

Do remember when you are using transfer dyes that the design will be reversed when it is printed onto the fabric.

Transfer paper can transfer a computer image from an inkjet printer onto a pale-coloured cotton, but some brands leave a plasticized surface, so will need stitching, or, perhaps, fabric bits added. See pictures on pages 76 and 78.

TRANSFERRING DESIGNS

PENCIL DRAWING

Using a hard (H) pencil to prevent excessive marking, the essential marks of a design can be made on the fabric. This method can be used if the work is going to be heavily stitched, coloured, appliquéd, etc. and at the end of the work the pencil marks will be covered, as the marks will not readily wash out. Pencil can also be used to trace the design onto vanishing fabric, as the fabric will disappear once the work is completed – though do use a hard pencil. Indelible pens can also be used on some vanishing fabrics.

VANISHING PENS

There are many vanishing pens on the market. The result produced by some of them can disappear in light (beware, this can happen overnight), while others need wetting, washing or removing with an eraser provided. If you are using the sort that needs wetting, make sure that this is appropriate to your design and methods. Note also that the marks may be fixed by ironing or can reappear with ironing. There is some question over certain types of these pens and their long-term effect on fabric, particularly if it is stored

Shadows by Cas Holmes. Paper, emulsion transfers, machine and hand embroidery.

in airtight conditions (inside a box, or framed). Ensure you are happy with the brand you are using, or that long-term preservation of the work is not an issue (use for quick samples, but not for fine exhibition pieces, for example).

TRANSFER PENCILS AND PAINTS
A design can be outlined with a transfer pencil or painted with

transfer paint onto a sheet of paper, greaseproof paper, or tracing paper, and then transferred onto the fabric using an iron. For transfer paints, the quality of the paper chosen (whether it is more or less absorbent) and the nature of the fabric (whether it is more or less synthetic) will have quite a marked effect on the brightness of the colours in the resulting transfer.

LIGHT BOXES AND WINDOWS
If you need to trace off a design onto a fabric that is not see-through, you can either use the tracing paper method (see page 164), or a light box or window. A light box is a box with a glass top that is lit from the inside. Tape the drawn design to the surface and the fabric over the top. You can now see the design through the fabric

and trace it off using your preferred pen or pencil. You can use a window in the same way as a light box, by taping the design and fabric to a window with good light and tracing off the design.

TRACING PAPER AND OUTLINE STITCH
Trace the outlines of the design onto a good-quality tracing or tissue paper. Place it on the fabric and secure it with pins or a few tacking (basting) stitches. Using the **darning foot,** work an **outline** running stitch over the drawn lines. This stitch may be done in a colour and thread that will later merge with the background, for example a white cotton thread on a matt white fabric ground (perhaps to be dyed later). This stitching may become part of the design: for example, two rows of metallic stitching can be used to outline a figure drawing, or changing colour where appropriate these first outline stitches can become part of your design. A vanishing thread could be used and vanished later on in the making process. For this to work it is best to use two rows and small stitches so that they don't pull up when you gently tear off the paper to leave the outline stitch.

TEMPLATES
See **templates.**

TRANSPARENT FABRICS
A wide choice of transparent fabrics is available: silk and nylon chiffon, cotton organza, silk organdie, polyester organdies and shimmer fabrics, some of which are 'shot' (the warp and weft are different colours). These transparent fabrics are easily available and have become very popular in general use.

They can be stitched on, perhaps delicately, to produce beautiful fabric in their own right, perhaps with **all-over designs.** They can be layered together and then areas cut out or cut through to create **shadow work** or **mola work.** A background can be built up of different see-through

Narbonne outline (as picture on page 112), worked on transparent fabrics cut out with a soldering iron, and then bonded with bonding powder.

colours, layering colours together a little like a watercolour, building up light and shade to describe an object – this is particularly effective for figure drawing.

Chiffon and organdie can be stretched and distressed by pulling with your fingers, or they can be stitched on the cross while pulling to create distortion.

Synthetic fabrics respond well to burning, either to finish edges or to create holes without the problem of fraying. Transparent fabrics can be burnt through to reveal other fabrics underneath, as the polyester transparent fabrics respond particularly well to **burnt cutwork** worked with a **soldering iron. Nets** can also be treated in exactly the same way.

When stitching, consider the importance of the colour of the bobbin thread if it is likely to show, and use a ballpoint needle for these fabrics. They are fine, so the finer the needle the better – use a 75 or 80 on these fabrics, unless you are using metallic threads.

Transparent fabrics also work well incorporated into vanishing fabric lace, as their delicacy can complement a finely stitched lace structure, yet provide areas of firmness to support the work.

Transparent fabrics can also be interesting when they are used in **trapunto quilting**, with objects of interest trapped behind.

TRAPUNTO QUILTING

A traditional method of quilting that involves stitching around a shape through two layers of fabric. The backing fabric behind the shape is then slit open and stuffing is added from the back of the work before the slit is stitched back together again. The backing needs to be firm so that the stuffing pushes out on the right (top) side of the quilting. The fabric on the top side should respond well to light – such as a pale or shiny fabric – so that the manipulation of the fabric has an effect as the work

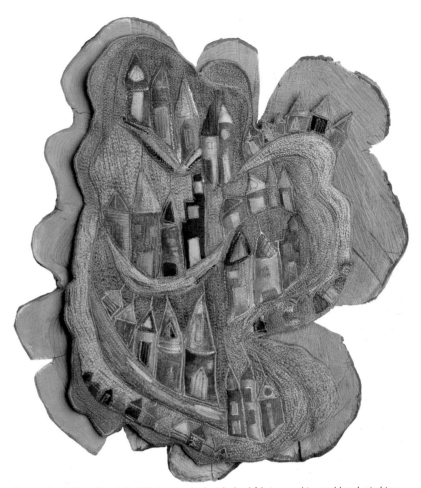

Fantasy Beach Huts II by Julie O'Brien, worked with dyed fabrics, machine and hand stitching, and trapunto quilting.

catches the light. The outlining stitches can be done by machine, but the sewing together of the slit must be worked by hand.

Using this traditional technique as a starting point, one can experiment with all kinds of variations. By using a see-through top fabric, the colour used in the stuffing could play a role – different coloured felts or dyed **tops** could be used. Different objects could be put into the sandwich: beads, buttons, found objects of any nature, made perhaps in ceramic or metal. The sandwich could be made of plastic or net. Objects can also be sandwiched between two layers of fabric and then stitched around to hold them in place. The advantage of adding them from the back after

the stitching has been worked is that their position is more secure, as they cannot move during the stitching process. For the more difficult items, there won't be problems with getting the work under the needle bar, or breaking the needle if it accidentally hits a hard object.

TRIANGLES

Triangles can be stitched together in **patchwork** or created with cutting and piecing techniques in Seminole patchwork.

In **free motion embroidery**, triangles can happen accidentally when trying to stitch small **circles** or **granite stitch** as a novice embroiderer. Very simply, if the machine speed isn't fast enough for

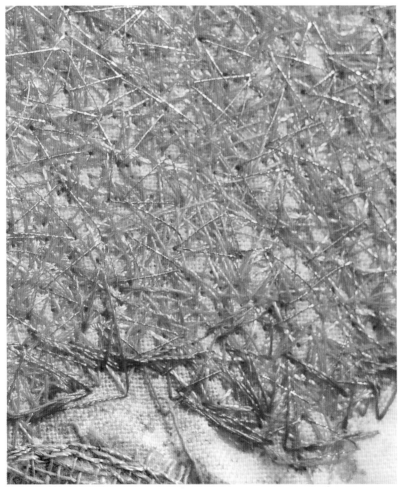

Hydrangea. Detail of machine stitched triangles with large stitches in free motion embroidery.

the speed that the hoop is being moved, the machine will make large stitches instead of small ones. So the movement you are making may well be circular, but the large stitches have a tendency to make triangles. Use a faster machine speed and slower movement to cure the problem. On the other hand, the large stitched overlapping triangular forms that emerge have a textural quality that could be useful.

TRIPLE NEEDLE
Like a twin needle, three needles are presented on the same shaft instead of two. A triple needle is threaded from three spools, placed on the two normally available spool holders. If you have an additional spool holder you can use a normal

spool for the third thread; if not, this can be threaded onto a bobbin and placed on the same holder as one of the spools. Two threads will go down one side of the tension wheel and one thread down the other: one thread to each needle. Triple needles do not create pintucks in the same way as twin needles do, but they can be used for decorative stitching.

If you are using **automatic patterns** with a specific stitch width it is essential to try out the complete pattern first, turning the machine by hand, to make sure that the needles will not hit the needle plate during the stitching. If this does occur you will have to use a narrower stitch, and then test the pattern again. Bear in mind that there is only one

bobbin thread for the three top threads that are stitching side by side. So if you don't want the surface of the fabric to be pulled by the stitching, use a slack tension on the top, and if necessary on the bobbin as well. The reverse side of the work can also be interesting, especially if you have used different colours for each of the threads on the three spools.

On many machines it is possible to select twin or triple needles up to a certain width, and the machine will set the appropriate width for any automatic pattern. Check your handbook for details.

TROUBLE SHOOTING
See **bird's nest, correct tension, needle breakage, thread breakage, threading the machine, uncontrolled spool off.**

TWIN NEEDLE
Twin needles are sometimes called double needles. They consist of two needles held in one shaft that will be held in the usual place in the machine. They are generally found in size 80 and 90 and come in various widths, stated in millimetres, which indicates the gap between the needles. You will find them in 1.6mm, 2mm, 3mm, and even 4mm (up to $^{1}/_{8}$ inch) sizes.

Twin needles can achieve interesting decorative effects with **automatic stitches**, in which case an embroidery foot suitable for zigzag or satin stitch is required. If used for pintucking there is a selection of **grooved feet** to choose from.

For decorative effects using straight lines, you will be able to stitch as normal. If you don't wish to create pintucks, use soft, slightly loose tensions top and bottom. The resulting stitching might be useful for **hand whipping**. When using **automatic, zigzag** or **satin** stitches, check that the width of stitch that you have chosen will work without the needles hitting the needle plate at the most extreme points in the design. On machines that have a twin needle button, this will ensure that the design will fit for twin needles, usually up to 2mm – see your handbook for details. If you don't have this facility, or the needles are wider than those allowed for, do the following check:

Put your twin needles in the machine, select the stitch and width you want, then, turning the machine wheel gently by hand, work through the whole of the design. Look carefully at the plate as you do so: the needles may enter, but may be touching the side of the plate and bending slightly. As you turn the wheel by hand this doesn't break them, but once the machine is running they will splinter.

Twin needles are expensive, so it's worth taking precautions to look after them. Use fairly loose tensions so that the fabric is not pulled up, because there is only one thread on the back holding these

two separate threads on the front. You can experiment with different colour choices – contrasting, harmonious colours, or close shades can give very different results. Note that the back of the work can often look interesting too, especially with **triple needles**.

For pintucking with twin needles, see **pintucking** – see also picture on page 14.

TWIST
The amount of twist in a thread will be one of the determining factors in its tensile strength. The others are the nature of the fibre itself (whether it is cotton, rayon, polyester, nylon or acrylic, for example) and the length of the fibres used in its production. Simply looking at a wide variety of threads and comparing them with each other will give you some idea of their comparative twists.

The greater the twist in the thread manufacture, the greater its strength. However, a high twist will affect the way the thread lies on the fabric, and the way in which it mixes with adjoining threads. High-twist yarns are useful for work where the effect is likely to be linear – quilting for example – but if a subtle blending of many colours is required it may be better to choose a thread with less twist, even if it is more fragile.

For computerized embroidery machines, a fairly highly twisted strong polyester thread is often recommended, but other threads can be used, generally without problems – it rather depends on the type of embroidery design the machine is being asked to produce.

TYVEK
Tyvek is a flexible, tough non-porous material used where such a

Detail of *Crazy Quilt* by Isabelle Girodet. The work consists of layers of fabric, straight stitch lines, burnt layered fabrics and rolled Tyvek beads incised with a soldering iron.

fabric is needed, for instance to bind legal documents and keep them secure.

It shrinks with heat, buckling and bubbling easily with heat from an **iron** or a with a **hot air tool**. If you use an iron, place the Tyvek between two sheets of **baking parchment** to avoid sticking. When using a hot air tool, do so on a heatproof, non-stick surface. Endless experiments can be tried: ironing on one side to make bubbles, turning over, and ironing again to turn the bubbles into holes. Its structure is fascinating, as are the results that can achieved. It can be dyed or painted before or after heat treatment – each method gives a different result. Acrylic paints, dyes or watercolours can be used. Waxed products can be used afterwards on the surface, metallic polishes added, and so on.

Like many popular techniques, it can look gimmicky if its use is not carefully integrated into the work with adequate stitching, colouring and design preparation. So enjoy experimenting, but think about the end result you are aiming for.

For stitching purposes use a darning foot and a sharp needle of a suitable size for the thread you are using. The Tyvek may tend to stick to the bed of the machine, so it's worth using a backing fabric. No hoop is required.

Many other commercial plastics can be used in the same way. Always use a mask when heat treating fabrics because of potentially dangerous fumes. See also picture on page 77.

UNCONTROLLED SPOOL-OFF

The tendency of certain threads to run more thread off the spool than can be used by the stitching process. The excess thread gets caught around the bottom of the spool holder and will at first cause the top tension to become tight, and then the top thread will break.

This problem is particularly noticeable with silky rayon threads

that can slip off the spool more easily. The cheaper ones are often not very well wound in the first place, but the delicious colours make them worth using. Metallic threads can also suffer from uncontrolled spool-off. The problem occurs more often on non-electronic machines, as the machine runs on a little after you take your foot off the pedal and doesn't stop so calmly. The controlled stop/start of electronic and computerized machines virtually eliminates this problem. Machines with horizontal spool holders are also less likely to suffer from uncontrolled spool-off.

To deal with the problem there are several things that you can do:

■ Look out for badly wound reels of thread. Try to rewind the last portion of thread if it is particularly untidy, or wind it onto a bobbin for use on the bobbin, or on the top of the machine.

■ If a thread is causing particular problems, look out for the change in the top tension which indicates that the thread is caught around the bottom of the spool holder. You should be able to catch it in time before it actually breaks, and rewind it. It'll save you re-threading the needle.

■ Try to keep your machine speed as even as possible. Stop and start gently, avoiding abrupt speed changes. This is especially important on non-electronic machines.

■ With a vertical spool holder, make sure you have a piece of felt on the base of the holder. All machines come with a perfect circle of felt with a hole cut in it for the spool holder. This helps immensely.

■ A piece of carpet cut out to imitate this piece of felt can have a greater effect than the felt, though it may increase the top tension a little, so look out for that.

■ Various products can be purchased to help you prevent uncontrolled spool-off. A metallic thread holder fits between the vertical spool holders and carries the thread off the top of the spool.

■ Vertical spool holders with hooks, holding various quantities of thread, and generally positioned behind the machine, can be purchased, generally for use with computerized embroidery machines. Stretchy nets that hold the spool prevent uncontrolled spool-off.

■ A rogue thread can be placed in a jar behind the machine which is threaded up as normal. The thread runs off as required and turns in the jar.

■ Note also that the larger cones of thread suffer less from this problem.

UNDER-STITCHING: AS A DECORATIVE TECHNIQUE

Different effects, particularly using colour, can be achieved by under-stitching before working the top layer of the embroidery. Using under-stitching in a complementary colour underneath the final colour, or a cool colour under a warm colour, or a warm colour under a cool one, is a technique much employed by pastel artists and it can have an interesting and enlivening effect on the final embroidery. Using straight lines of stitching in an opposing direction to the final work is most effective, but you may also like to experiment with different **fillings, zigzag** and other textures.

This is a very useful technique when working with **vanishing fabric**, because the nature of the fabric requires some sort of weaving or lace structure in order for it to hold together once the fabric has been vanished. By stitching an under-stitching in a carefully chosen colour, different from the final layer but offering a warm/cold contrast,

Collioure au Soleil by the author. Worked on hot water vanishing fabric in layers of stitching. Different colours are used in the bobbin to add to the overall colourful effect.

or in harmony with the final colour, the embroidery will be richer in effect. The under-stitching should be worked in a different direction from the final layer, as it will serve to create a 'woven' structure to the embroidery once the vanishing fabric has been vanished.

Under-stitching can also be effective if it is worked in a metallic thread to create a subtle amount of glitter on the top surface of the piece of embroidery.

When working on scrim and muslin, a layer of under-stitching in open zigzag can pull the fabric apart, making a textural surface for

the future embroidery, but also offering some stability to the whole surface of the work. Again, the colours can be carefully chosen for maximum effect.

UNDER-STITCHING: COMPUTERIZED MACHINE EMBROIDERY

Also known as underlay stitches. These first stitches of the design, often in a large open zigzag, will stabilize the design area and make sure that the base fabric is secured to the stabilizer (if it is not a bonded one). These underlay stitches will help to hold the whole design in

shape on the fabric during and after the stitching process.

It's quite interesting to use only this part of a given design, on a pile fabric for instance, as a starting point for something creative. Depending on how they are laid down they may also help some areas of the embroidery to be raised slightly above the surface.

UPPER TENSION

The tensions used to control the tension or tightness of the top spool thread. The presser foot lever must be lowered for the upper tension to be engaged. See **tension settings**.

VANISHING FABRIC

There are now many vanishing fabrics to choose from: **dissolvable film, hot water vanishing fabric, magic film, Solusheet, Soluweb, vanishing muslin, vanishing paper** – all have their uses. As a general rule, cold water dissolvables leave a residue in the fabric that can leave a little or a lot of stiffness. This may be useful: if not, the finish can be improved by washing in hand-hot water, then in fabric softener. Hot water vanishing fabrics leave no residue, but need to be boiled, which may cause difficulties in the choice of fibres used on it. Muslin requires the use of a hot iron, an oven or a hot air tool, which can damage some fibres (dissolving from the back can help), but leaves no residue.

Dissolvable and vanishing fabrics can offer openness to structures, to create lace or new fabrics. Layers of additional stitching to create extra texture and depth can be added to existing embroidery, or three-dimensional bits and pieces can be made and added. Raised work or stumpwork techniques can be adapted for use with vanishing fabrics, or fully three-dimensional forms such as boxes, bowls and jewellery. Pictures made entirely on vanishing fabric can create their own edges to leap out of the usual rectangular format. The fact that the bobbin thread may be visible allows more colours to be incorporated and underlying threads can thus add more depth and interest to such pictures.

Any fabric created on vanishing fabrics will have to hold together once the fabric has been dissolved. An underlying structure of a grid or circles will do this, but may not always be appropriate to the total design. Even if you use a grid structure to start with as a security measure, try to develop structures that are relevant to your final piece. Practising different patterns of stitches can be useful. When you are stitching on a normal fabric, if two threads appear to touch on a given drawn line, this is sufficient. However, on vanishing fabric if two threads are meant to touch this will affect the whole structure of the final fabric, so make sure that they do cross over so that the work will hold together. Satin stitch is only a closed zigzag, and with the fabric removed it will become a straight line, it is therefore necessary to work it over several rows of straight stitching so that it will hold together. Heavy areas of overlapping open zigzag can work, although there may be the occasional hole where the threads don't inter-link.

Working with tension techniques needs careful thought and planning. Bear in mind that it is the position of the fabric between the looser tension techniques that allows the loops created to have a form. If the fabric is removed, the copious amounts of loose thread and loops will make for a disorganized tangle of threads and an unclear design. Whip stitch, or whip stitch cord and cable stitch, will work well and can be used as a **gimp thread,** which is a thicker thread used in lacemaking to pick out shape and stabilize a design. Any other tension technique, such as feather stitch, can be worked on vanishing fabric as long as there is an existing surface of stitching or applied fabrics.

For specific techniques see **boxes, broderie anglaise, creating fabrics, cutwork, jewellery, lace edges, lacy effects, openwork, stumpwork.**

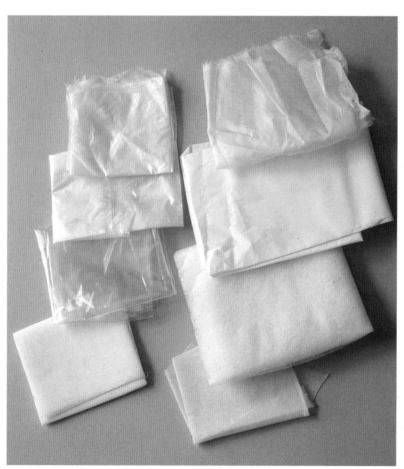

Examples of vanishing fabric. Clockwise from top right: Hot water vanishing fabric, vanishing paper, Soluweb, vanishing muslin, Solusheet, dissolvable film in heavy, medium and light weights.

VANISHING MUSLIN

Vanishing muslin was originally used to provide a strong support for industrial Irish machine embroidery, thus avoiding the need for a hoop, and this was a boon to early art college embroidery students, who found new and exciting uses for this fabric. It can be painted or embroidered and left intact, with the knowledge that after a certain amount of time exposed to air and light it will no longer disappear. Areas that you do wish to get rid of can be ironed away, or a whole piece can be foil-wrapped and placed in a medium-hot oven. It will also vanish under a blast from a **hot air tool** – probably the simplest way. The disadvantages of this fabric have always been the small pieces of burnt fibre that have been difficult to eliminate even by brushing or rolling between sticky hands. This has made it less suitable for pastel or white embroidery, as the burnt fibres can be very visible. A new product called Heataway seems to do away with this problem, as it is much easier to eliminate all of the burnt fibres. The advantage of vanishing muslin is that once vanished, the quality of the lace or stitching is exactly that of the fibres you have used, with no residue to cause hardening or starching of fibres.

Working on this fabric is relatively easy, although do be careful with tensions that are not overtight. If using tension techniques such as whip stitch, be careful that the bobbin has been sufficiently loosened, and that you are not just relying on a tight top tension, as this can damage the fabric. As the fabric is fairly stiff, you do not have to use a hoop to stitch on it, which could damage these delicate fibres – this can be useful if you want to work on large areas. Although the ironing or heat process involved might damage certain fibres, rayon, cotton and metallic threads all stand up pretty well, although the brilliant metallic quality can be lost. Iron from the back for best results.

American alternating current irons can have a problem with this product as they do not produce enough heat, so use an oven or hot air tool if you have problems.

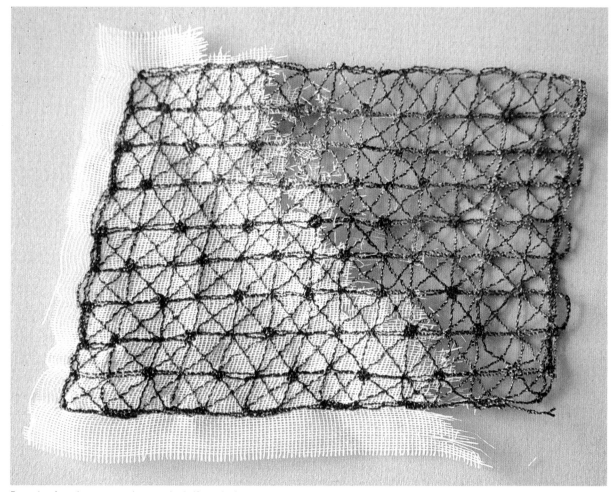

Example of stitching on vanishing muslin, half vanished.

VANISHING PAPER

A cellulose-based paper product that disappears when washed out under a cold tap. It can be stitched on and vanished like any other vanishing fabric. It is stiff, so doesn't require a hoop, but as with any paper, it can tear as it is being stitched, so the quality of the stitching becomes quite variable, just as in the first attempts at **guipure lace**, which were on paper. Its disappearance can be inhibited with gesso or nail varnish, so it could be painted on and required areas left as paper.

VANISHING THREAD

A clear thread that disappears in cold water, it is sold for tacking (basting) seams together. It is excellent for creating **moss stitch**, and can also be used to **transfer a design** onto a fabric with marks that can be got rid of afterwards.

VARIEGATED THREADS

A variegated thread is a thread that changes colour within the same spool of thread, for example in different pastel shades, harmonious but different greens with blue/greens, yellow and orange with red, and so on. These threads can be a little obvious if they are used on their own, but used with care they can be useful as they offer a greater quantity of colour more quickly than just plain threads. If you look at the needle and just above it to see what colour is coming through next, you will be able to move to an area of the design where that colour is appropriate, and thus be able to avoid unsightly stripes. Mix the thread into a surface with lots of other colours, or one that picks up on one of the colours in the variegated thread. Use the variegated thread in the needle with a plain thread that picks up on one of the colours in the variegated thread. This can be useful for straight stitch fillings or even satin stitch. See also **shaded threads**.

Organism by Lesley George. Silk/viscose velvet dyed with Procion dye. Metallic transfer foils are added with bonding glue. The detail around the top is made from foiled synthetic velvets applied with free motion stitching. Some pieces have been machined and burnt away with a soldering iron before applying. Pieces of machine-embroidered stocking wiggle around the appliqué; these are hand beaded into place for an encrusted look. The beads on the main garment are hand 'whipped' onto machine stitching. The edges are satin stitched. The whole garment was stabilized with Stitch and Tear while it was being embroidered.

VELVET

Velvet has a cut pile which gives the fabric its beautiful, rich surface. There are different qualities of velvet and velveteen, with different-length piles, and different draping qualities. Velvets can be dyed, or etched with devoré techniques using special pastes to give texture to the surface. For this the pile needs to be a cellulose fibre (rayon or cotton) on a silk ground.

It is necessary to take certain precautions when stitching velvet. If the stitching is worked directly into the velvet surface, it will be lost in the pile, so to ensure that this does not happen, a topping fabric can be used. A fine cold water vanishing fabric placed on top of the velvet will ensure that the stitching does not bed into the surface. The topping can be washed away afterwards.

This method of keeping the stitching from being lost into the surface of a fabric can also be used for towelling and corded fabrics.

VERMICELLI STITCH

A meandering line that wiggles in and out and backwards and forwards. It can be worked in lines or cover whole areas. It is particularly nice worked in a **whip stitch cord** for extra texture, or in quilting, where it can be used to flatten a background, leaving the areas of the design unstitched and standing proud of the background. On some modern machines it can be found as an automatic linear pattern in the **automatic stitches**. See also **stippling** and **crazy stitch**.

VILENE

Vilene is a useful non-woven fabric, available in white or black, to use as a **backing** or **stabilizer** to strengthen a fabric to keep it from puckering where they may be areas of heavy stitching. Some Vilenes can be glued to the fabric by ironing, as one side may have glue on it. Gluing backing fabrics can be particularly useful if there is to be heavy stitching on a stretch fabric, as it prevents the fabric from stretching out of shape during the stitching process.

Vilene is also very useful in dressmaking to strengthen collars and cuffs. See also **pelmet Vilene**.

VOIDING

Leaving an area unstitched that becomes the design itself. This technique is most often used in quilting where whole background areas are quilted with circles or vermicelli, leaving a blank, soft quilted area that has the design shape but is void of stitching. Voiding may also be appropriate in fabric colouring techniques such as stencilling, printing or silk painting. See also **negative shapes**.

WADDING

See **quilt wadding**.

WALKING FOOT

Available for most machines, a walking foot ensures a good top feed for the top fabric so that seams will match perfectly. It can prevent uneven feed while topstitching, and when using vinyl, plastics and leather. It also prevents the marking that an ordinary foot might leave, and stops unsightly puckers appearing on quilting. The foot may come with a **quilting guide** to ensure the maintenance of parallel lines during stitching.

Muse by Janice Liley, while a student at Opus School of Textiles. Worked on a dyed background with stitched fabric frame. Vermicelli stitching in the background.

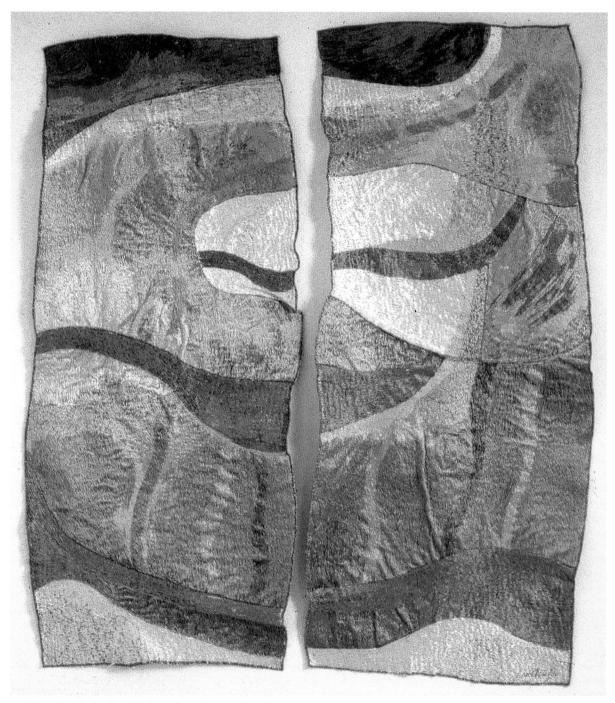

Landfall, wallhanging by Carol Naylor in floss threads with cable stitch.

WALL HANGINGS

Making textile pieces in tapestry or canvas work is an historic aspect of textile art. It was particularly useful for insulating chateau walls before central heating, and making large rooms feel cosy and quieter.

Textiles as hangings have other functions too, most notably as a way of exhibiting pieces that do not have a format suitable for picture framing. A textile hanging can be very large, undulating instead of flat, or even with areas in relief or three-dimensional. Another advantage of exhibiting a textile as a wall hanging is that the true quality of the colours and textures can be appreciated in a way that is not possible if the work is placed under glass. It can also make a room feel warmer!

WATERCOLOUR

Watercolour paint can be a useful medium to take with you, along with your crayons and sketchbook – travel sets are available that take up very little space. A disadvantage is that unless you are particularly experienced, the paint can lack the textural qualities of other drawing techniques that will help you to define the textural qualities to use when embroidering.

A way round this is to use mixed media: watercolours can be used with pen, pencil (wet or dry) and with water-soluble crayons. Try using them on a very textural watercolour paper with oil pastels. Watercolours can also be used as a quick colour technique for colouring fabric. Although they are not fast to water or washing, the colours will be as light resistant as they would be on paper – and that will depend on the quality of the watercolours. See pictures on pages 143 and 148.

WAVE STITCH

An **automatic stitch** is available on many machines which has the appearance of waves. The needle works from left to right across the width available, while feeding forward at the same time – not unlike a **three-step zigzag**, except that the edges are rounded off. It can be used with the feed dog up and a foot on, but you can also set it, then use it for free motion embroidery.

If you don't have a wave stitch available, you can nevertheless achieve the same appearance in free motion embroidery by imitating the movement yourself. It's useful for working over areas of small pieces of appliqué to blend them, or moving colours gradually from one colour zone to another, as layers of different colours can be added. It can be used in much the same way as a 'drunken wiggle', which sometimes has harsher edges and is a little less rhythmic. It can also create an interesting open structure on vanishing fabrics.

Doorway at Roussillon by the author. Worked on hot water vanishing fabric. The wall surround is worked in wave stitch, allowing for an open, shabby feel of peeling stucco.

WEAVE STITCH

A free motion embroidery filling using straight stitch. Draw a number of vertical lines, taking care not to make the points loopy, but keeping the turning points as points. Then draw a number of horizontals in the same way. The hoop movement is backwards and forwards a few times, then from side to side a few times. Move along the vertical or horizontal row a little more each time so that the new set of stitching is in a different area. Keep working to fill, or half fill in the background. Other colours can be introduced, or

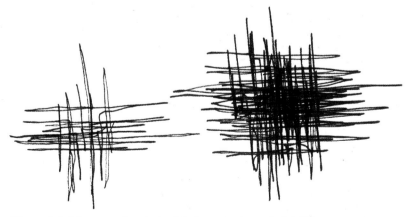

Weave stitch, left open and worked solidly. It can also be worked at 45°.

this can be an interesting fill with a **variegated** or multicoloured thread. With this method you can completely fill a background, or it can be used to **integrate** pieces of applied fabric and merge them into the background. See pictures on pages 41 and 154.

WHIPPED SATIN STITCH

A whip stitch technique can be worked with a satin stitch or open zigzag, bringing in a greater degree of colour and texture in a fairly haphazard way as the threads pull through to the top in loops on either side of the zigzagging top thread. A whipped satin stitch can be quite effective for producing the texture of wood or bark in an embroidery. For details of how to create a whip stitch see below.

WHIP STITCH

Whip stitch is where small loops of thread are brought to the surface of the work using a tight top tension, often in conjunction with a loosened bobbin tension. See **tension techniques** for the methods involved in setting it up on the machine.

The textured result in the stitching can add a bolder appearance to the line if it is virtually covered by the bobbin thread. Depending on the colour contrasts used, a broken appearance can be given to the line and the colour result modified by using colours a shade darker or lighter than the top thread, with larger stitches. Colour contrasts or harmonies can also be used. See **colour circle.**

Many stitch patterns and fillings can be used for this technique: curving stitches will pull the bobbin thread through more for a greater effect, while circles or granite stitch, vermicelli and 'drunken wiggle' will all create an effect. Satin stitch and zigzag can also be used. A fast machine speed will result in less thread being pulled through to the top. The speed at which you move the hoop will also have an effect:

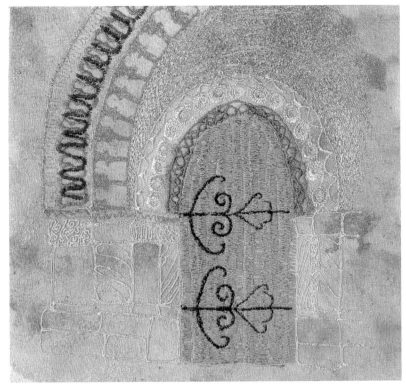

'Church Door', by the author. A collection of tension techniques from whip stitch to heavy whip stitch and a whipped satin stitch door.

more thread will be pulled through if you move faster, particularly if you are working in curves.

Whip stitch can be created using any threads you choose. However, if you are relying on an increased top tension rather than on a loosened bobbin tension, it is best to use a stronger thread on the top, perhaps a cotton thread, polyester, or the 30s rayon threads which have a heavier twist than the 50s. Pulling through metallic threads is a little more difficult as they resist the fabric, so you will need a greater top tension and/or a looser bobbin tension than normal to create the same effect with a metallic thread. The effect can be worth it, particularly for **colour spotting.** Using a metallic thread for a whip stitch is a good way of adding a little bit of glitter interest to an embroidery without overdoing it.

Because less thread is pulled through to the surface (as opposed to **feather stitch**), whip stitch can be used to good effect on vanishing fabrics without too much concern. A whip stitch that pulls even more thread through to the surface of the fabric because the bobbin tension has been loosened a little more, yet is not as loose as a feather stitch, can be referred to as a **heavy whip stitch.** Lumps and bumps can be included if the needle stays stitching in one place from time to time, but don't overdo it or the top thread is more likely to break.

A whip stitch with very little bobbin thread coming through to the surface, created simply by tightening the top tension, can be very useful as a way of introducing more colour into an area – see **colour spotting.** The top thread may also be taken out after stitching a whip stitch or **feather stitch** to create **moss stitch.** A whip stitch stitched in even very small stitches and completely covered by the bobbin thread is called a **whip stitch cord,** or corded whip stitch.

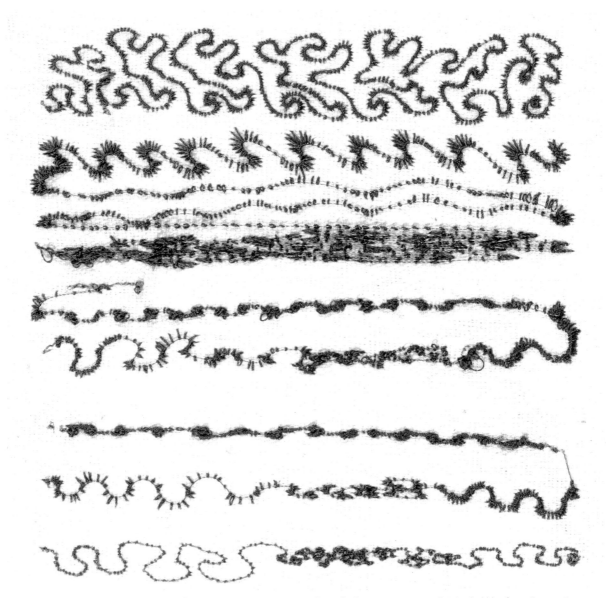

Example of whip stitch, whip stitch cord, heavy whip stitch, and whip stitch worked at an uneven speed giving bobbles from time to time. Four different tension adjustments were made to work this sample.

WHIP STITCH CORD

A **whip stitch** stitched with very small straight stitches is called a whip stitch cord, or corded whip stitch. Set up a whip stitch as described above, with a tight top tension and a loose bobbin tension, so that the bobbin thread easily covers the top thread, though without loose loops. The stitches should literally be one next to another as in satin stitch, so that the top thread is entirely covered

with loops and is not visible at all. Staying on the spot can cause bobbles, but be careful: if you stay too long on one spot the top thread can break. Extra-thick top threads can be used, such as buttonhole twist, to give a more raised quality. This lovely decorative stitch works well with **'drunken wiggle'**, **crazy stitch**, **vermicelli**, **circles** and on **edges**. It can also be used with a **gimp thread** on **vanishing fabric lace**, or for a **whip stitch edge**.

WHIP STITCH EDGE
See **edges**.

WHITEWORK
Refers to embroidery that is colourless and worked with white or unbleached cotton or linen thread. There are many traditional whitework hand embroidery techniques, but the term most specifically applies to fine pure white stitching on fine lawn or sheer fabrics. The poor pay and working

conditions of the whitework embroiderers in Ireland and Scotland have been well documented. Their poverty and conditions were not in the least alleviated by the advent of hand machines and Schiffli machines, which produced the same kind of work, some types quickly becoming known as Swiss embroidery.

Types of whitework with fine lines, padded satin stitch and delicate tracery are still produced on the industrial market today, and programs exist for domestic computerized embroidery machines. The notion of all-white or one-colour embroidery can be fascinating, and it's worth giving full attention to a sample piece all in white to see just what textures can be achieved with different stitches, and the use of matt and shiny threads on a fine fabric ground.

Fabric manipulation or iridescent surfaces (see **metallic transfer film** and **metallic threads**) could be a way of developing the techniques still further.

WIDE SATIN STITCH
The width of satin stitch available on any given machine is dictated by the hole or throat in the needle plate and the capacity of the swing needle. The number on the width control dial or on the push button control indicates the width in millimetres and is generally from 4 to 6. On some computerized machines the throat in the needle plate, and the capacity of the swing needle, exceeds the width given on the width control. This is very simply because for a very wide zigzag the tensions have to be very carefully adjusted (use a loose tension – otherwise the fabric will pucker), and it will be best to use a stabilizer under the fabric, such as Vilene or **Stitch and Tear**. With these imperatives in mind, some manufacturers have preferred to leave the very wide satin stitches as programmable, rather than programmed.

Wider zigzags can also be created using a **jump stitch** if your machine has a **tacking (basting)** facility.

WIRE AND WOOD
Wire can easily be incorporated into any embroidery around the edges or even in the middle of work, to add form and structure to the piece. This allows the embroidery to be sculpted once it has been finished. Small pieces can be made for **stumpwork**; larger sculptural pieces, such as vessels, boxes, bowls or jewellery,

may also benefit from the inclusion of wire. It can be placed in seams or pintucks, or covered on ordinary fabric or incorporated by working a satin stitch or zigzag stitch over the wire to hold it in place. You can risk incorporating it with ordinary free motion straight stitching over it if you want its inclusion to be less noticeable, but there is a greater risk of hitting the wire with the needle. Wire can obviously be used in vanishing lace and fabric techniques and **needlemade lace**.

Shows the stitching of the cocktail sticks into place on the existing triangles for *When You Find Your Way to the Sea*. Worked on Soluweb. The straight lines on the Soluweb are where several offcuts from previous projects have been stitched together to be reused.

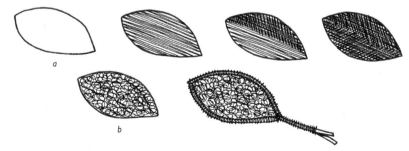

Working leaves or petals over wire on vanishing fabric. First draw an outline with straight stitch (a). The outline is filled with small circles to resemble needlemade lace (b). Straight stitches are used to create a flatter, leaf-like surface. A wire is satin stitched into place once the leaf is finished.

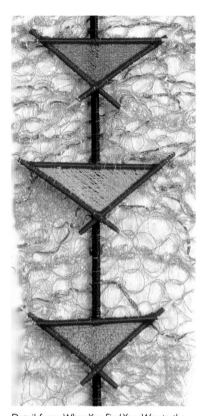

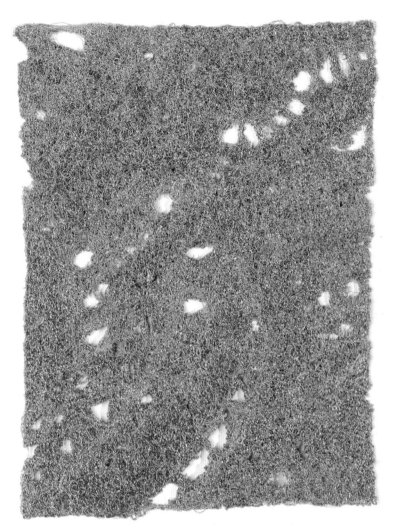

Detail from *When You Find Your Way to the Sea* worksheet. The boats are first worked as triangles on cold water vanishing fabric. While not dissolved, the cocktail sticks are applied with a satin stitch worked with free motion embroidery. The kebab stick used for the mast was covered with a machine satin stitch. The boats were stitched onto the mast by hand. The background is made with two layers of plastic film, ironed together with hand stitched threads sandwiched in between. The sandwich is then stitched with circles in free motion embroidery.

Lacy fabric created with the Sfumato program on the Janome 10000. The black stitching created as a base on the program was simply left out. As the program generally stitches in a sort of vermicelli stitch and this doesn't hold together on vanishing fabrics, worker stitches in small circles with a gold thread were added all over the piece once it was stitched. The worker stitches serve to integrate the whole into a luxurious gold setting, but also work to hold the embroidery together. The programming of this embroidery can be seen on page 136.

Any type of wire can be used, from covered florist's wire (being green this may be useful) to thick electrician's 2.5mm (¹⁄₈ inch) or even larger – this gives a good solidity to the work. Be careful not to hit the wire with the needle. If the wire is fine, the needle may push it into the bobbin race of the machine, which may cause damage if you don't stop working as soon as it happens. A thicker and stronger wire will break the needle, which could be considered preferable.

Copper or coloured wire, or heat-treated copper can also be left visible on the surface of the work, in between stitching, for its decorative effect, or it could become part of the structure of the work itself and moulded, twisted, woven or coiled as an incorporated decoration.

Another interesting way of incorporating strong forms for sculpture, in pintucks, seams or for stitching over with a satin stitch, is to use cocktail or wooden kebab sticks.

WIREFORM
See **mesh.**

WORKER STITCHES
Stitches that do not necessarily play a prominent role in a piece of embroidery, but are essential in integrating the different surfaces involved in the work, or helping with colour movement. Machine worker stitches might include: **crazy stitch, 'drunken wiggle', open zigzag, straight running stitch, vermicelli, wave stitch, weave stitch.**

WORKSHEET

Although a worksheet may be similar to a **design sheet** in appearance, it is essentially a working space on a large sheet of paper where ideas can flow and develop, perhaps following through to a conclusion. Several worksheets may follow a theme and eventually lead to a project, with technical samples and all the requirements to be able to work it. It may also include a number of dead ends (or they could be redeveloped later) or drawings and samples that do not become part of the final project. If you need to illustrate a proposal for a commission, or create a design sheet for an exam, you may have to choose the most pertinent parts and rework them onto a design sheet.

A worksheet can be a very effective way of 'brainstorming ideas', and is better than a sketchbook, in which when a new page opens, the old page closes. On a single worksheet, or series of worksheets, all the ideas are there and can continue to have an influence on the development of the main theme. If you have a studio with enough wall space, pin them up as you go.

WRAPPED EDGES

Unworked edges of stitched pieces or even solid vanishing fabric embroideries can have their edges wrapped on the machine to give a soft but solid edge, often a little irregular in appearance.

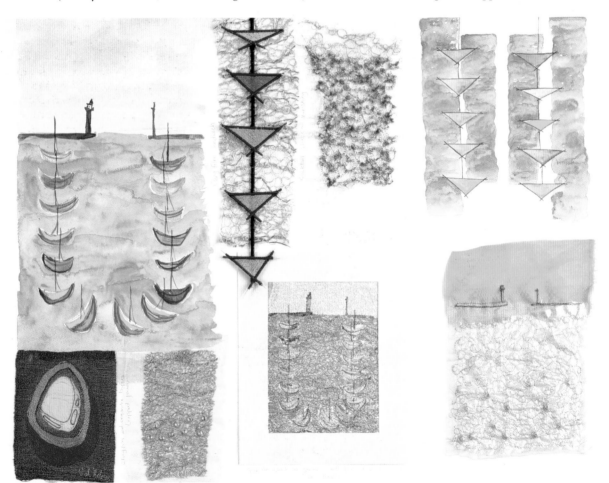

When You Find You Way to the Sea, worksheet by the author. From an original watercolour done in the port of Mèze, on the basin of Thau, which has a small access into the Mediterranean in southern France. The watercolour was influenced by an exhibition including the work of Dufy seen that morning, and my ideas about Mèze. The work developed in response to the image. Details are included on pages 124, 178 and 179. Bottom left: Boat worked on hot water vanishing fabric. Next: layers of plastic film with hand threads sandwiched between them, stitched with circles, then applied to a polyester organdie with jewels from a broken bracelet sandwiched with circular machine stitching. Next: see page 124. Next: polyester organdie with iridescent metal transfer bonded, layered onto an iridescent fabric and stitched with a wave stitch and circles, incorporating beads to manipulate the surface. Top row: watercolour. Next: see pages 178 and 179 Next: bubblewrap stitched in circles with feather stitch. Top right: proposition for installation. Hanging pieces of plastic film treated as on page 179. Boats worked on kebab sticks for an increase in scale, attached to a cord or wire mast.

Tile: Xpandaprint centre with free embroidery worked with a spring needle. The edges of the fabric are wrapped with stitching. Mounted on a raku-fired ceramic tile. By the author.

Wrapping the edge of a solid fabric or embroidery with free motion embroidery: at right-angles to the edge (left), at 45° to the edge (middle), with cross-hatching (right).

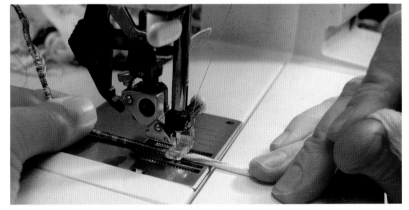

Wrapping cords on the sewing machine.

Use free motion embroidery, but working with a darning foot, and with a straight stitch setting. Work over the edge and into the fabric with a straight machine line, cross-hatching or a circular movement. Different colours on the bobbin and top thread will produce a different result, or the tensions could be offset for an interesting effect. A zigzag stitch can also be used.

WRAPPING THREADS AND CORDS

Cords can be wrapped by placing them under the darning foot and using a zigzag stitch that is wide enough to fall on each side of the cord to be wrapped. A closed zigzag or satin stitch could be used to entirely cover the cord with the embroidery thread, or an open zigzag to allow the cord to show through if this is of interest. A mixture of the two can also be interesting, allowing the cord to show through here and there.

Place your left hand holding the cord behind the needle to pull the cord through, and guide it into place with your right hand. Be careful to use a sufficiently wide zigzag. The thickness of the cord that you can wrap on your machine will therefore depend on the width of zigzag that it will do.

The cord to be wrapped does not have to be a unique thread. Try putting a quantity of handstitch or knitting threads together in a

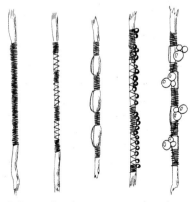

Different ideas for wrapping cords with zigzag and satin stitch.

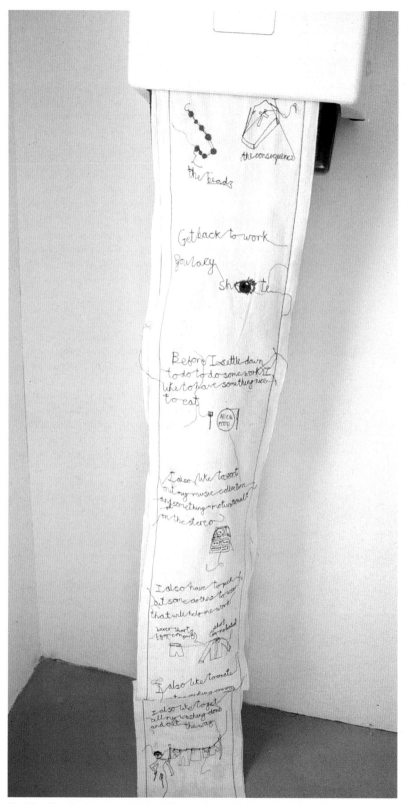

Hand Towel by Elizabeth Lucy Wells, while a student at Goldsmiths College, University of London.

chosen colour range, or with varying textures, and binding these together with an open zigzag. If they become a little unruly, you can just twist them a little as you guide them under the foot, so that the zigzag can wrap them by going into the machine on each side of the cord rather than going through the middle of them.

Beads may also be threaded on a strong thread and included in the cord. Leave space in between the beads on the thread and wrap the thread like the others, allowing a bead to be included from time to time along its length.

Your finished cord can be applied to other embroidery, or it can be used in soft furnishing, fashion garments or jewellery decoration.

WRITING FREEHAND

Although there are many machines with writing and lettering programs incorporated, if you really want to say something personal it's rather nice to use your own handwriting. Writing included on work is inevitably personal, as it will express your own ideas about the subject. It may be a poem, and even if the poem is not your own, it is still you who chose it. Diaries, letters, quotes, notes and signatures become more expressive if they are created with your handwriting.

With a good free motion embroidery technique acquired from practising **circles**, **vermicelli** and **straight stitching** in lines in different directions, you should be able to master a joined-up alphabet. Work in a hoop and keep your hands in the correct position on the edge of the hoop for good manipulation and control. After a few goes you will relearn all the methods of making your writing totally joined up (much easier for machine embroidery) and you will probably be surprised to find that your writing by machine is (frighteningly!) similar to your writing by hand – now you can sign your embroidery work!

XPANDAPRINT

Xpandaprint is a non-toxic medium for printing and painting, which is expanded by the application of heat to give a raised three-dimensional effect. This can then be coloured in a variety of ways and is soft to the touch so it can be stitched without damaging the needle. It also fuses the fabric, which becomes rubberized. It is therefore non-fraying, so shapes and holes can be made without having to worry about the edges.

It comes in the form of a white paste (almost clear when applied, but white again once expanded) that can be applied in a number of ways, depending on the desired effect. It is best applied thinly – more can always be added later. It can be spread, printed, painted in a directional way, stencilled and so on. The type of fabric used, whether it is rough or smooth, will also have an effect on the result, so it is necessary to experiment. It can be cured in an oven, with an iron (between layers of baking parchment), or using a hot air tool. Instructions are usually supplied when you buy the product.

It can be coloured with fabric paint, metallic fabric paints, acrylic paint, pastels, inks, felt pens or even shoe polish! The result can be a bit harsh, so stitching is essential to make the surface your own.

For free motion embroidery the fabric may be put in a hoop to keep it taut. If this is not appropriate, the best solution is to use **Stitch and Tear** or some other **stabilizer** as a backing and use a **darning foot** as the surface to be stitched into is soft. Use a ballpoint needle to stitch with. Bits of fabric or chiffon may be added to the surface to improve its 'textile' quality (otherwise it's a little rubbery). Try stitching into the flat areas, or overlaying the raised areas with **long stitches** (slow speed). See also **puff paint** and **dimensional paint**, and the pictures on pages 49 and 181.

YOUNG EMBROIDERERS

For nearly 30 years the Embroiderers' Guild has had a group especially for Young Embroiderers under 18 years of age. For a time the group was known as the Young Textile Group, but it has now found its former name once again, in reference to the fact that these are young stitchers who will hopefully go on to be members of the Embroiderers' Guild. There is an ideas and news magazine for members, as well as day schools organized at both local and national levels.

Young embroiderers are obviously essential for the future of embroidery, and children can be very enthusiastic about textiles and art. Even if they may have difficulty in completing pieces of work, it must be remembered that many adults suffer from this too! Although embroidery stitches can be learned – and cross stitch projects are popular as presents for young children – I feel that this rather takes us back to the role of our ancestors in inculcating our girl children with the gentile feminine arts, and keeping them out of mischief. Children can be so creative when they are allowed to be, and encouraged. Drawing skills are learnt through repetition and

Xpandaprint on cotton ground with whip stitch cord, heavy whip stitch and colour spotting using a heavy whip stitch and fast machine movement. The edges are wrapped with a light whip stitch tension.

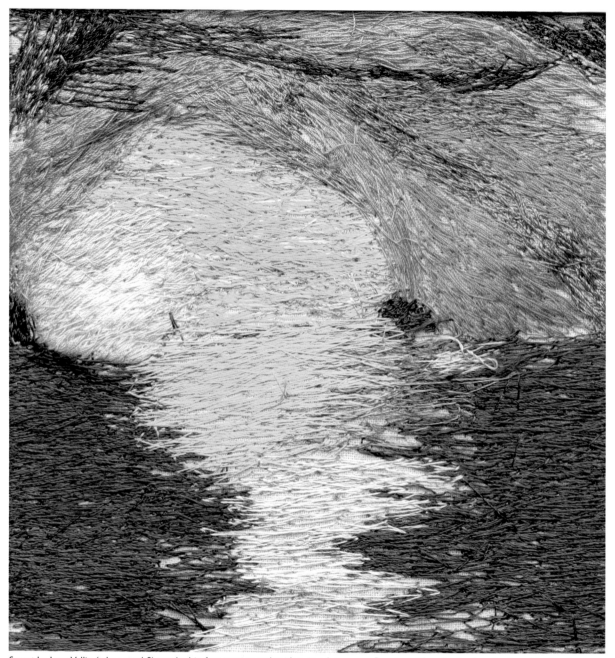

Sunset by Lucy Vallin (when aged 8), worked in free motion embroidery in a hoop on a Bernina with a darning foot in place. No drawing was done before the embroidery was begun.

practice, and are not inborn, and when a child finds that his/her work is valued, he/she will continue to work and produce better and better drawings or objects.

Although free motion embroidery is perhaps a little dangerous for very small children (for the machine and the child),

from the age of seven or eight there should be no problem at all, as long as the child is supervised. I prefer to insist on a hoop and a darning foot being used, which ensures more protection for small hands. A child notices easily the relationship between drawing on a piece of paper and drawing with a sewing

machine, and is not bothered by the notion that with the sewing machine it is the 'paper' (fabric) that moves and not the 'crayon' (needle), which stays in its place. Starting off with the first few stitches yourself is a good idea at first. Check the threading of the machine if you allow the child to do

Computerized embroidery by Joanne Vallin (when aged nearly 5). The castle was digitized from a scan of Joanne's drawing into the Sfumato program. The densities of the stitching were adjusted within the program to achieve the scribble effect of Joanne's drawing. Joanne pressed all the buttons to make the machine (a Janome) work. The dragon was drawn freehand onto a graphic tablet (Joanne's first attempt at drawing directly into the computer) in the Janome customizer program. She then chose the stitches and colours – and signed the embroidery!

it, and be around to listen for problems, such as the foot lever not being lowered! Before getting involved in other textile issues such as dyeing, appliqué, other technical surface creations or even designing, simply give the child a blank piece of fabric and allow him/her to draw freely to get the handle of the machine and to discover this extraordinary mark-making device without too many preconceptions. You may be surprised at how well things can turn out!

Even for very small children the machine can be fascinating. I have held one of my daughters at the age of three on my knee and allowed her to move the ring as I operated the foot pedal. We based the work on a drawing that she had done, so

Le Pull et Mini-jupe de Margot by Fanny Viollet. Detail of the picture on page 111.

that I had a clue about how she was planning to move the hoop. Slightly older children may wish to do things on their own, so automatic stitches and patterns with a foot and feed dog engaged can be used safely to create embroideries.

If you have a computerized embroidery machine, ask the child to do a drawing using just four to six felt-tip pens. The result can be scanned into the computer and will then make an embroidery. A small child will love watching it being stitched and pressing the start/stop button!

YOUR OWN THING!

It sounds obvious, but when you work with sketch and ideas books, worksheets and sampling, the work you create can really be your own and an expression of the things you need or wish to express.

ZIGZAG

A zigzag stitch is worked with a **swing needle** by setting a **stitch width** on the control panel of your machine and using a **stitch length** of more than 1mm. If a shorter stitch length is set, the result will be close to a **satin stitch**. The stitch can now be stitched with the foot on and feed dog engaged. The zigzag can be used as a decorative stitch on its own, or for **applying thread, cord and ribbon**. It can also be useful for finishing off the edges of seams if your machine doesn't have an **overlock** stitch capability.

Similarly, a zigzag can be created in **free motion embroidery** by selecting a stitch width and moving the **hoop** fairly rapidly to produce

the stitch. It is very important to use a correct hand position on the hoop so that the stitch length can be controlled.

You can experiment with different widths of zigzag on top of each other and side by side. Work from side to side for a **sideways zigzag** or **stem stitch**. Try moving in circles or moving slower and faster to change the density of the zigzag.

When the stitch length is small, or the movement of the hoop is slight, a **satin stitch** is produced.

ZIGZAG FILLINGS

There are many ways of filling in or **colouring in** an area with zigzag stitches. **See encroaching satin stitch, satin stitch blocks** and **sideways zigzag**. There are also various **straight stitch fillings** that work well when employed with a zigzag or satin stitch. **Circles or granite stitch, crazy stitch, 'drunken wiggle', vermicelli** and **weave stitch** all create interesting results. See also **bead stitch, bullion knots, french knots, open zigzag, seed stitch, whipped satin stitch.**

ZIPPER FOOT

A long, slim foot with a notch on each side, so that the needle can go into the fabric very close to the foot while the foot is held tight against a zip. The needle can be placed to the left or right of the foot by changing the needle position, using the appropriate button or knob. The foot is also useful if putting piping cord into a strip of fabric, as it will hold the stitching tight against the piping cord for an attractive, neat finish.

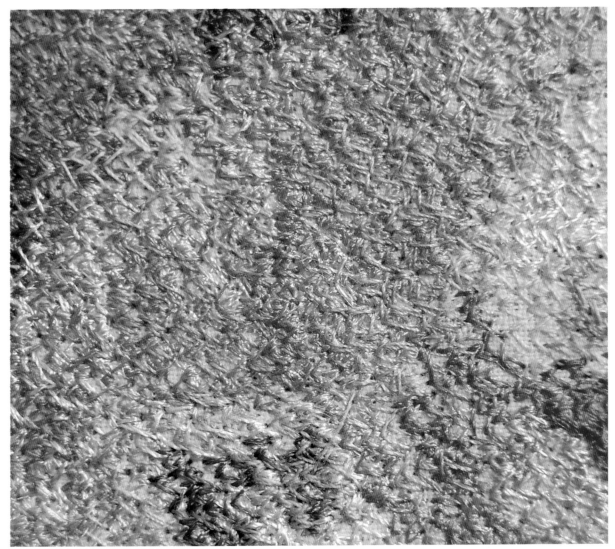

Layers of zigzag taken from oil pastel drawing of a hydrangea.

Hydrangea drawing in oil pastel.

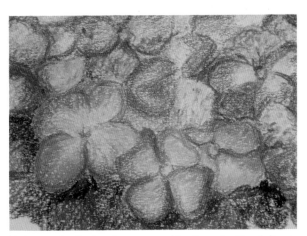

Hydrangea drawing in soft crayon, used for the embroidered slip on page 144.

Appendix on Embroidery Machines

If you're reading this book and considering making an investment in a computerised embroidery machine, I can probably assume that you already have a normal sewing machine. My first piece of advice is: don't trade it in! Using a computerised embroidery machine for ordinary free motion embroidery seems something of a waste, because the wear involved on any parts could prove expensive, although computerised machines are as robust as any other machine, and are certainly capable of free motion embroidery. The main reason for not trading in your old machine is that it is useful to be able to do free motion embroidery on it while your computerised embroidery machine is working away next to you. Many embroidery designs can take hours (the small piece on page 124 took about 3 1/2 hours, not including thread changes). So you can be present to change the threads or rethread if the thread snaps, but at the same time be working on something else.

For the creative embroiderer these machines are probably most interesting as starting points for further work. The surfaces they create can offer a base for further embroidery, spot motifs can be made for inclusion in other pieces, and lace or other structures can also be made and adapted to creative pieces. The personal side can be approached whilst your embroidery machine continues to work on its own.

The whole point of computerised machines for the creative embroiderer is to be able to create designs yourself. Although some simple machines are available at a relatively modest price, if they only work from preset designs this is not really interesting. To create your own designs you will need three things: a computer, a program to design for your machine (more of that later) and a computerised embroidery machine that is capable of taking designs from your computer, either through a direct connection, a USB key, a CD or memory card.

The programs that come with your machine in the package are pretty expensive so make sure they suit you. You may need the program that goes with your machine to upload the design into your machine if it has a direct link, but for the designing itself you can choose from a variety of programs, some available on the internet, that are perhaps cheaper and just as good or better for what you require. Many programs are capable of saving your design into different file types so that they will be suitable for different machines, and you will be able to select the hoop size for your machine on these general programs just as you can on the special program for your machine. This area is worth investigating as there is lot of money to be saved in buying the programs that will suit you first time. It is the program that will ensure the success of your embroidery and not necessarily the machine itself – all of these machines are capable of following the given instructions and of creating nice stitches – although the speed of production can change from one to another.

The other major influence in the choice of your machine may be the size of the hoop available. Check that what is on offer is a true design size. Some machines have big hoops but which have to be turned around and manipulated, and will accept different motifs but not a whole design. As we move on the top end of the market offers larger and larger usable hoop sizes but these machines are very expensive. Also available are embroidery only machines. It is true that when these machines are sewing and embroidery machines, all the best features are included in these top of the range models so that the machine embroiders automatically but is also an excellent sewing machines. This obviously adds to the cost and you can now buy embroidery only machines that look like sewing machines but only do embroidery. These machines are economical and a good solution if you already have a sewing machine that you are perfectly happy with. With the advances in the domestic market semi-industrial machines with large hoop sizes and several needles (perhaps 6 or 8) are now becoming more affordable for the embroiderer who really wants to pursue this area.

For all these machines, their abilities are changing all the time, you may not have the budget for regular machine changes so make sure you get the best choice for your budget in the first place. You may also consider whether your machine allows manufacturers updates, and whether these are included in the package or are paid for as and when on offer.

Choosing to invest in such a machine is a big step, and I would consider the priorities to be: hoop size – the bigger you can design the more versatile will be your machine; good tension – it will be automatic, but it is best if you can override this, both for computerised embroidery, (this can be fun see page 36), and if you are using the machine for free motion or ordinary stitching and finally, ease of sending a design from the computer to the machine.

Once mastered these machines can be a very useful addition to our creative tools. But we do need to master this technology and not be its slave. It's relatively easy to design the stock flat designs so popular on children's clothing and tablecloth edgings, but creative embroiderers will not be taken in by that kind of work – only experimenting and through spending time with these machines and the more advanced programs can other more interesting work emerge.

Corrections and updates

This book was first published in 2003, when the last few type only pages were deliberately included so that I would be able to easily add anything that I felt was particularly important in subsequent reprints. Although the general information about machine embroidery doesn't really change that much, as a professional embroiderer and teacher one is always making discoveries of new materials or new ways of using old ones. Here are a few extra words to add to the Encyclopedia, and a few additions to existing words.

Aquabond

This is a sticky backed cold water dissolvable fabric. The fabric itself resembles vylene dissolvable, also known as **solusheet** or solufleece. It is presented on a brown paper backing which easily peels off to reveal its sticky surface. The fact that this is sticky is very useful for sticking on fabrics to create an **appliqué** or **crazy patchwork** without a final backing – held together uniquely with the stitching that will be added to hold it. Threads can also be placed in exactly the desired position and stitched into place. This technique can be used to create a woven type surface with interesting yarns and threads, simply by placing the threads in one direction to form a warp and stitching in the other to form a weft. The fabric can also be used to hold down fibres such as **silk** or **wool tops** or throwster's waste etc., whilst they are stitched. For ease of use I tend to only take off the backing where I wish to stick down the threads, fibres or fabrics I wish to use. You can score a line through the paper, the required shape and size with a needle or pin, and remove the protective paper from this area. Some people find it difficult to stitch with loose fibres, though threads or fabrics are easier. If you

do get bothered by fibres getting caught around the foot or needle a topping of light weight dissoluble film can be added. I prefer not to do this as it is easier to see colours and textures without and thus to have a real appreciation of the finished result.

Embellisher

Dry needle felting has been popular in textiles for some time, being somewhat easier and less messy than soap and water felting. The results are different and I'm not going to start any arguments here! However because of the popularity of this technique which consists of sticking rough needles into wool again and again so that the fibres become enmeshed and felted together, it seems inevitable that a machine should be invented to replace the hand work. Although attachments can be bought for some sewing machines, these are expensive in themselves and less convenient that a machine destined only to be used as an embellisher. For one thing the very nature of the fixed foot and large hole seems to encourage needle breakage.

These machines generally consist of five to seven rough felting needles held in place (individually interchangeable needles are better and more economic) and an adjustable foot which can be lower or higher according to the thickness of fabrics and fibres being passed under the machine. There should also be a little collecting box for fluff. The machine has no mechanism under the needle, so fluff from the felting process should not be a problem, though check regularly for blockages. This is another argument for an Embellisher machine over an attachment.

So what can they actually be used for? The process of needle felting will enmesh the fibres of one fabric or fibre into another if they are suitable fibrous, and from this premise on one can experiment. The most obvious is felt or wool fibres onto felt. But many surfaces can successfully be used if they have enough fibre content to hold the fabric being felted into it. Even if the fabric felted could be torn away it might be an interesting way of applying it, and further stitching on a normal machine can be added. Braids and threads can be applied. Patterned fabrics can give interesting results from the back. Silk paper can form an interesting surface to felt into. Polyester and nylon voiles create superb effects if needle punched. Once these fabrics are held down all over their surface burning with a heat tool can produce very interesting results. Punching voiles onto an unwoven synthetic surface such as **lutradur** (see below) will not attach them. You can them pull them off and use these fabrics for appliqué and other surfaces as they will be manipulated and changed. Working fibres such as wool, but even silk, and cotton and linen with cotton, heavily into a dissolvable surface such as **solusheet** and then dissolving it will make a sort of paper surface a little like silk paper. These surfaces once dissolved can receive further embellishing or stitching. Many examples of work done on these machines are relatively heavy and come from the felting tradition, by turning it around with fine fibres on dissolvable surfaces, or fine fabrics applied and manipulated the results can be lightweight and quite different.

Hot water dissolvable fabric

The new hot water dissolvable fabric has a different formula from those formerly written about in this book. The HWDF now available will disappear at around 70°C and will shrivel and shrink evenly to produce interesting effects to any work on it or fabrics applied to it at about 40–50°C. This makes it more versatile than its forerunner which had to be boiled in order to disappear.

Lutradur

A product recently discovered by textile artists. It is a polyester non woven fibre available in a number of weights (30, 70, 100 and 120g per m2) which comes to us from the building industry where it is used as a damp-proof membrane. In can be cut with a modelling knife, scissors or soldering iron, it can be holed or cut roughly with a heat tool. Some sources of this product seem to bubble as well as hole if heated with a heat tool. If you prefer it to remain flat it can be pinned out with drawing pins on a wooden board and holed more easily; and it will remain beautifully flat. You can also try the same technique with **tyvek** and **acrylic** and polyester **felt**.

Lutradur colours beautifully. You can use transfer dyes for synthetics, acrylic paint, inks, watercolours, crayons and watercolour crayons, and most other things you can think of. When painting the colours bleed easily when wet, this can be avoided by applying a **gesso** primer before painting, but the surface will become harder and loose its transparency.

It takes stitching easily and the heavier weights (70 upwards) work very well without a hoop. You may find that the stitching manipulates or pulls it out of shape more than you would wish. Although it can be ironed, it cannot be pulled back into shape in the usual way, so if you don't want this result, you use several layers of fabric (2 x 70g for instance) when stitching and it will loose its shape considerably less.

Quilting machines

A recent innovation in the domestic market are machines destined solely for quilting. They have a very long arm, and can be used for free motion embroidery or ordinary sewing but will only do a straight stitch. They generally work at twice the speed of an ordinary machine (around 1600 stitches per minute) and create a very beautiful straight stitch because fewer compromises have been made in the production of this stitch. Compromises necessary it would seem when the machine is also expected to deal with zigzag and width stitches.

A frame is also available for such machines which permits them to sit astride a roller mechanism on which the prepared quilt has been stretched, thus a huge quantity of quilt can be seen and stitched at a time. These vary in size, but can include the whole of the length of the quilt, although the quilt is rolled around the frame so not all of the width can be viewed and stitched at the same time. The whole machine can move up and down the surface of the exposed part of the rolled quilt, and backwards and forwards within the limitations of the long arm of the machine by means of two handle bars which the operate can move easily. A button in front controls machine speed. Preset quilt patterns can even be 'drawn' onto the fabric by following an infra red light as you stitch.

This is obviously an excellent tool for professional quilters, but its speed also makes it an interesting drawing tool for embroiderers as it replicates the speed of the Irish machine. Unfortunately it is only a straight stitch tool.

Sizoflor

Like a fine lutadur, this fabric has made its appearance in the decorative industry for window decoration, wrapping flowers and so on. For this reason one can find cast offs for free, or different colours at a reasonable price by the metre. The colours tend to change with the seasons and fashion. It responds very quickly to a heat tool so do be cautious. The resulting fabrics can be fascinating to include in your work. It can be torn, cut with a soldering iron and layered as it is very transparent.

Twin needles

Now available in 6mm width for machines that have at least a 6mm width available. But do be careful when using them. If you wish to use automatic stitches, this will only be possible if your machine has a 9mm width available. Check as before: see **Twin needles**.

Machine-made cords, ribbons and appliqué on a dyed surface, by Roma Edge.

Recommended Reading

Beaney, Jan and Jean Littlejohn. *Stitch Magic*. Batsford, 1998.

Campbell-Harding, Valerie and Maggie Grey. *Layers of Stitch*. Batsford, 2001.

Edmonds, Janet. *Embroidered Boxes*. Search Press, 2002.

Edwards, Joan. *Machine Embroidery: Dorothy Benson and the Embroidery Department of the Singer Sewing Company.*

Hedley, Gwen. *Surfaces for Stitch*. Batsford, 2000.

Holmes, Val. *The Machine Embroiderer's Workbook*. Batsford, 1991.

Risley, Christine. *Machine Embroidery, a Complete Guide*. Studio Vista, 1973.

Twigg, Jean. *Embroidery Machine Essentials*. Krause Publications, 2001.

Artstraws, plastic canvas, and polymer clay are all available from art or hobby shops, and glue guns from hardware stores. Bondaweb (fusible webbing) is available from haberdashers

Dick Blick Art Materials
PO Box 1267
Galesburg, IL 61402-1267
Mail order: 1-800-447-8192
www.dickblick.com

Embroidery Adventures
email: reliker@embroideryadventures.com

Gerber EZ-Liner Diaper Liners,
800-4-GERBER (diaper liners)

Impress Me, www.impressmenow.com
(Impress Me stamps)

Kunin Felt, 380 Lafayette Road,
Hampton, NH 03842, USA
tel: 800-292-7900
(zappable felt)

Meinke Toys, PMB#411, 55 E Long Lake Rd, Troy MI 48085, USA
tel: 248-813-9806, fax. 801-991-5983
email: meinketoy@mindspring.com
(most supplies)

Nancy's Notions, www.nancysnotions.com
(Flower Stitcher)

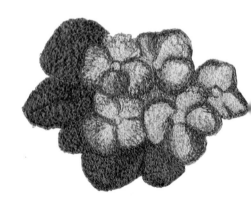